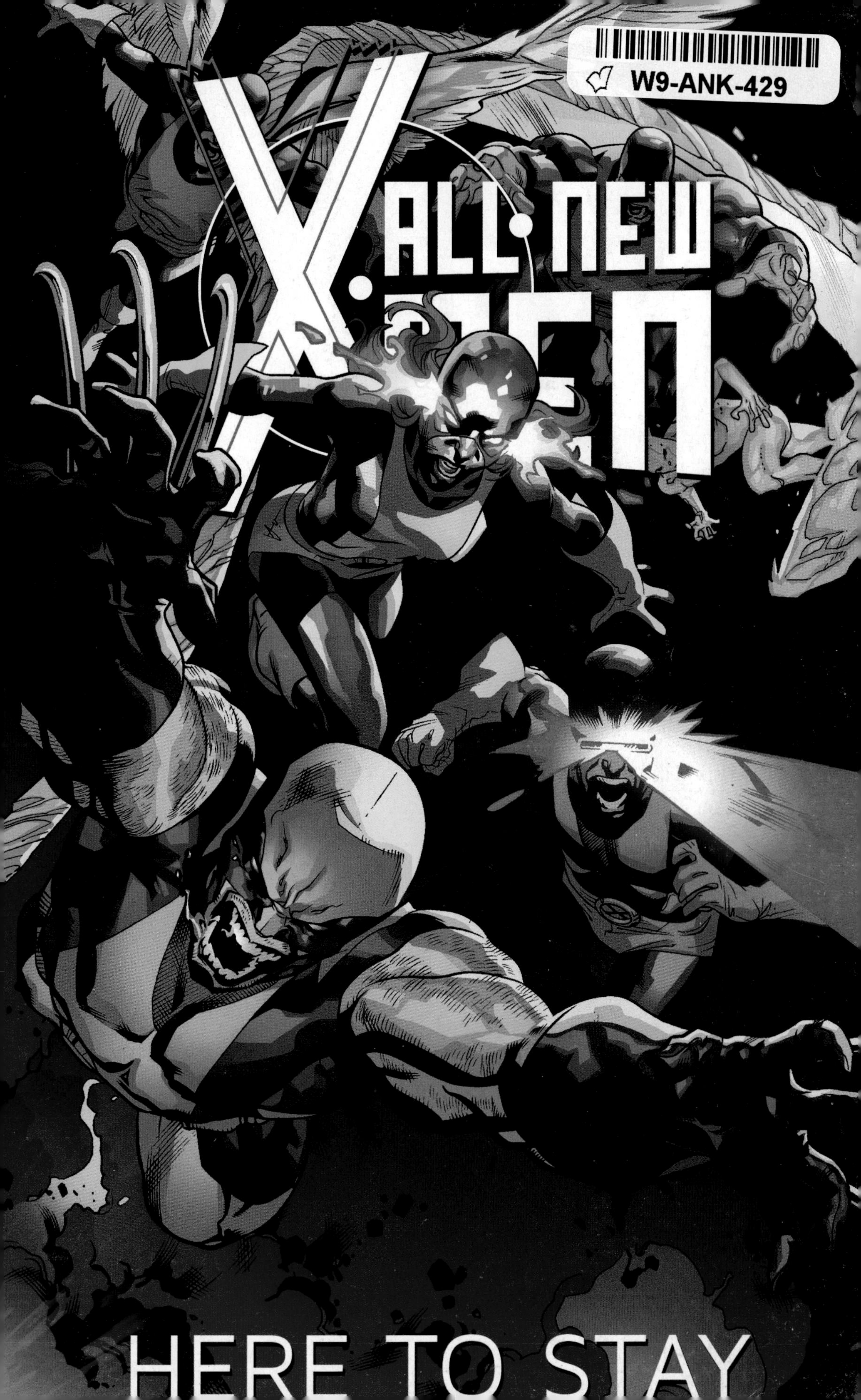
ALL-NEW X-MEN
HERE TO STAY

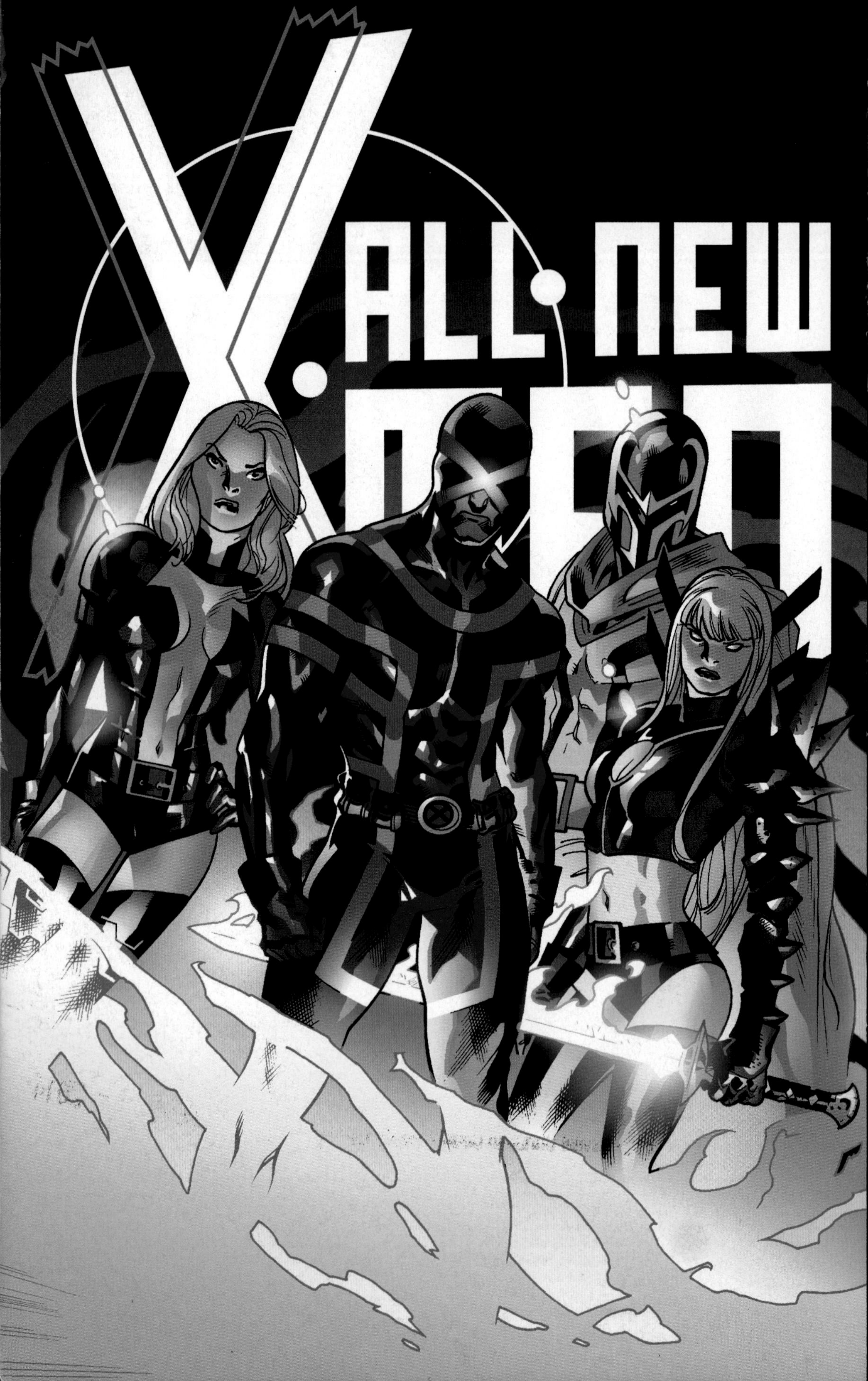

X
ALL·NEW

BEAST
FRANK McCOY

MARVEL GIRL
JEAN GREY

CYCLOPS
SCOTT SUMMERS

ANGEL
WARREN WORTHINGTON III

ICEMAN
BOBBY DRAKE

HERE TO STAY

BRIAN MICHAEL
BENDIS
WRITER

DAVID
MARQUEZ
ARTIST, #6–8

STUART
IMMONEN
PENCILER, #9–10

WADE VON
GRAWBADGER
INKER, #9–10

MARTE
GRACIA
WITH RAIN BEREDO (#9–10)
COLORISTS

VC'S CORY
PETIT
LETTERER

COVER ART: STUART IMMONEN, WADE VON GRAWBADGER & MARTE GRACIA

JORDAN D.
WHITE
ASSISTANT EDITOR

NICK
LOWE
EDITOR

COLLECTION EDITOR: **JENNIFER GRÜNWALD**
ASSOCIATE MANAGING EDITOR: **ALEX STARBUCK**
EDITOR, SPECIAL PROJECTS: **MARK D. BEAZLEY**
SENIOR EDITOR, SPECIAL PROJECTS: **JEFF YOUNGQUIST**
SVP PRINT, SALES & MARKETING: **DAVID GABRIEL**
BOOK DESIGNER: **RODOLFO MURAGUCHI**

EDITOR IN CHIEF: **AXEL ALONSO**
CHIEF CREATIVE OFFICER: **JOE QUESADA**
PUBLISHER: **DAN BUCKLEY**
EXECUTIVE PRODUCER: **ALAN FINE**

MAR - - 2014

Hopkinsville Christian County Public Library

ALL-NEW X-MEN VOL. 2: HERE TO STAY. Contains material originally published in magazine form as ALL-NEW X-MEN #6-10. First printing 2014. ISBN# 978-0-7851-6638-2. Published by MARVEL WORLDWIDE, INC., a subsidiary of MARVEL ENTERTAINMENT, LLC. OFFICE OF PUBLICATION: 135 West 50th Street, New York, NY 10020. Copyright © 2013 and 2014 Marvel Characters, Inc. All rights reserved. All characters featured in this issue and the distinctive names and likenesses thereof, and all related indicia are trademarks of Marvel Characters, Inc. No similarity between any of the names, characters, persons, and/or institutions in this magazine with those of any living or dead person or institution is intended, and any such similarity which may exist is purely coincidental. **Printed in the U.S.A.** ALAN FINE, EVP - Office of the President, Marvel Worldwide, Inc. and EVP & CMO Marvel Characters B.V.; DAN BUCKLEY, Publisher & President - Print, Animation & Digital Divisions; JOE QUESADA, Chief Creative Officer; TOM BREVOORT, SVP of Publishing; DAVID BOGART, SVP of Operations & Procurement, Publishing; C.B. CEBULSKI, SVP of Creator & Content Development; DAVID GABRIEL, SVP Print, Sales & Marketing; JIM O'KEEFE, VP of Operations & Logistics; DAN CARR, Executive Director of Publishing Technology; SUSAN CRESPI, Editorial Operations Manager; ALEX MORALES, Publishing Operations Manager; STAN LEE, Chairman Emeritus. For information regarding advertising in Marvel Comics or on Marvel.com, please contact Niza Disla, Director of Marvel Partnerships, at ndisla@marvel.com. For Marvel subscription inquiries, please call 800-217-9158. **Manufactured between 1/17/2014 and 2/24/2014 by R.R. DONNELLEY, INC., SALEM, VA, USA.**
10 9 8 7 6 5 4 3 2 1

Born with genetic mutations that gave them abilities beyond those of normal humans, mutants are the next stage in evolution. As such, they are feared and hated by humanity. A group of mutants known as the X-Men fight for peaceful coexistence between mutants and humankind. But not all mutants see peaceful coextistence as a reality.

X ALL NEW X MEN

The Beast used a time machine to bring the original five X-Men (Cyclops, Marvel Girl, Iceman, Beast and Angel) to the present.

He hoped their presence would convince the adult Cyclops — who killed Professor Xavier while posessed by a cosmic force and is now leading a revolutionary team alongside Magneto — to change his ways.

The original X-Men are shocked to find a world that is the opposite of the one Xavier had envisioned. The young Jean Grey called a vote and her team decided to stay until they can make Xavier's dream a reality.

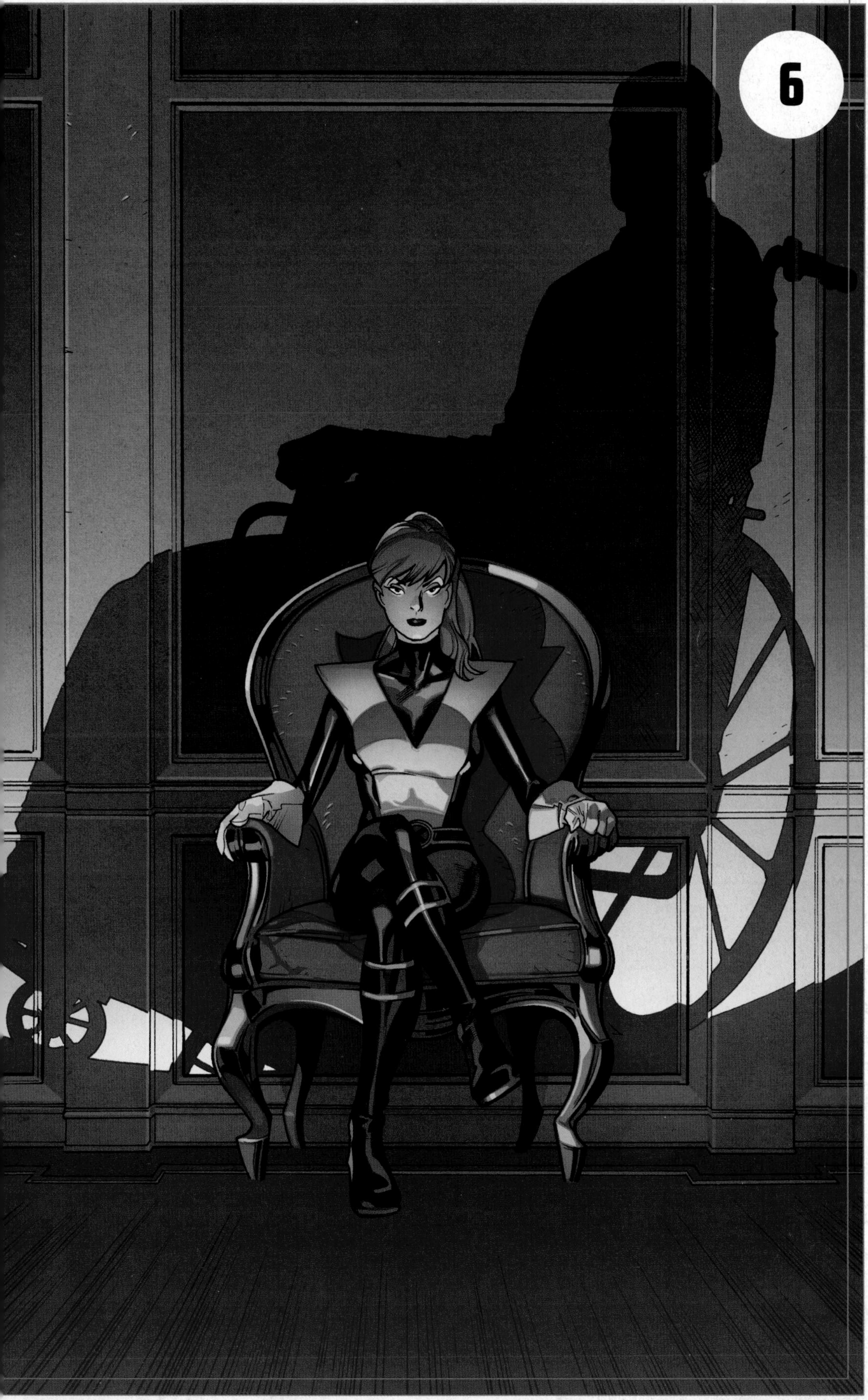
6

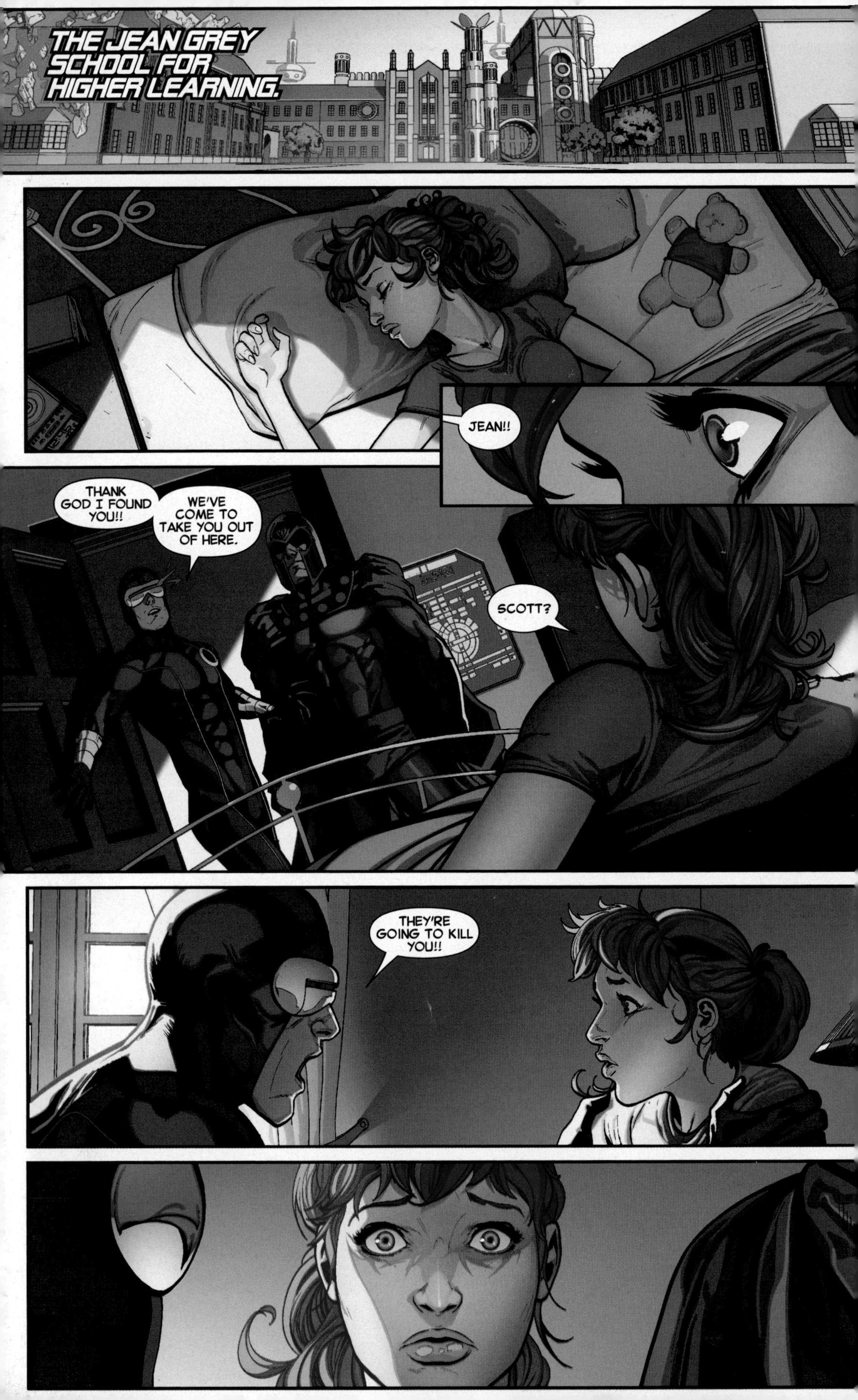
THE JEAN GREY SCHOOL FOR HIGHER LEARNING.
JEAN!!
THANK GOD I FOUND YOU!!
WE'VE COME TO TAKE YOU OUT OF HERE.
SCOTT?
THEY'RE GOING TO KILL YOU!!

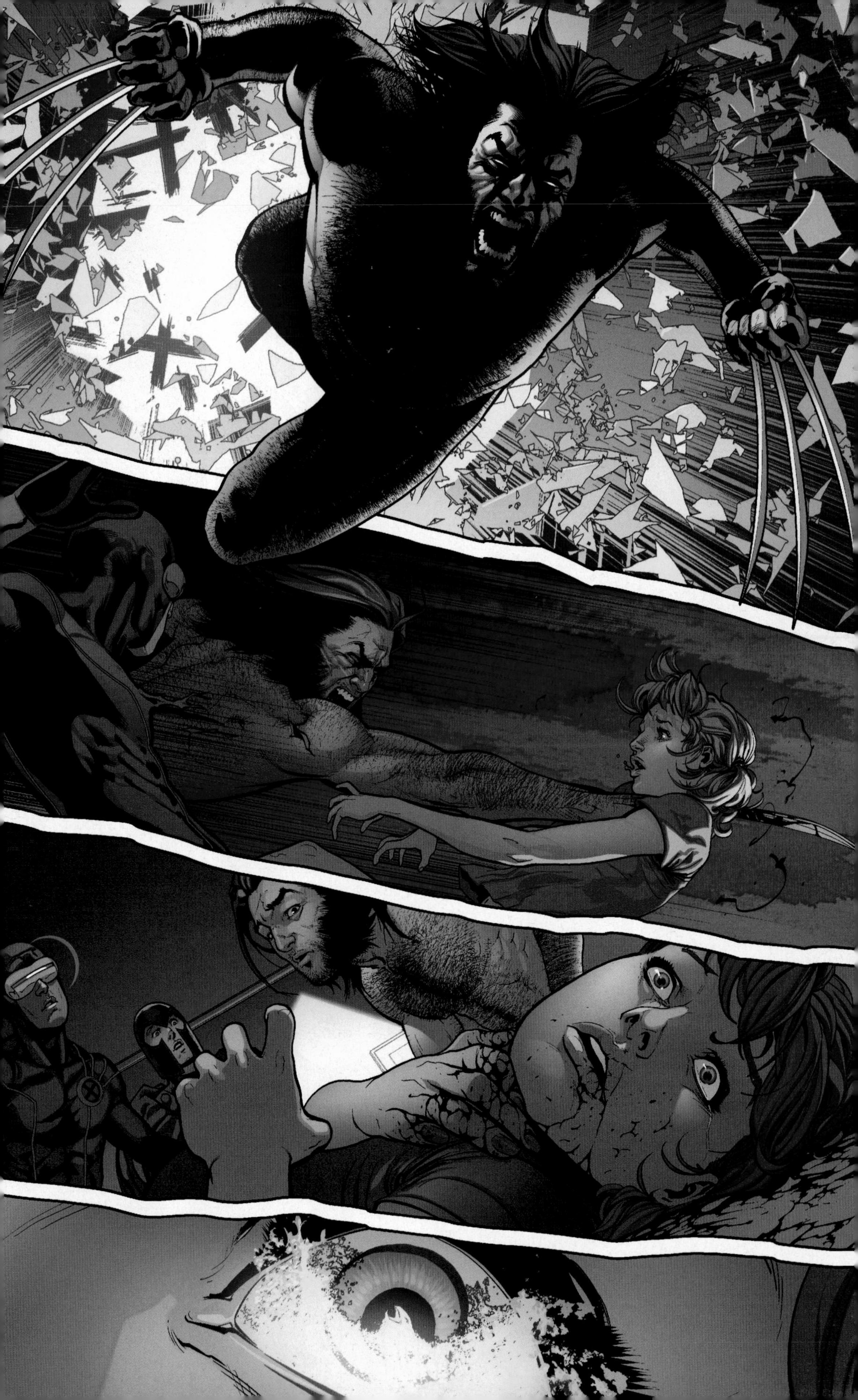

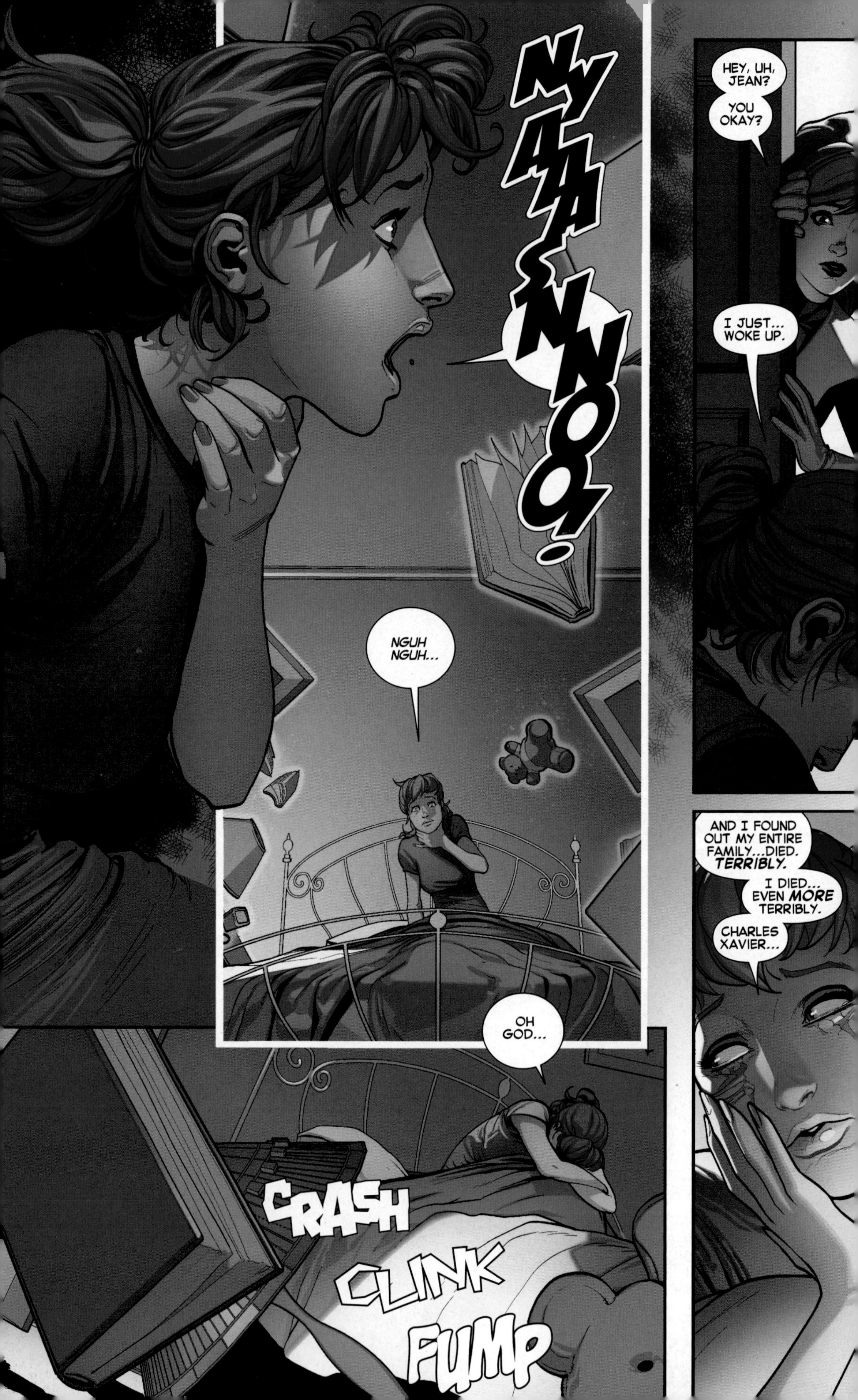
NYAAAASNNNOOO!
NGUH NGUH...
OH GOD...
CRASH
CLINK
FUMP
HEY, UH, JEAN?
YOU OKAY?
I JUST... WOKE UP.
AND I FOUND OUT MY ENTIRE FAMILY...DIED. TERRIBLY.
I DIED... EVEN MORE TERRIBLY.
CHARLES XAVIER...

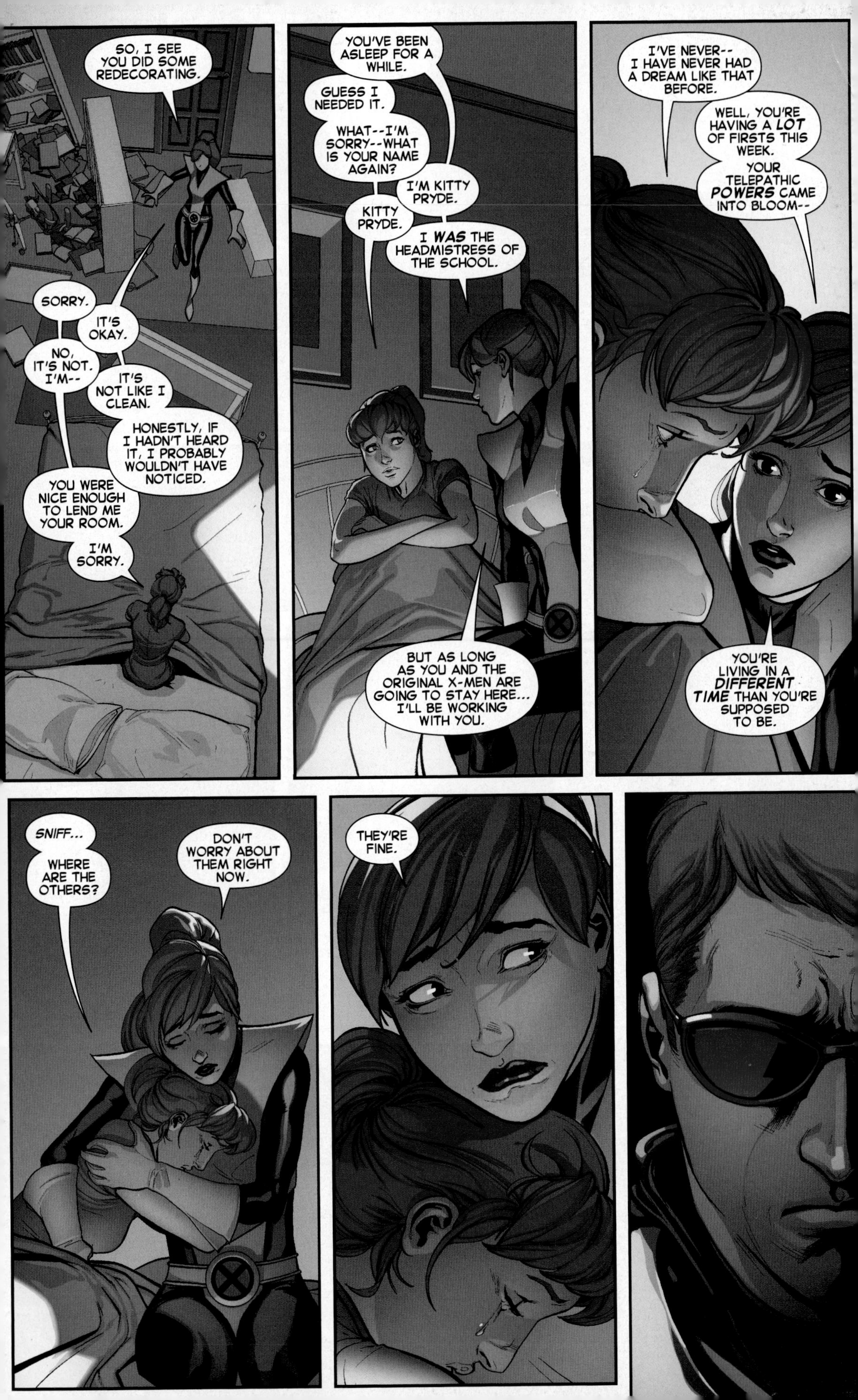
SO, I SEE YOU DID SOME REDECORATING.
SORRY.
IT'S OKAY.
NO, IT'S NOT. I'M--
IT'S NOT LIKE I CLEAN.
HONESTLY, IF I HADN'T HEARD IT, I PROBABLY WOULDN'T HAVE NOTICED.
YOU WERE NICE ENOUGH TO LEND ME YOUR ROOM.
I'M SORRY.
YOU'VE BEEN ASLEEP FOR A WHILE.
GUESS I NEEDED IT.
WHAT--I'M SORRY--WHAT IS YOUR NAME AGAIN?
I'M KITTY PRYDE.
KITTY PRYDE.
I *WAS* THE HEADMISTRESS OF THE SCHOOL.
BUT AS LONG AS YOU AND THE ORIGINAL X-MEN ARE GOING TO STAY HERE... I'LL BE WORKING WITH YOU.
I'VE NEVER-- I HAVE NEVER HAD A DREAM LIKE THAT BEFORE.
WELL, YOU'RE HAVING A *LOT* OF FIRSTS THIS WEEK.
YOUR TELEPATHIC *POWERS* CAME INTO BLOOM--
YOU'RE LIVING IN A *DIFFERENT TIME* THAN YOU'RE SUPPOSED TO BE.
SNIFF...
WHERE ARE THE OTHERS?
DON'T WORRY ABOUT THEM RIGHT NOW.
THEY'RE FINE.

IT'S A FUNNY THING--

YESTERDAY I WAS THE LEADER OF THE X-MEN...

THAT WAS *YESTERDAY.*

AT LEAST TO ME.

IF YOU'LL EXCUSE ME.

HOW?

HOW COULD I *BE* THIS THING?

HOW COULD I HAVE *DONE* THIS?

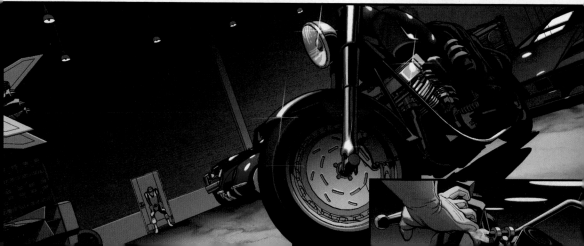

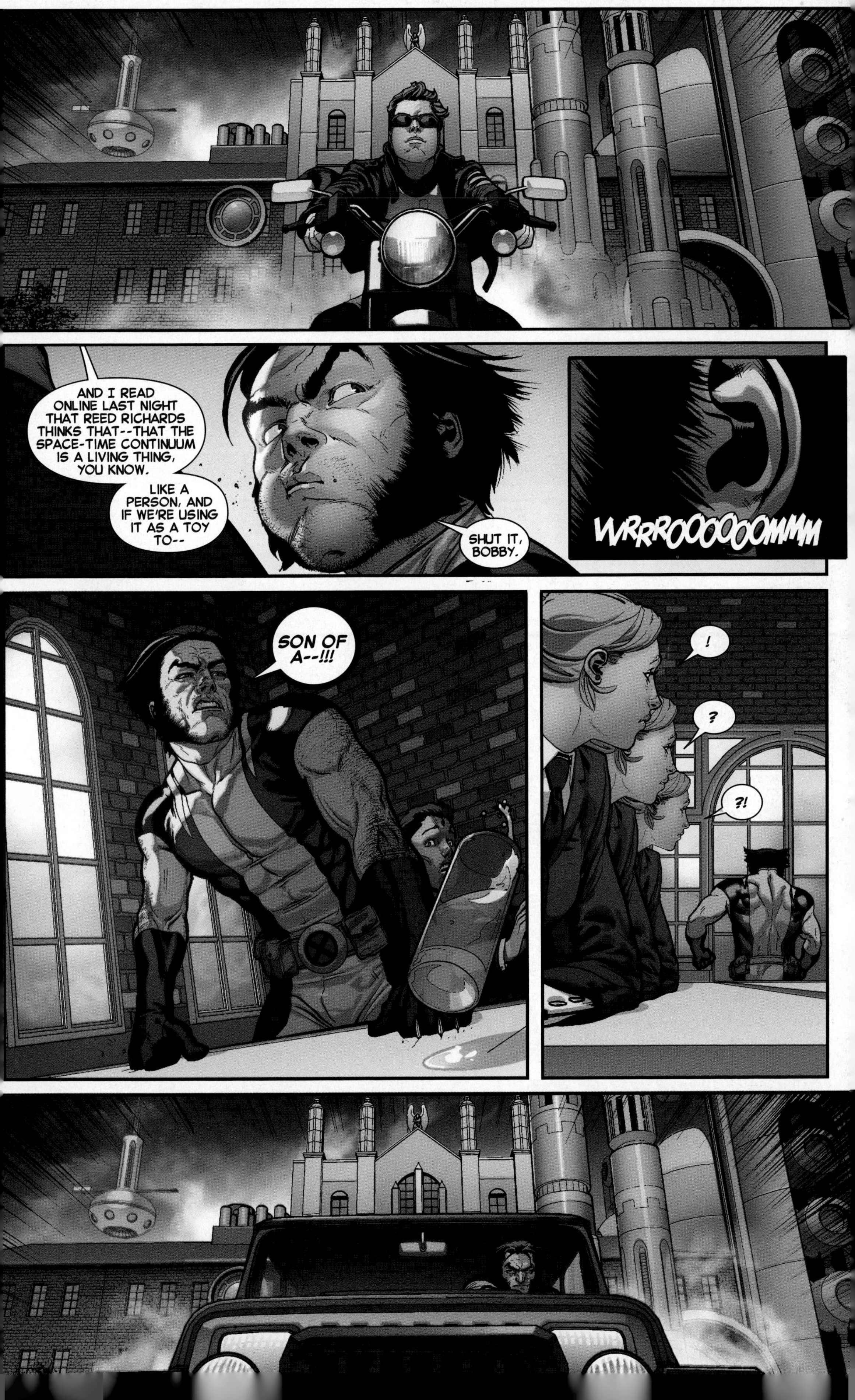
AND I READ ONLINE LAST NIGHT THAT REED RICHARDS THINKS THAT--THAT THE SPACE-TIME CONTINUUM IS A LIVING THING, YOU KNOW.
LIKE A PERSON, AND IF WE'RE USING IT AS A TOY TO--
SHUT IT, BOBBY.
VVRRROOOOOOOMMM
SON OF A--!!!
!
?
?!

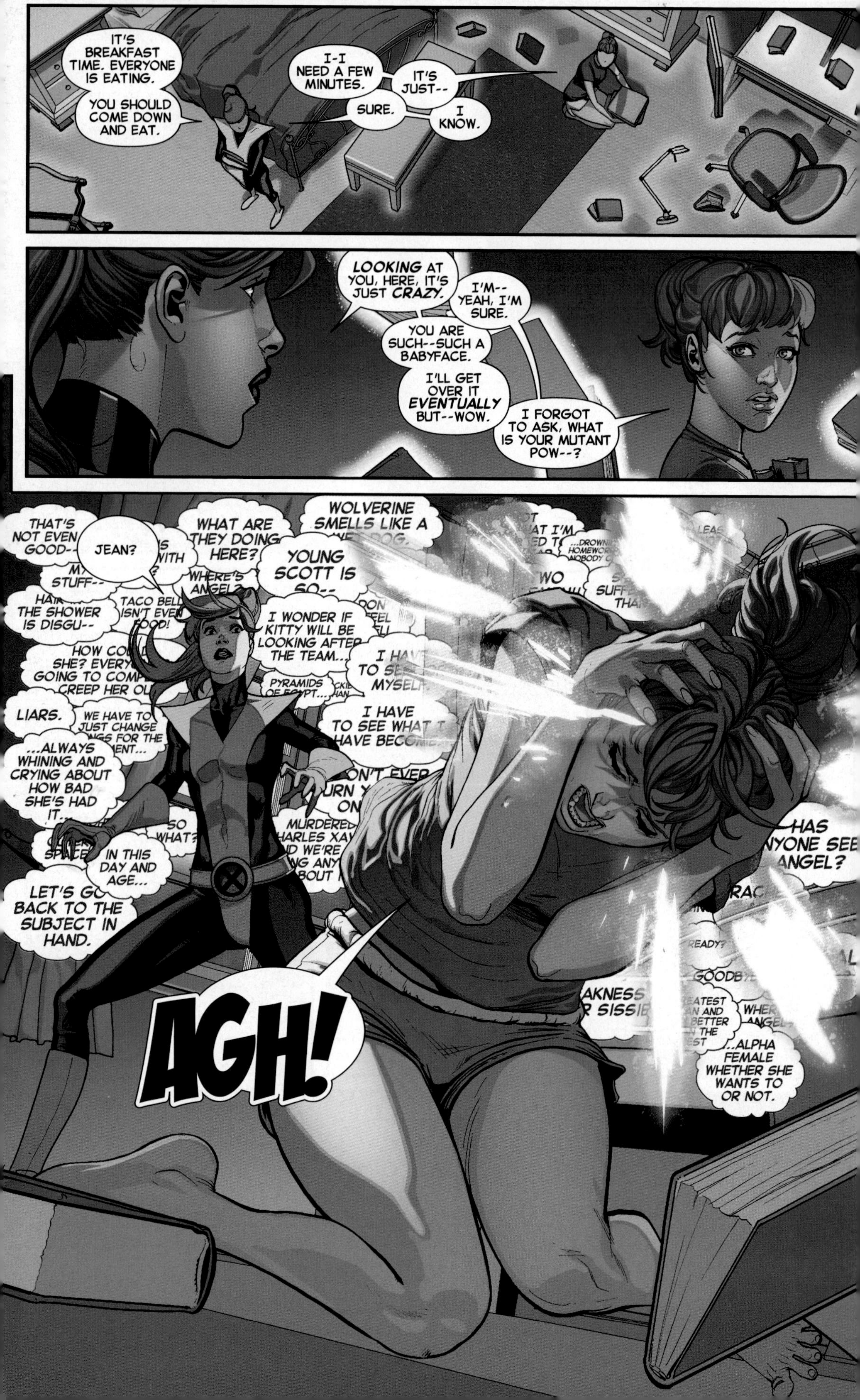

IT'S BREAKFAST TIME. EVERYONE IS EATING.
YOU SHOULD COME DOWN AND EAT.
I-I NEED A FEW MINUTES.
IT'S JUST--
SURE.
I KNOW.
LOOKING AT YOU, HERE, IT'S JUST CRAZY.
I'M-- YEAH, I'M SURE.
YOU ARE SUCH--SUCH A BABYFACE.
I'LL GET OVER IT EVENTUALLY BUT--WOW.
I FORGOT TO ASK, WHAT IS YOUR MUTANT POW--?
JEAN?
THAT'S NOT EVEN GOOD--
WHAT ARE THEY DOING HERE?
WOLVERINE SMELLS LIKE A
YOUNG SCOTT IS SO--
THE SHOWER IS DISGU--
TACO BELL ISN'T EVEN FOOD!
I WONDER IF KITTY WILL BE LOOKING AFTER THE TEAM...
LIARS.
I HAVE TO SEE WHAT I HAVE BECOME.
...ALWAYS WHINING AND CRYING ABOUT HOW BAD SHE'S HAD IT...
SO WHAT?
IN THIS DAY AND AGE...
LET'S GO BACK TO THE SUBJECT IN HAND.
HAS ANYONE SEEN ANGEL?
READY?
GOODBYE
...ALPHA FEMALE WHETHER SHE WANTS TO OR NOT.
AGH!

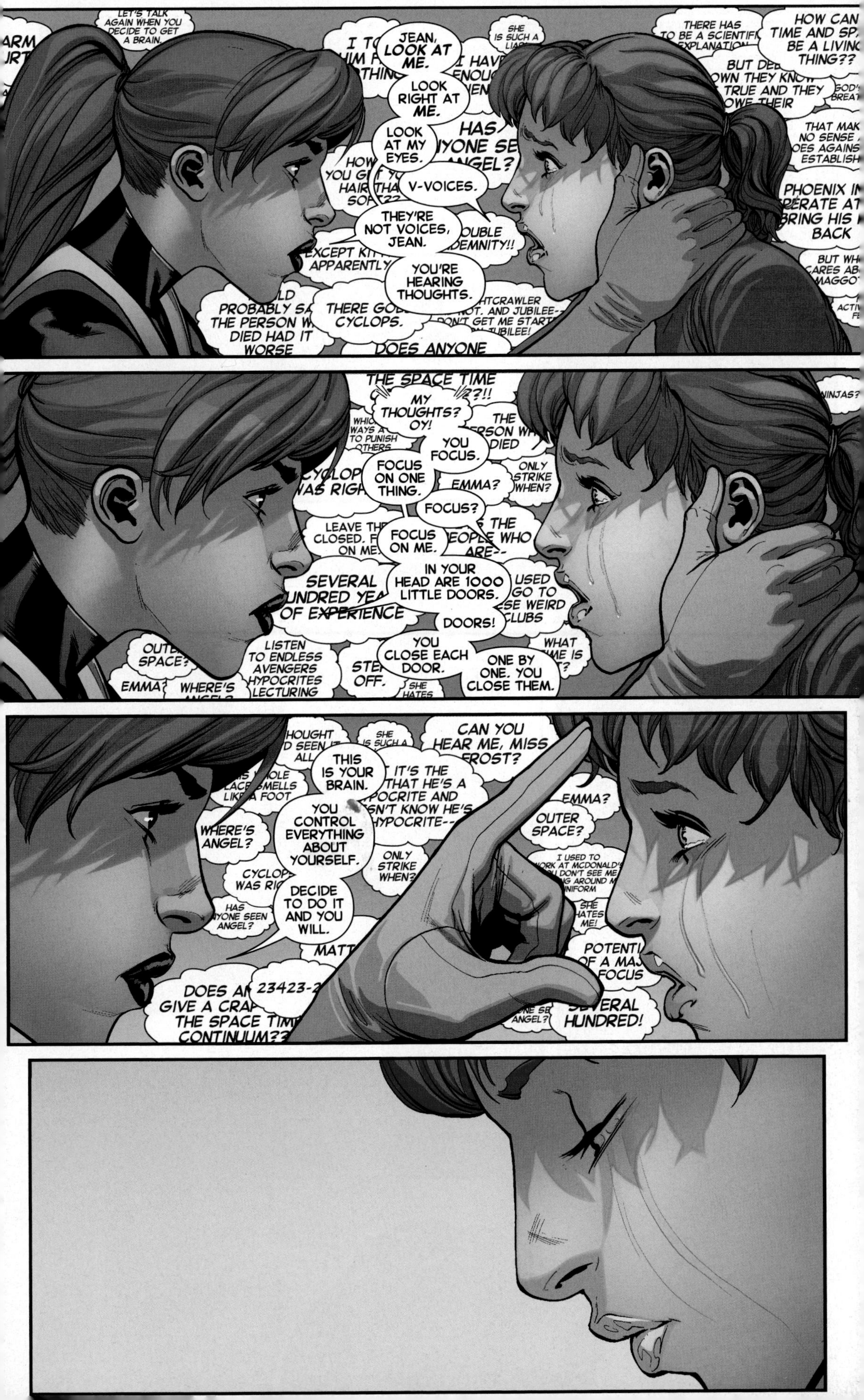
LET'S TALK AGAIN WHEN YOU DECIDE TO GET A BRAIN.
SHE IS SUCH A LIAR
HOW CAN TIME AND SPACE BE A LIVING THING??
JEAN, LOOK AT ME.
LOOK RIGHT AT ME.
LOOK AT MY EYES.
V-VOICES.
THEY'RE NOT VOICES, JEAN.
YOU'RE HEARING THOUGHTS.
EXCEPT KITTY APPARENTLY
THERE GOES CYCLOPS.
PHOENIX IN
BACK
THAT MAKES NO SENSE
DIED HAD IT WORSE
DOES ANYONE
THE SPACE TIME
MY THOUGHTS? OY!
YOU FOCUS.
FOCUS ON ONE THING.
FOCUS?
FOCUS ON ME.
IN YOUR HEAD ARE 1000 LITTLE DOORS.
DOORS!
YOU CLOSE EACH DOOR.
ONE BY ONE. YOU CLOSE THEM.
NINJAS?
ONLY STRIKE WHEN?
EMMA?
SEVERAL
OF EXPERIENCE
CLUBS
OUTER SPACE?
LISTEN TO ENDLESS AVENGERS HYPOCRITES LECTURING
OFF.
CAN YOU HEAR ME, MISS FROST?
THIS IS YOUR BRAIN.
YOU CONTROL EVERYTHING ABOUT YOURSELF.
DECIDE TO DO IT AND YOU WILL.
WHERE'S ANGEL?
EMMA?
OUTER SPACE?
ONLY STRIKE WHEN?
SHE HATES ME!
HAS ANYONE SEEN ANGEL?
FOCUS
HUNDRED!
GIVE A CRAP
CONTINUUM??
23423-2

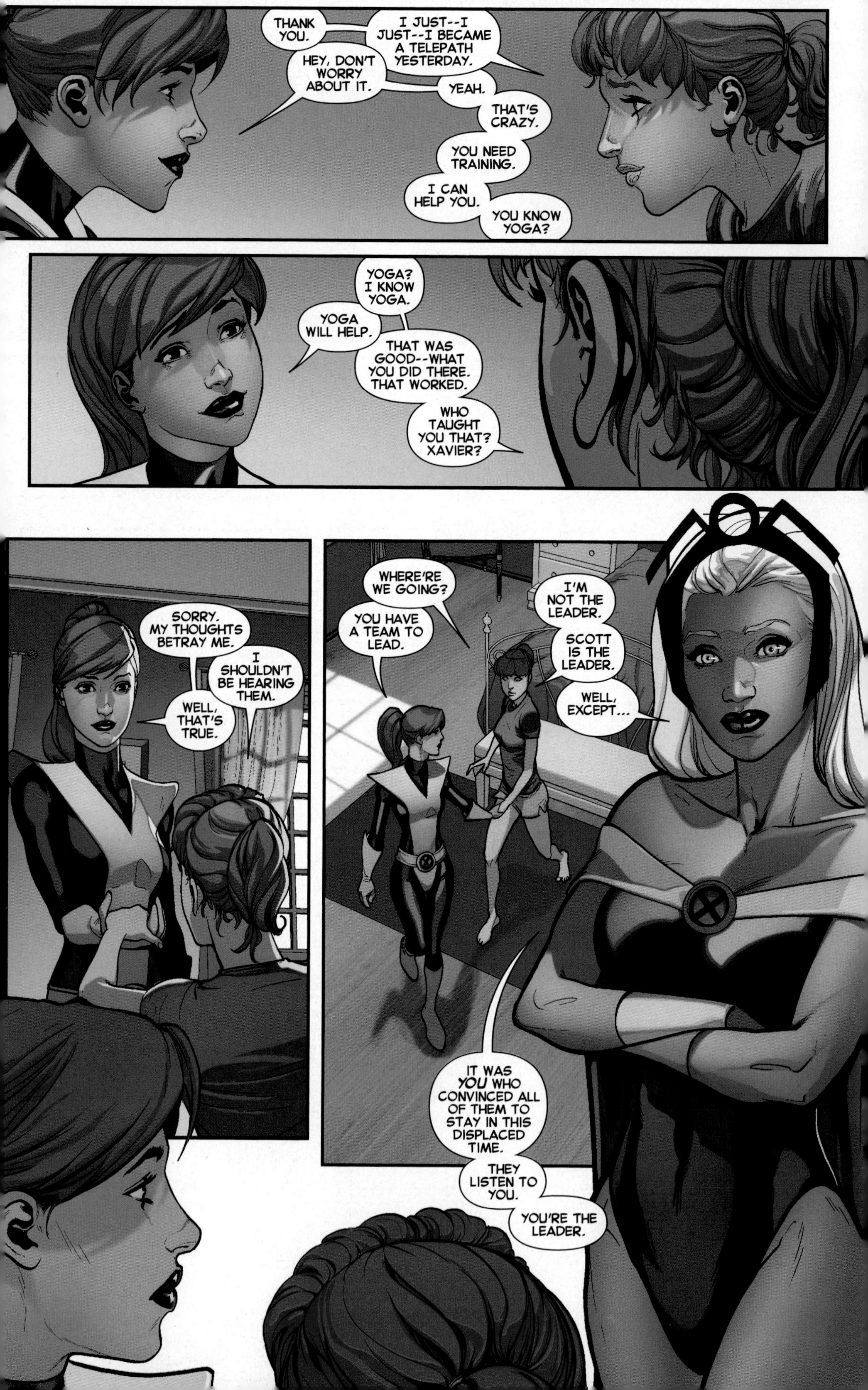
THANK YOU.
I JUST--I JUST--I BECAME A TELEPATH YESTERDAY.
HEY, DON'T WORRY ABOUT IT.
YEAH.
THAT'S CRAZY.
YOU NEED TRAINING.
I CAN HELP YOU.
YOU KNOW YOGA?
YOGA? I KNOW YOGA.
YOGA WILL HELP.
THAT WAS GOOD--WHAT YOU DID THERE. THAT WORKED.
WHO TAUGHT YOU THAT? XAVIER?
SORRY. MY THOUGHTS BETRAY ME.
I SHOULDN'T BE HEARING THEM.
WELL, THAT'S TRUE.
WHERE'RE WE GOING?
YOU HAVE A TEAM TO LEAD.
I'M NOT THE LEADER.
SCOTT IS THE LEADER.
WELL, EXCEPT...
IT WAS YOU WHO CONVINCED ALL OF THEM TO STAY IN THIS DISPLACED TIME.
THEY LISTEN TO YOU.
YOU'RE THE LEADER.

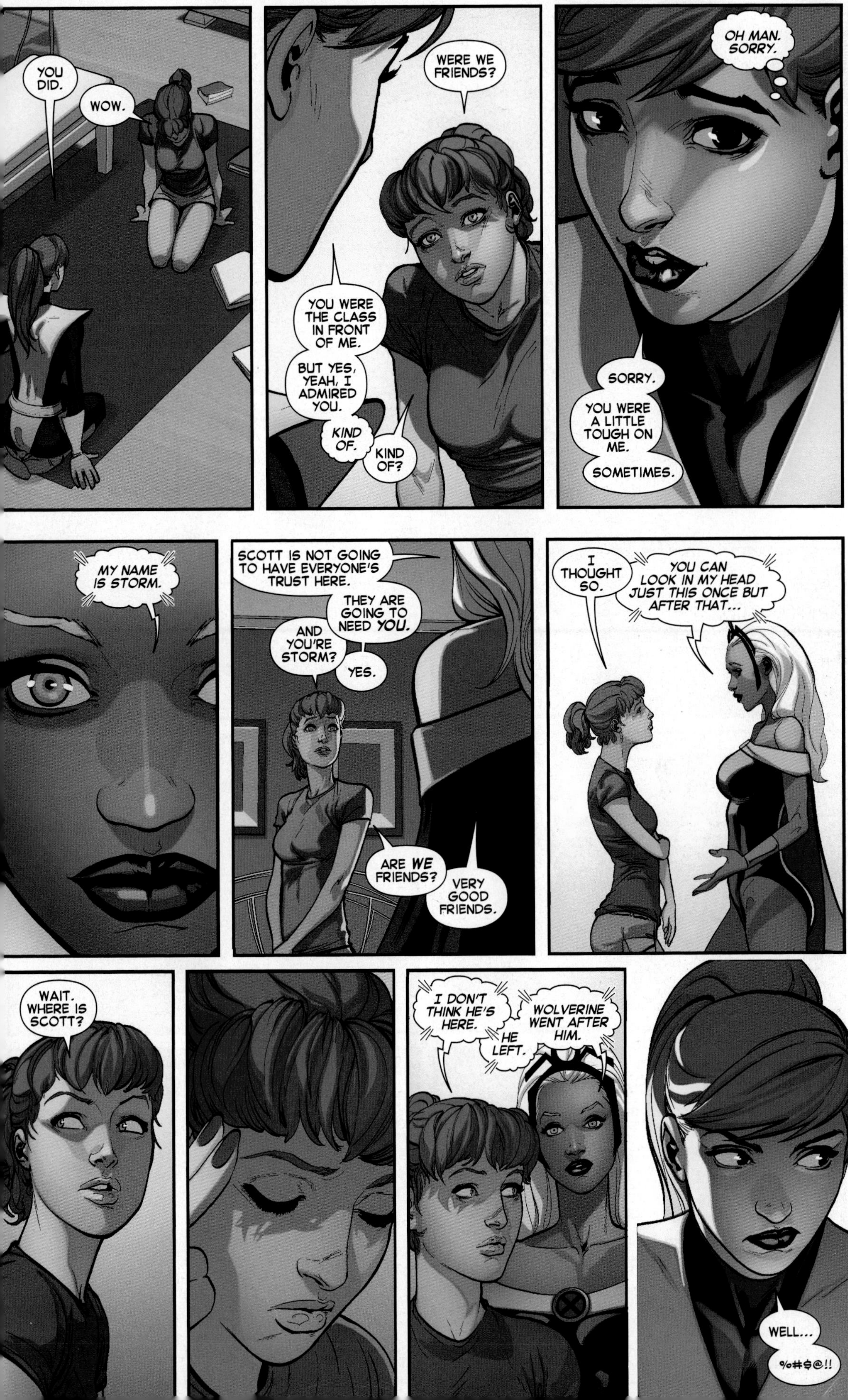
YOU DID.
WOW.
WERE WE FRIENDS?
YOU WERE THE CLASS IN FRONT OF ME.
BUT YES, YEAH, I ADMIRED YOU.
KIND OF.
KIND OF?
OH MAN. SORRY.
SORRY.
YOU WERE A LITTLE TOUGH ON ME.
SOMETIMES.
MY NAME IS STORM.
SCOTT IS NOT GOING TO HAVE EVERYONE'S TRUST HERE.
THEY ARE GOING TO NEED YOU.
AND YOU'RE STORM?
YES.
ARE WE FRIENDS?
VERY GOOD FRIENDS.
I THOUGHT SO.
YOU CAN LOOK IN MY HEAD JUST THIS ONCE BUT AFTER THAT...
WAIT. WHERE IS SCOTT?
I DON'T THINK HE'S HERE.
HE LEFT.
WOLVERINE WENT AFTER HIM.
WELL...
%#$@!!

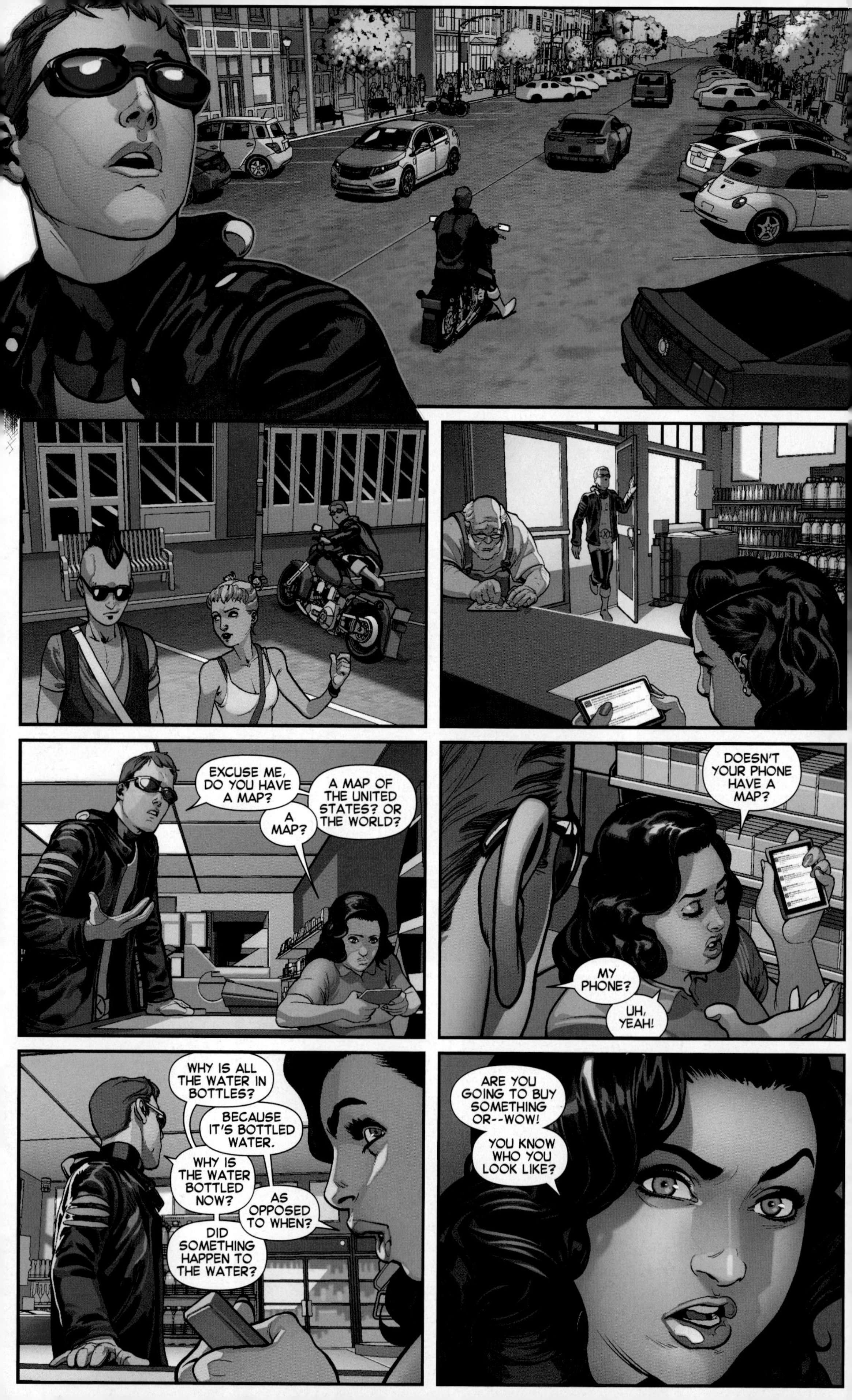

EXCUSE ME, DO YOU HAVE A MAP?
A MAP?
A MAP OF THE UNITED STATES? OR THE WORLD?
DOESN'T YOUR PHONE HAVE A MAP?
MY PHONE?
UH, YEAH!
WHY IS ALL THE WATER IN BOTTLES?
BECAUSE IT'S BOTTLED WATER.
WHY IS THE WATER BOTTLED NOW?
AS OPPOSED TO WHEN?
DID SOMETHING HAPPEN TO THE WATER?
ARE YOU GOING TO BUY SOMETHING OR--WOW!
YOU KNOW WHO YOU LOOK LIKE?

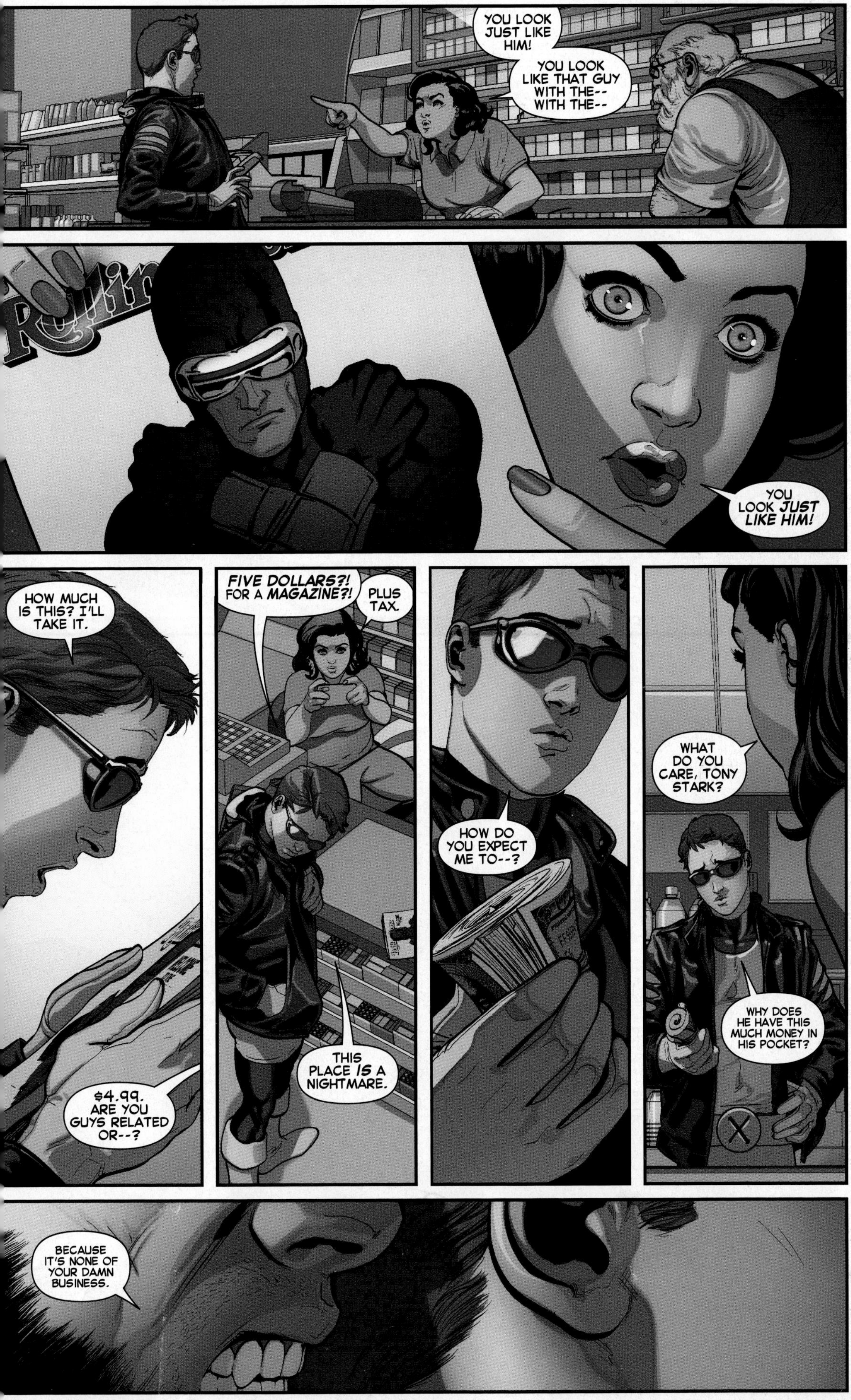
YOU LOOK JUST LIKE HIM!
YOU LOOK LIKE THAT GUY WITH THE-- WITH THE--
YOU LOOK JUST LIKE HIM!
HOW MUCH IS THIS? I'LL TAKE IT.
$4.99. ARE YOU GUYS RELATED OR--?
FIVE DOLLARS?! FOR A MAGAZINE?!
PLUS TAX.
THIS PLACE IS A NIGHTMARE.
HOW DO YOU EXPECT ME TO--?
WHAT DO YOU CARE, TONY STARK?
WHY DOES HE HAVE THIS MUCH MONEY IN HIS POCKET?
BECAUSE IT'S NONE OF YOUR DAMN BUSINESS.

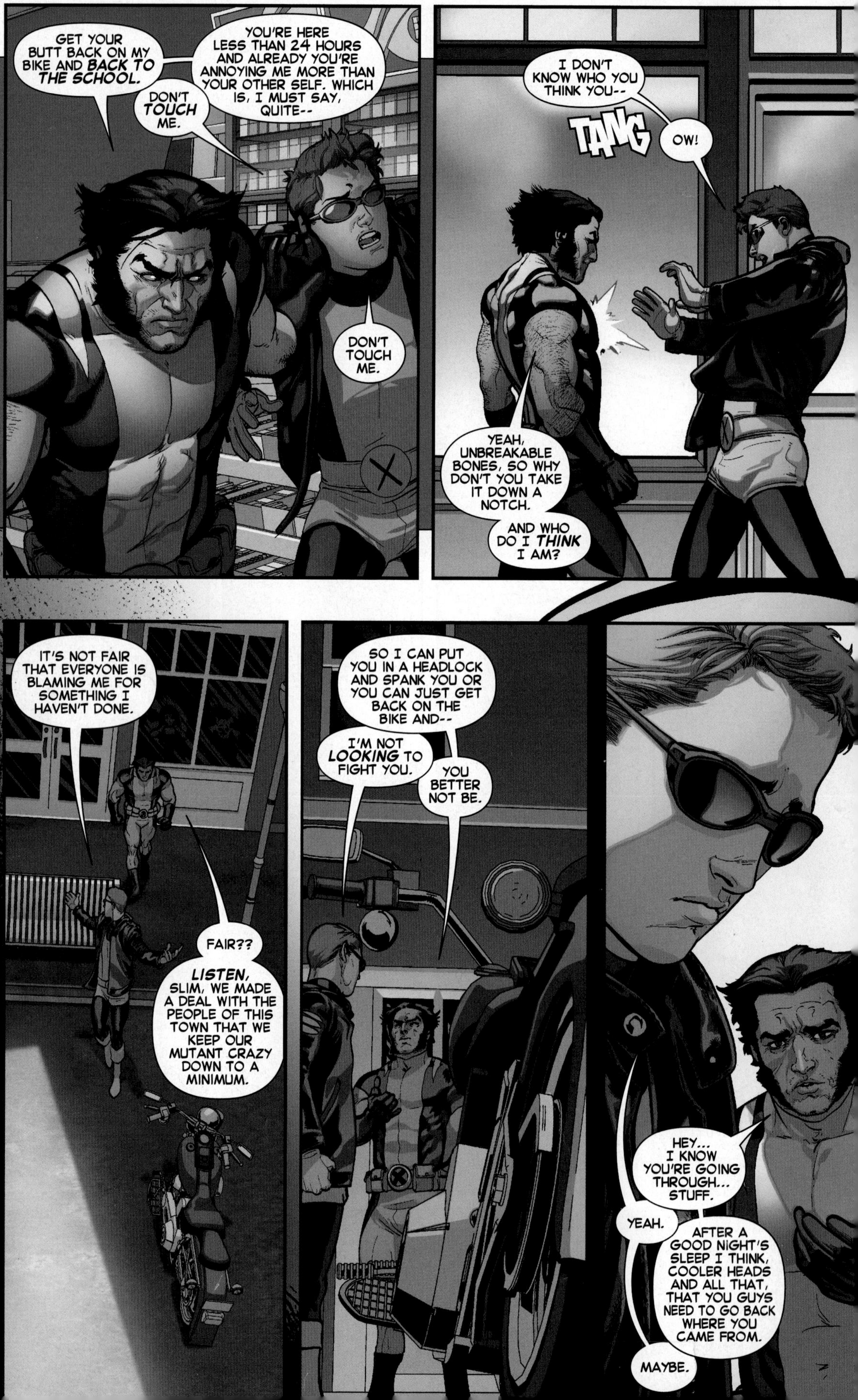
GET YOUR BUTT BACK ON MY BIKE AND BACK TO THE SCHOOL.
YOU'RE HERE LESS THAN 24 HOURS AND ALREADY YOU'RE ANNOYING ME MORE THAN YOUR OTHER SELF. WHICH IS, I MUST SAY, QUITE--
DON'T TOUCH ME.
DON'T TOUCH ME.
I DON'T KNOW WHO YOU THINK YOU--
TANG
OW!
YEAH, UNBREAKABLE BONES, SO WHY DON'T YOU TAKE IT DOWN A NOTCH.
AND WHO DO I THINK I AM?
IT'S NOT FAIR THAT EVERYONE IS BLAMING ME FOR SOMETHING I HAVEN'T DONE.
FAIR??
LISTEN, SLIM, WE MADE A DEAL WITH THE PEOPLE OF THIS TOWN THAT WE KEEP OUR MUTANT CRAZY DOWN TO A MINIMUM.
SO I CAN PUT YOU IN A HEADLOCK AND SPANK YOU OR YOU CAN JUST GET BACK ON THE BIKE AND--
I'M NOT LOOKING TO FIGHT YOU.
YOU BETTER NOT BE.
HEY... I KNOW YOU'RE GOING THROUGH... STUFF.
YEAH.
AFTER A GOOD NIGHT'S SLEEP I THINK, COOLER HEADS AND ALL THAT, THAT YOU GUYS NEED TO GO BACK WHERE YOU CAME FROM.
MAYBE.

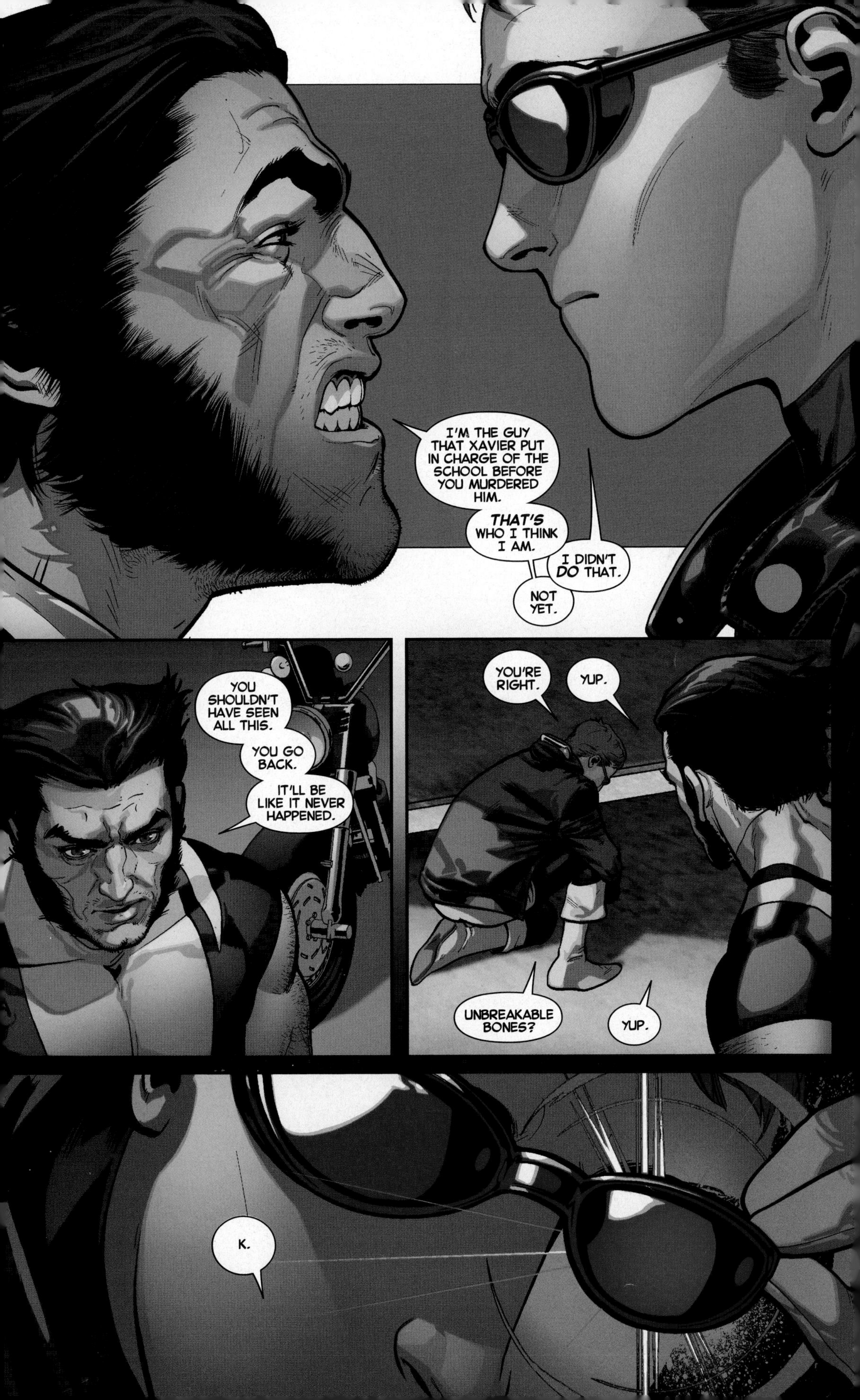
I'M THE GUY THAT XAVIER PUT IN CHARGE OF THE SCHOOL BEFORE YOU MURDERED HIM.
THAT'S WHO I THINK I AM.
I DIDN'T *DO* THAT.
NOT YET.
YOU SHOULDN'T HAVE SEEN ALL THIS.
YOU GO BACK.
IT'LL BE LIKE IT NEVER HAPPENED.
YOU'RE RIGHT.
YUP.
UNBREAKABLE BONES?
YUP.
K.

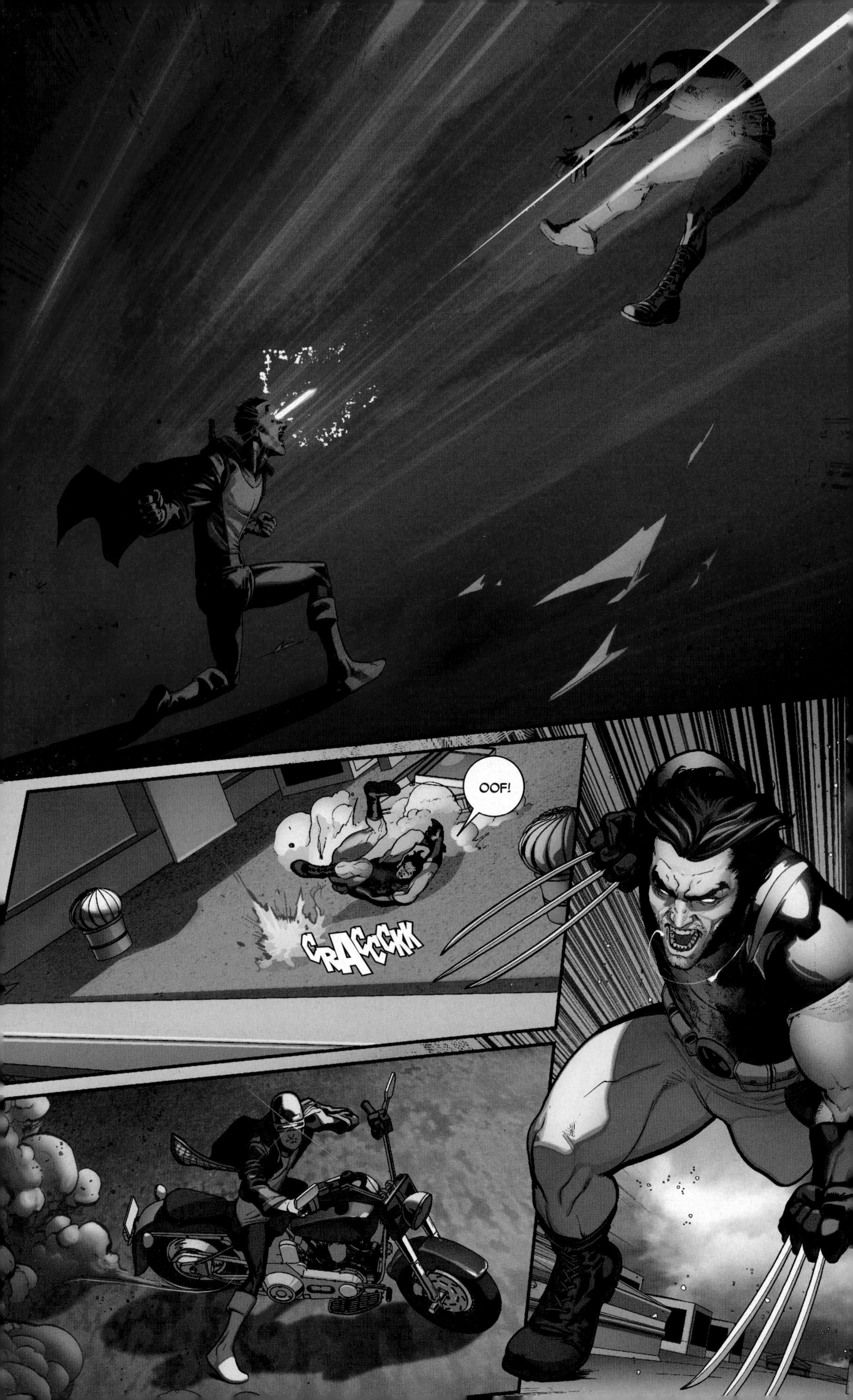
OOF!
CRACCCKK

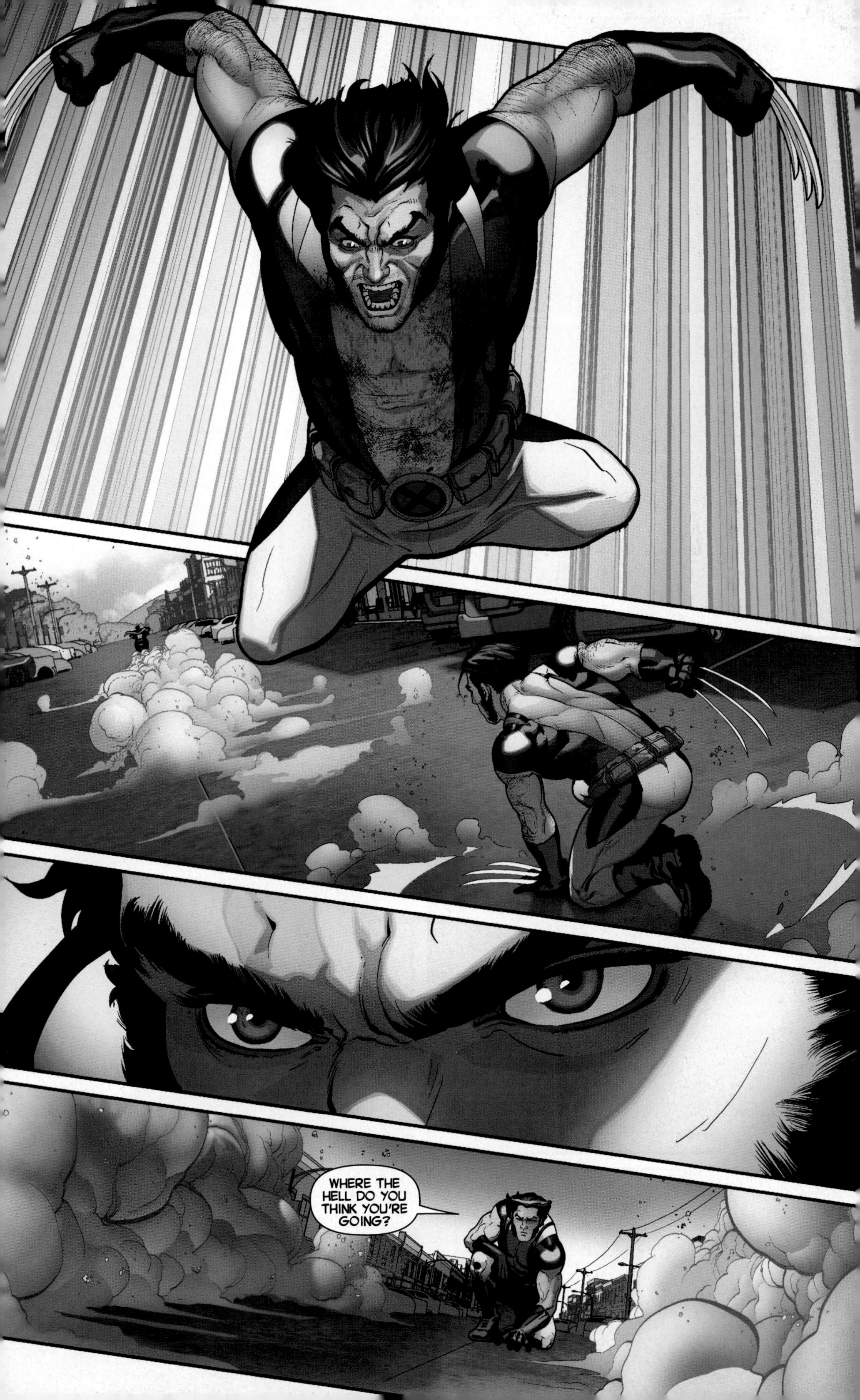
WHERE THE HELL DO YOU THINK YOU'RE GOING?

I HAVE TO SEE FOR MYSELF.

I HAVE TO SEE WHAT I HAVE BECOME.

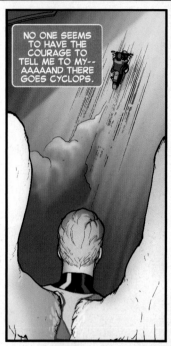

NO ONE SEEMS TO HAVE THE COURAGE TO TELL ME TO MY-- AAAAAND THERE GOES CYCLOPS.

SURE, LEAVE ME HERE, SCOTTIE.

I DON'T WANT TO BE HERE IN THE FIRST PLACE AND NOW YOU LEAVE ME HERE.

YOU GUYS STICK ME HERE AND YOU DON'T EVEN--

HUH-- OKAY.

WHAT IS--?

AM I NUTS OR DID THE GROUND JUST BURP?

WHAT HAS HAPPENED TO THE SCHOOL? WHAT HAS HAPPENED TO THE--?

WELL, THIS IS... UNEXPECTED.

OH MY GOD...

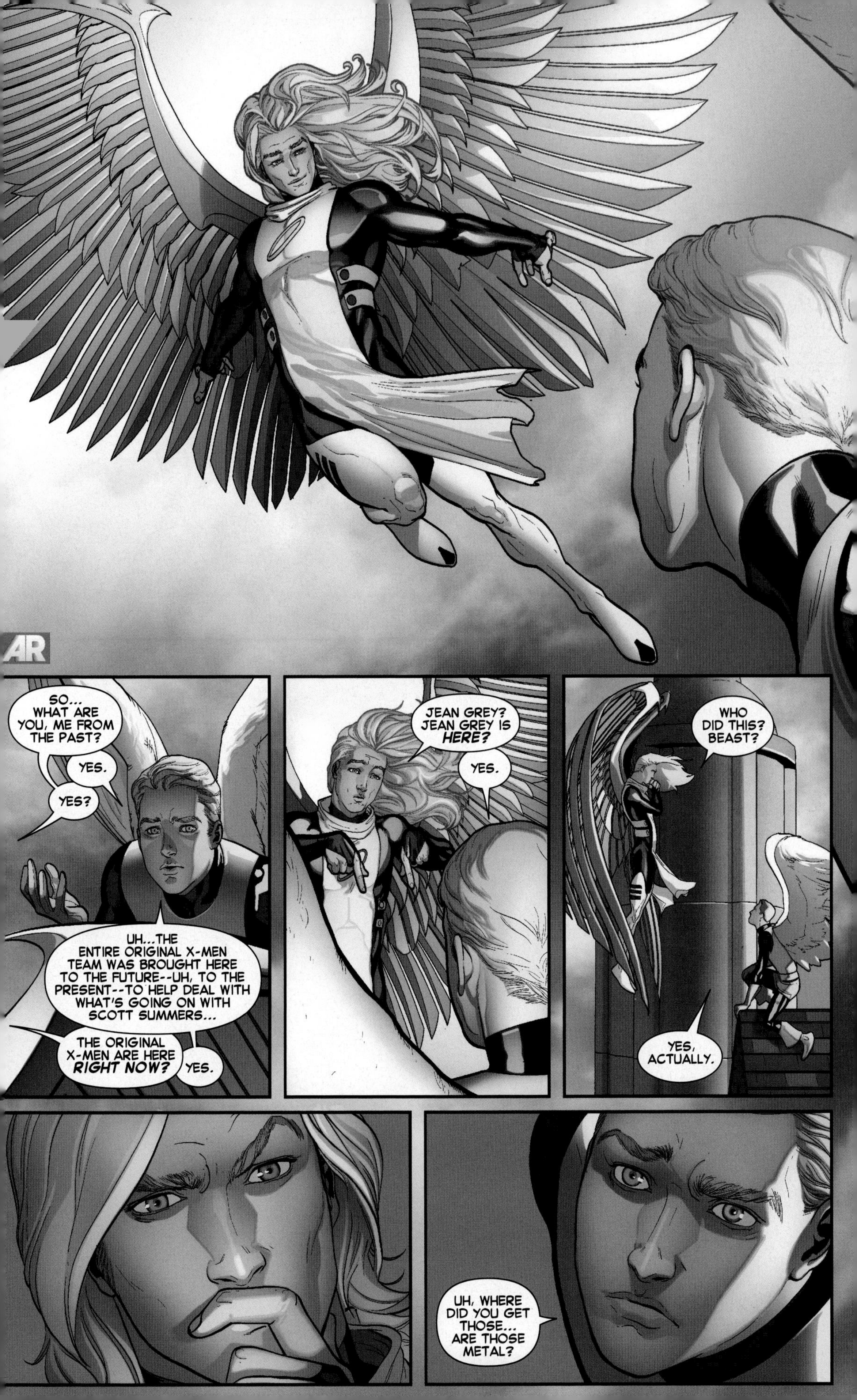
AR
SO... WHAT ARE YOU, ME FROM THE PAST?
YES.
YES?
UH...THE ENTIRE ORIGINAL X-MEN TEAM WAS BROUGHT HERE TO THE FUTURE--UH, TO THE PRESENT--TO HELP DEAL WITH WHAT'S GOING ON WITH SCOTT SUMMERS...
THE ORIGINAL X-MEN ARE HERE RIGHT NOW?
YES.
JEAN GREY? JEAN GREY IS HERE?
YES.
WHO DID THIS? BEAST?
YES, ACTUALLY.
UH, WHERE DID YOU GET THOSE... ARE THOSE METAL?

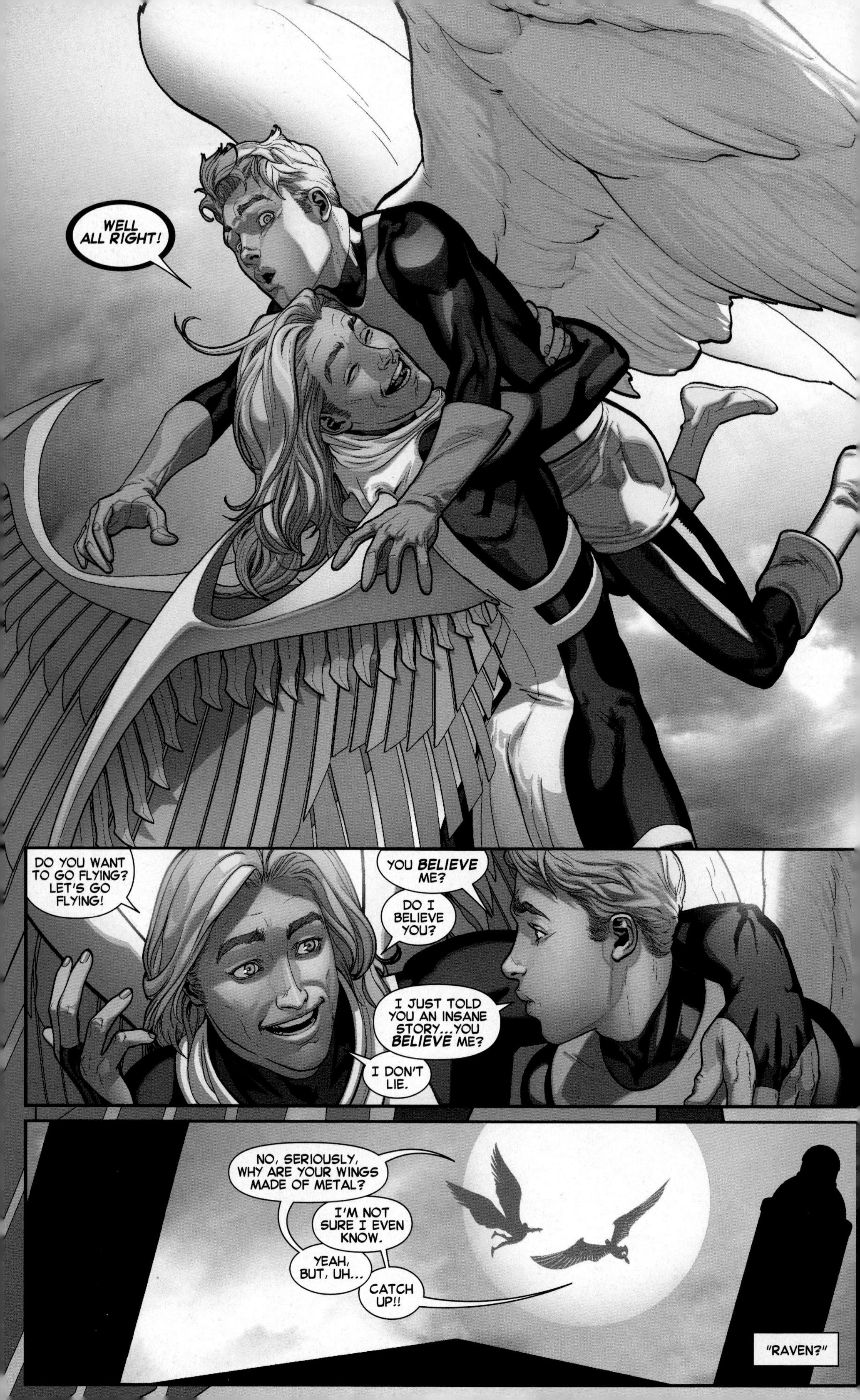
WELL ALL RIGHT!
DO YOU WANT TO GO FLYING? LET'S GO FLYING!
YOU BELIEVE ME?
DO I BELIEVE YOU?
I JUST TOLD YOU AN INSANE STORY...YOU BELIEVE ME?
I DON'T LIE.
NO, SERIOUSLY, WHY ARE YOUR WINGS MADE OF METAL?
I'M NOT SURE I EVEN KNOW.
YEAH, BUT, UH...
CATCH UP!!
"RAVEN?"

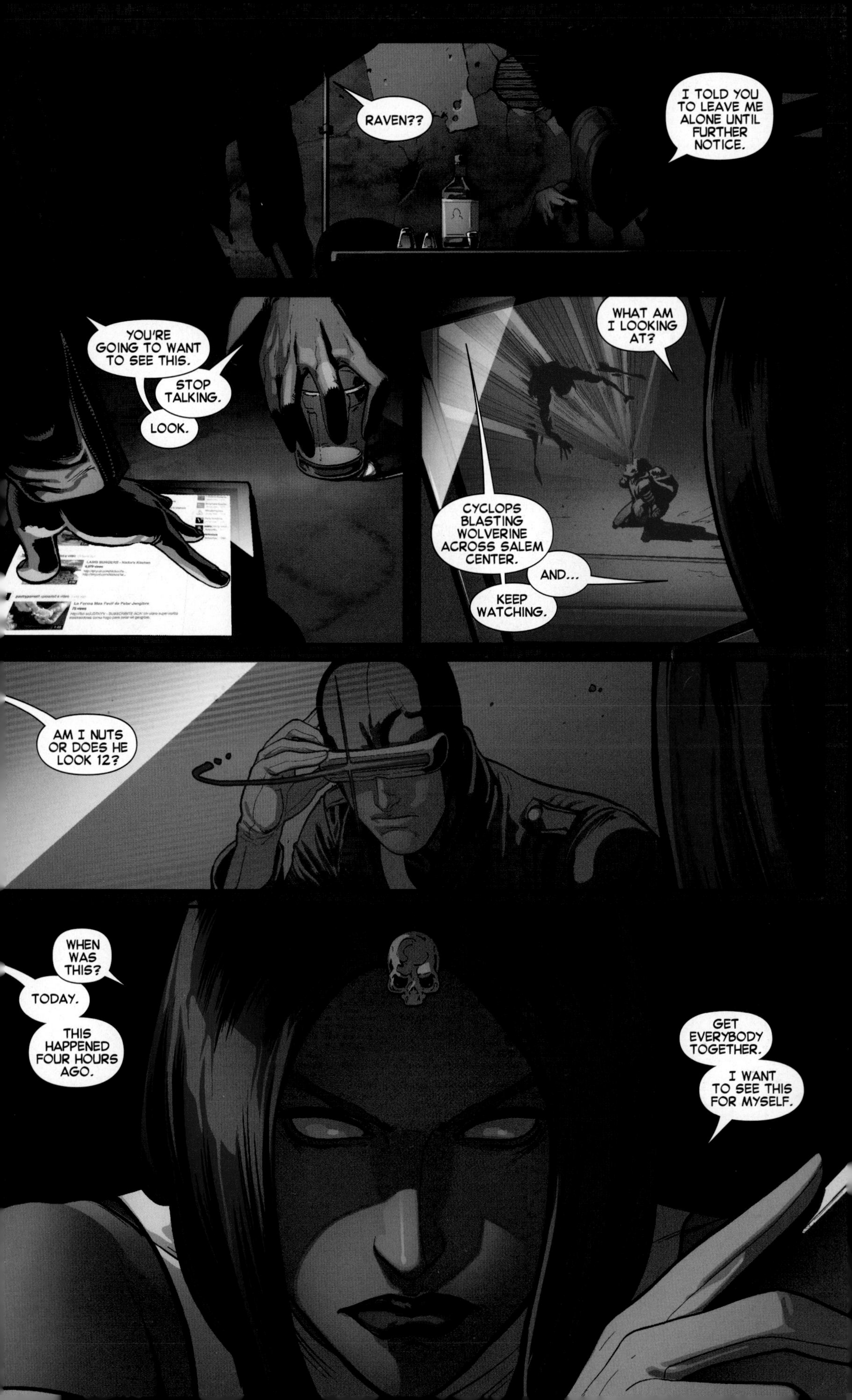
RAVEN??
I TOLD YOU TO LEAVE ME ALONE UNTIL FURTHER NOTICE.
YOU'RE GOING TO WANT TO SEE THIS.
STOP TALKING.
LOOK.
WHAT AM I LOOKING AT?
CYCLOPS BLASTING WOLVERINE ACROSS SALEM CENTER.
AND...
KEEP WATCHING.
AM I NUTS OR DOES HE LOOK 12?
WHEN WAS THIS?
TODAY.
THIS HAPPENED FOUR HOURS AGO.
GET EVERYBODY TOGETHER.
I WANT TO SEE THIS FOR MYSELF.

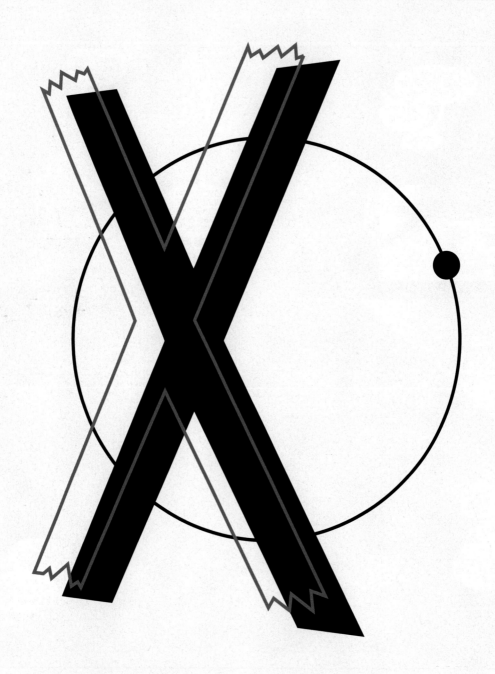

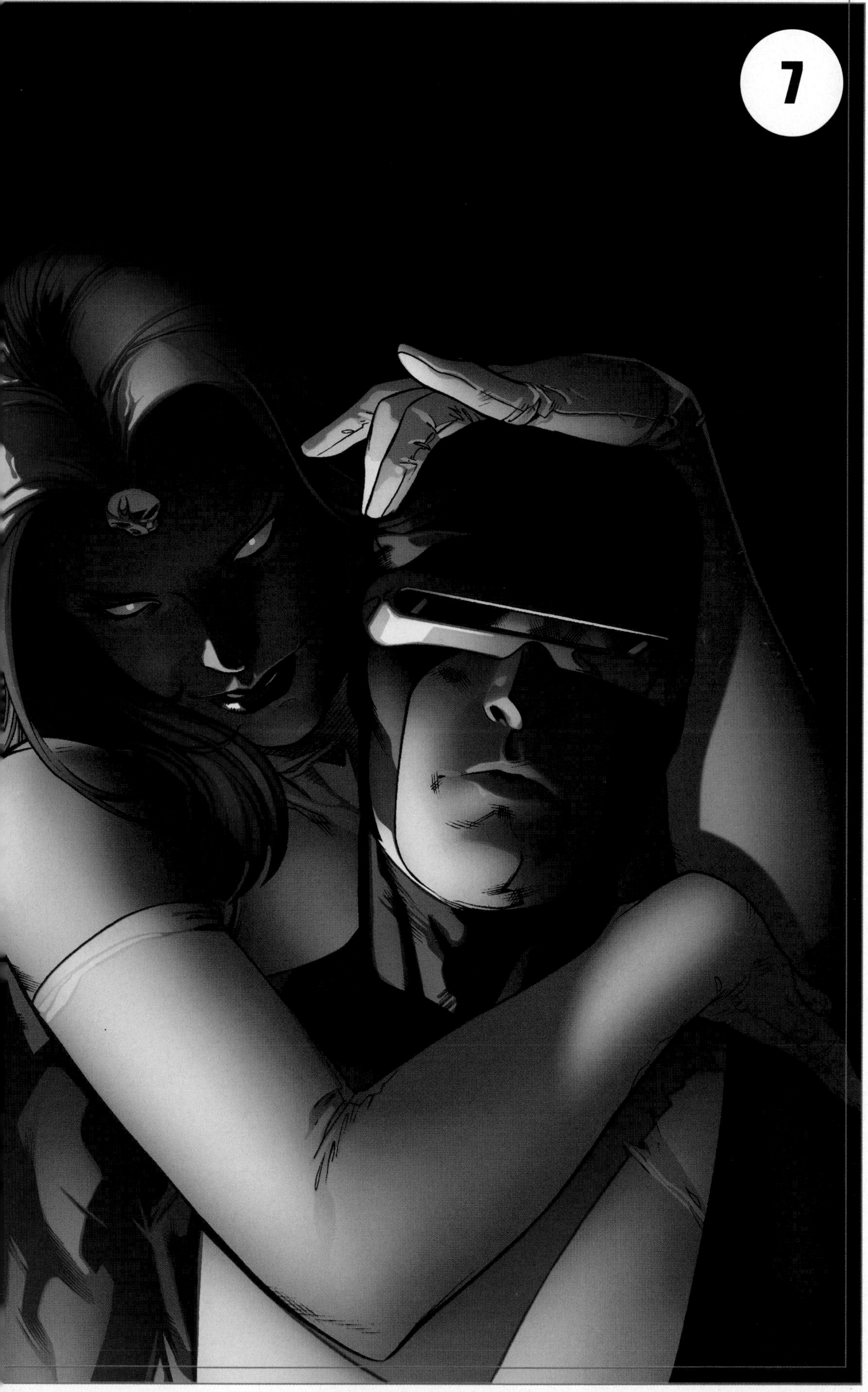
7

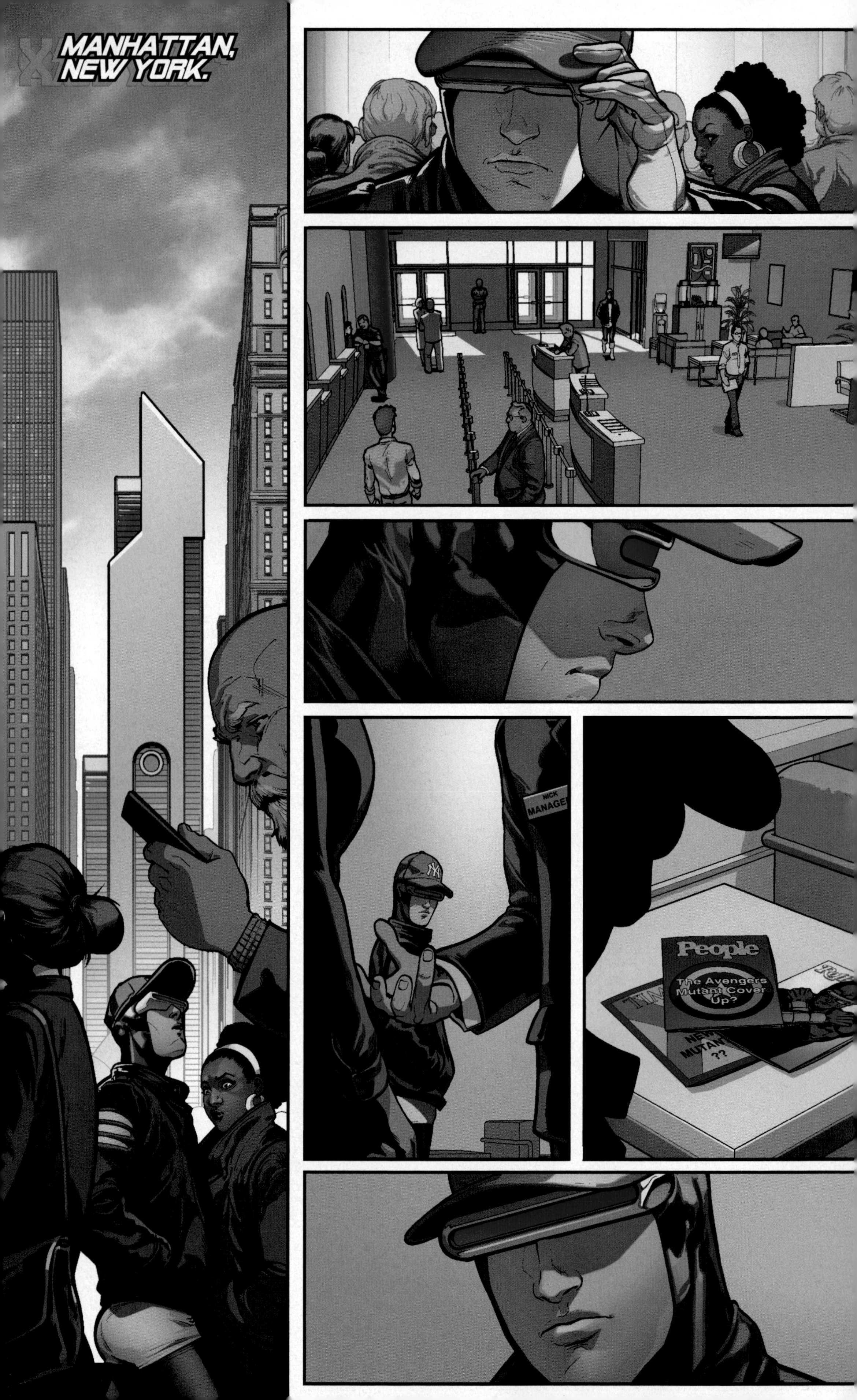
MANHATTAN, NEW YORK.
NICK
MANAGE
People
The Avengers Mutant Cover Up?
NEW MUTANT ??

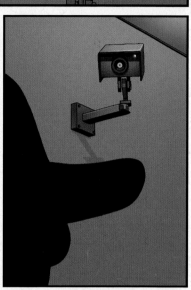

CAN I HELP YOU?

I NEED HELP WITH ONE OF THE SAFETY DEPOSIT BOXES.

SURE. DID YOU BRING YOUR KEYS?

I DIDN'T, ACTUALLY.

DO YOU HAVE TWO FORMS OF IDENTIFICATION?

WELL, SORT OF.

I'M SURE WE CAN--

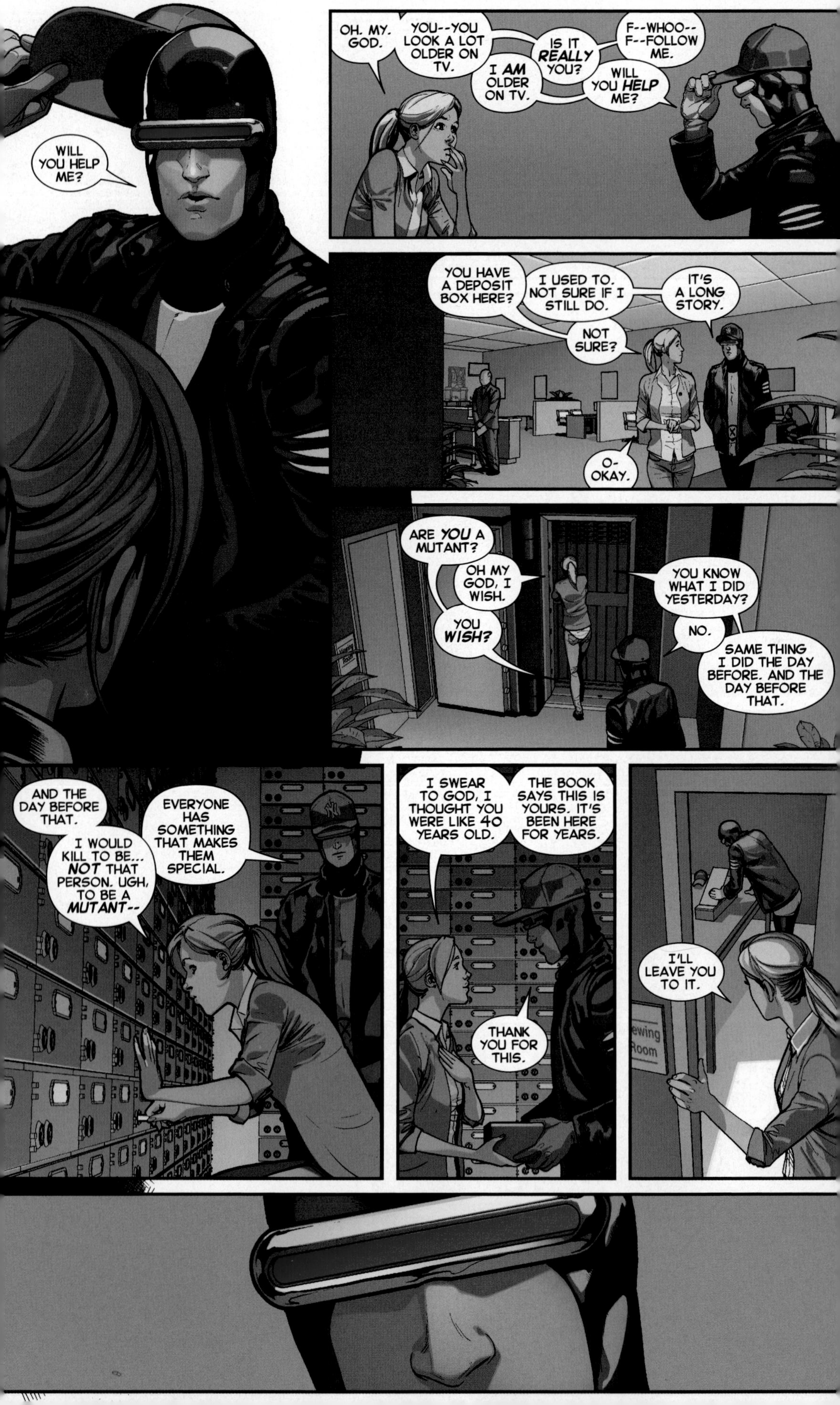
WILL YOU HELP ME?
OH. MY. GOD.
YOU--YOU LOOK A LOT OLDER ON TV.
I AM OLDER ON TV.
IS IT REALLY YOU?
F--WHOO-- F--FOLLOW ME.
WILL YOU HELP ME?
YOU HAVE A DEPOSIT BOX HERE?
I USED TO. NOT SURE IF I STILL DO.
NOT SURE?
IT'S A LONG STORY.
O- OKAY.
ARE YOU A MUTANT?
OH MY GOD, I WISH.
YOU WISH?
YOU KNOW WHAT I DID YESTERDAY?
NO.
SAME THING I DID THE DAY BEFORE. AND THE DAY BEFORE THAT.
AND THE DAY BEFORE THAT.
I WOULD KILL TO BE... NOT THAT PERSON. UGH, TO BE A MUTANT--
EVERYONE HAS SOMETHING THAT MAKES THEM SPECIAL.
I SWEAR TO GOD, I THOUGHT YOU WERE LIKE 40 YEARS OLD.
THE BOOK SAYS THIS IS YOURS. IT'S BEEN HERE FOR YEARS.
THANK YOU FOR THIS.
I'LL LEAVE YOU TO IT.

AGH!

OH... THAT'S BETTER.

THANK YOU, SCOTT SUMMERS.

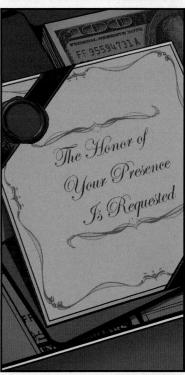

The Honor of Your Presence Is Requested

WHAT IS GOING ON WITH YOU, ALL OF A SUDDEN?

YOU HAVE NO IDEA WHO IS IN THERE RIGHT NOW...

WHO IS IN WHERE?

THE SAFE DEPOSIT BOX ROOM.

WHO?

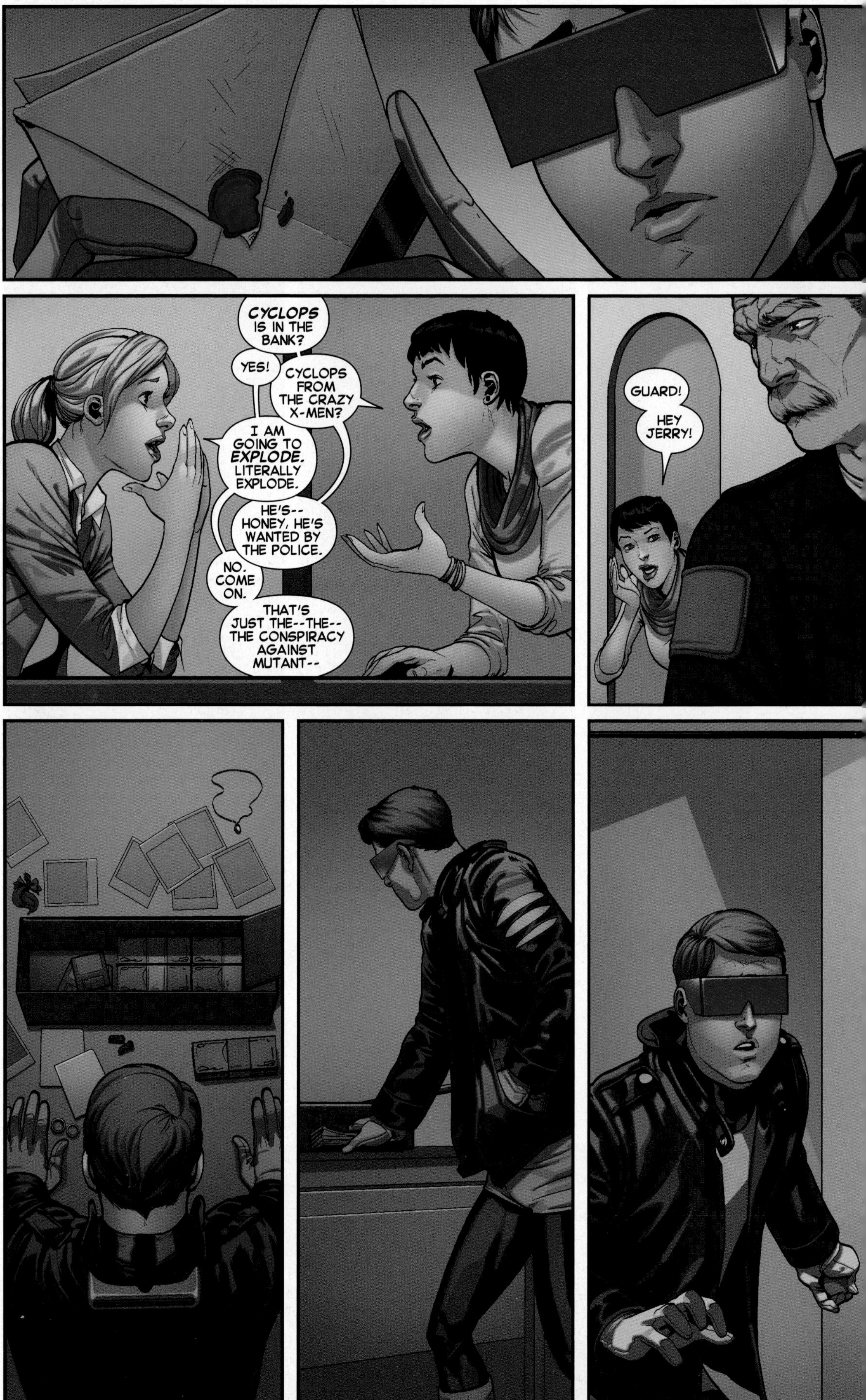
CYCLOPS IS IN THE BANK?
YES!
CYCLOPS FROM THE CRAZY X-MEN?
I AM GOING TO EXPLODE. LITERALLY EXPLODE.
HE'S-- HONEY, HE'S WANTED BY THE POLICE.
NO. COME ON.
THAT'S JUST THE--THE-- THE CONSPIRACY AGAINST MUTANT--
GUARD!
HEY JERRY!

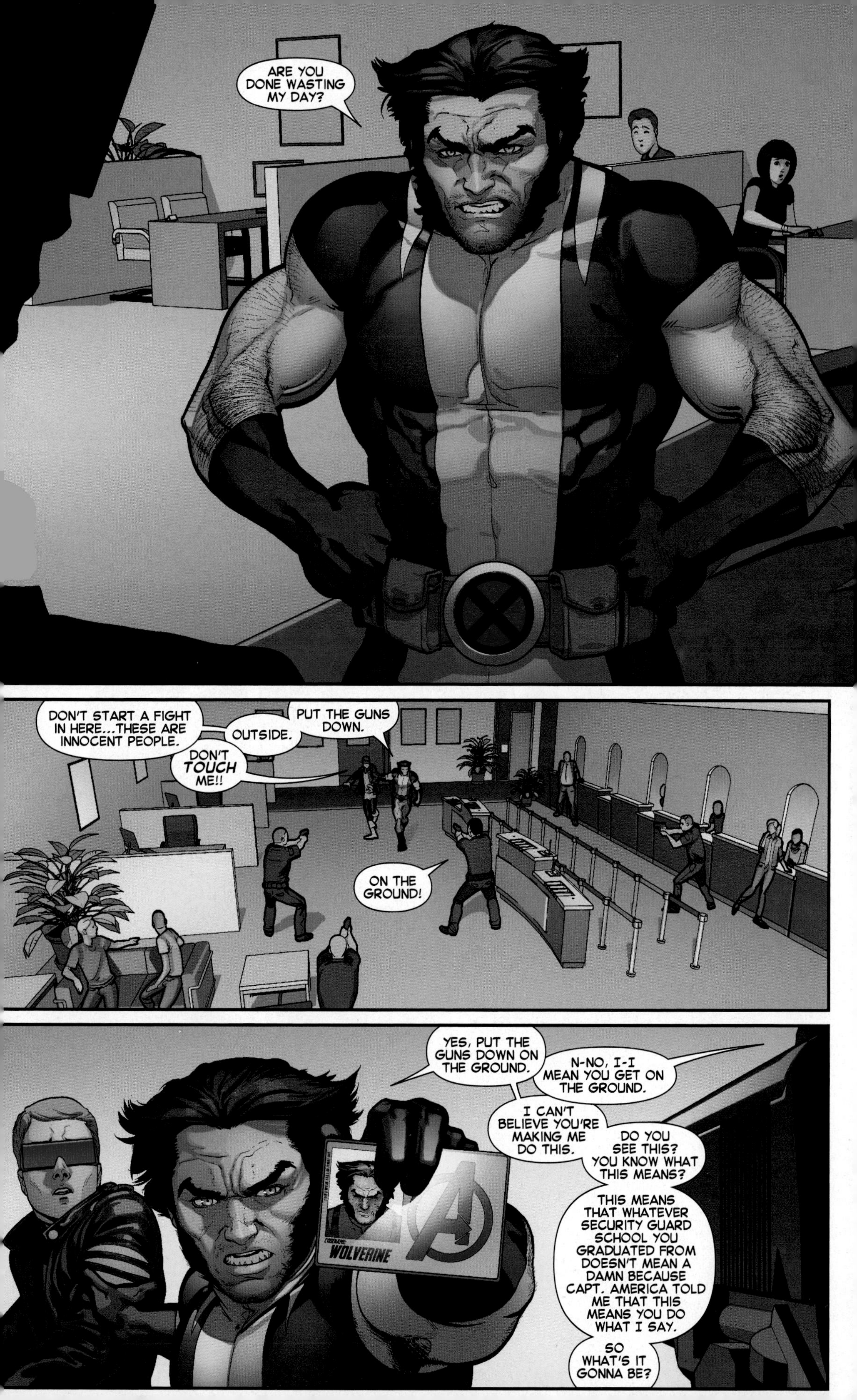
ARE YOU DONE WASTING MY DAY?
DON'T START A FIGHT IN HERE...THESE ARE INNOCENT PEOPLE.
OUTSIDE.
PUT THE GUNS DOWN.
DON'T *TOUCH* ME!!
ON THE GROUND!
YES, PUT THE GUNS DOWN ON THE GROUND.
N-NO, I-I MEAN YOU GET ON THE GROUND.
I CAN'T BELIEVE YOU'RE MAKING ME DO THIS.
DO YOU SEE THIS? YOU KNOW WHAT THIS MEANS?
THIS MEANS THAT WHATEVER SECURITY GUARD SCHOOL YOU GRADUATED FROM DOESN'T MEAN A DAMN BECAUSE CAPT. AMERICA TOLD ME THAT THIS MEANS YOU DO WHAT I SAY.
SO WHAT'S IT GONNA BE?
WOLVERINE

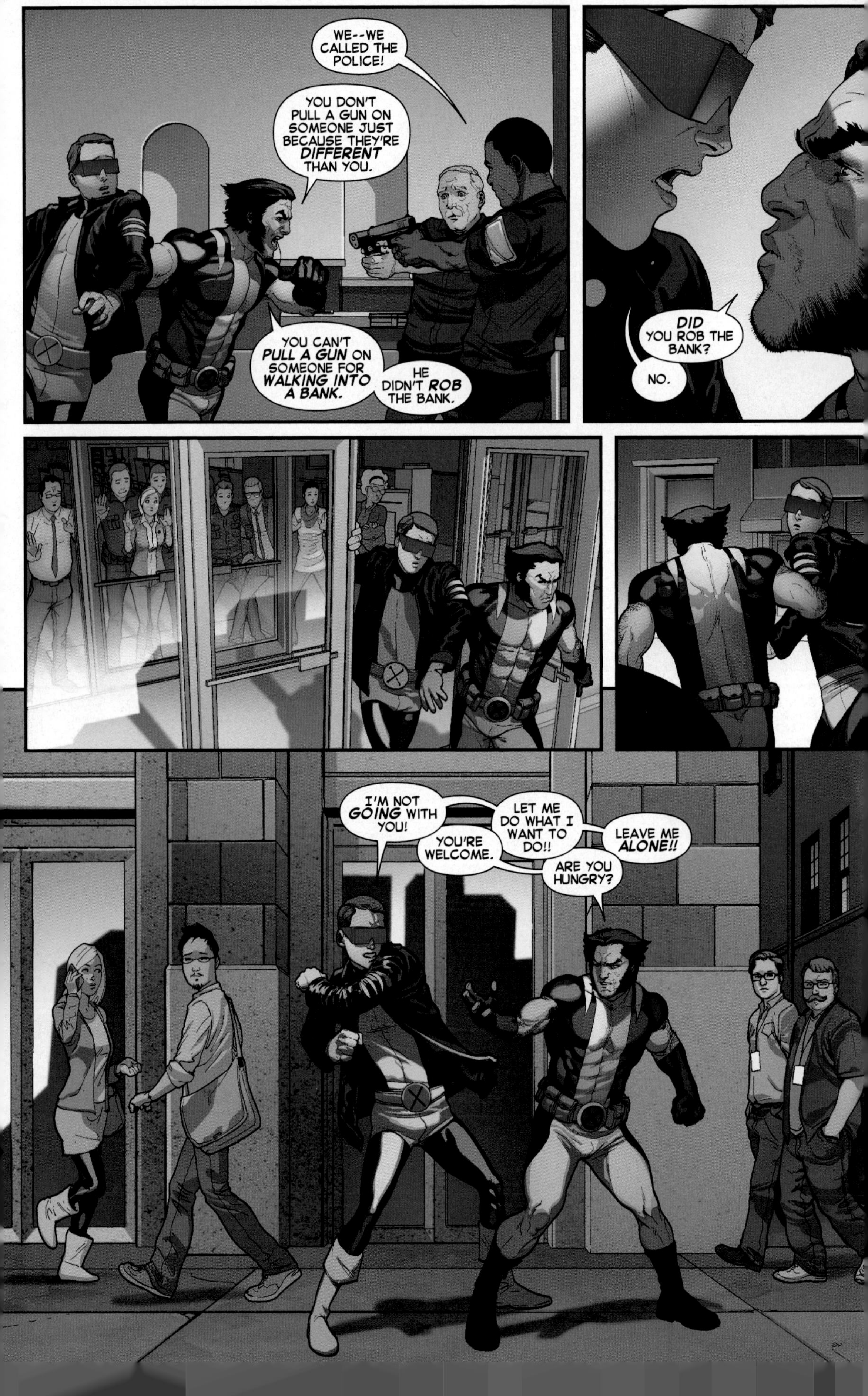

YOU DON'T PULL A GUN ON SOMEONE JUST BECAUSE THEY'RE DIFFERENT THAN YOU.
WE--WE CALLED THE POLICE!
YOU CAN'T PULL A GUN ON SOMEONE FOR WALKING INTO A BANK.
HE DIDN'T ROB THE BANK.
DID YOU ROB THE BANK?
NO.
I'M NOT GOING WITH YOU!
LET ME DO WHAT I WANT TO DO!!
LEAVE ME ALONE!!
YOU'RE WELCOME.
ARE YOU HUNGRY?

SEE, *HE* DIDN'T ROB THE BANK.

SO HERE'S THE DEAL: WE ARE LEAVING.

IF YOU *SHOOT* ME, IT WON'T HURT *ME* AND I WILL CUT OFF YOUR HANDS.

I'LL GO BACK TO WHEREVER I CAME FROM AND YOU WON'T HAVE *HANDS.*

SCOTT, DARLING, NOT EVERYTHING IS WHAT IT SEEMS TO BE.

WHAT DOES THAT MEAN?

C'MERE.

LET *GO* OF ME!!

JUST-- I NEEDED SOMEONE YOU WOULD BELIEVE AND SOMEONE THEY WOULD BE AFRAID OF...

HE WAS MY ONLY CHOICE, REALLY...

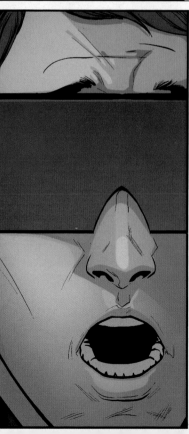

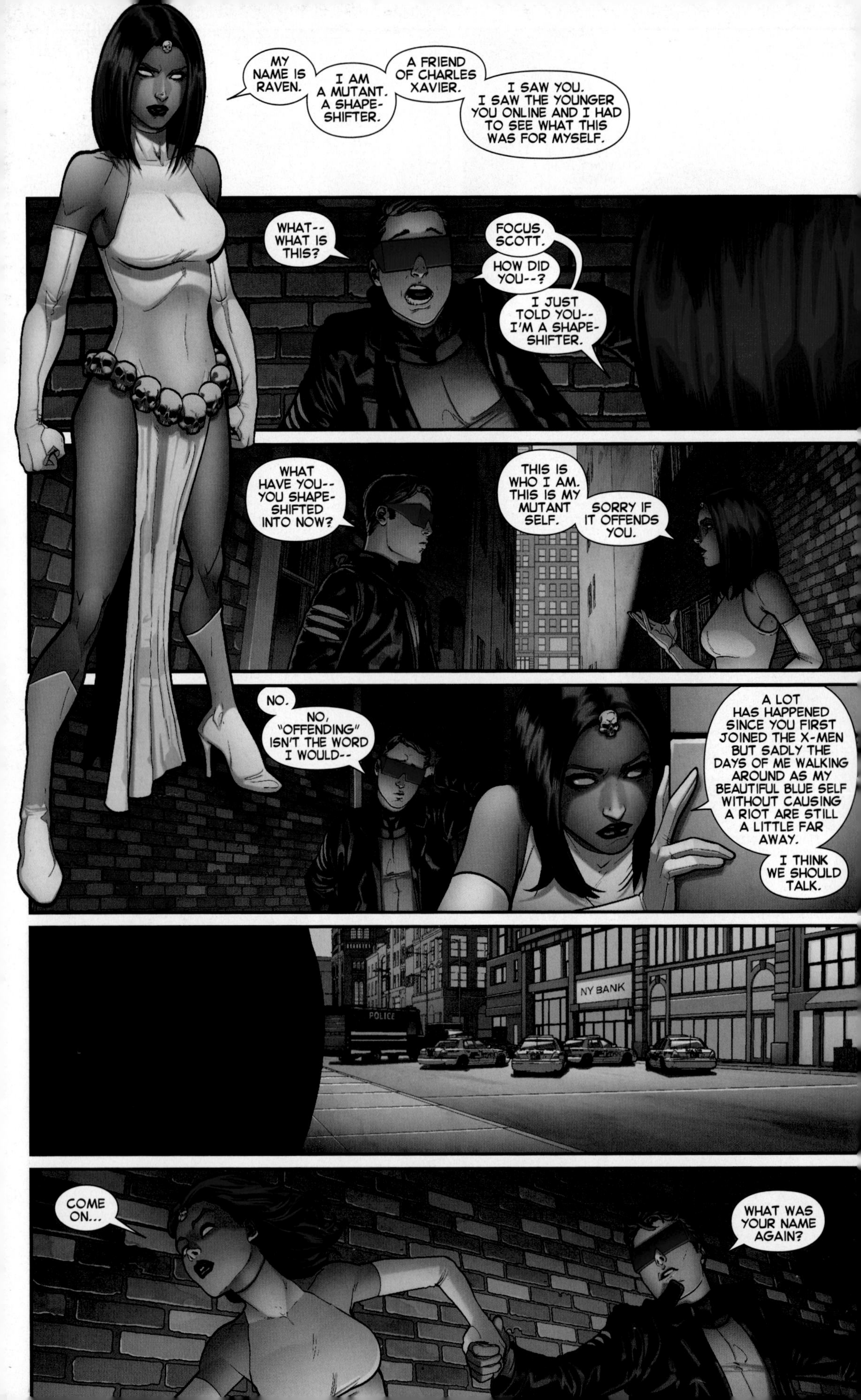
MY NAME IS RAVEN.
I AM A MUTANT. A SHAPE-SHIFTER.
A FRIEND OF CHARLES XAVIER.
I SAW YOU. I SAW THE YOUNGER YOU ONLINE AND I HAD TO SEE WHAT THIS WAS FOR MYSELF.
WHAT-- WHAT IS THIS?
FOCUS, SCOTT.
HOW DID YOU--?
I JUST TOLD YOU-- I'M A SHAPE-SHIFTER.
WHAT HAVE YOU-- YOU SHAPE-SHIFTED INTO NOW?
THIS IS WHO I AM. THIS IS MY MUTANT SELF.
SORRY IF IT OFFENDS YOU.
NO.
NO, "OFFENDING" ISN'T THE WORD I WOULD--
A LOT HAS HAPPENED SINCE YOU FIRST JOINED THE X-MEN BUT SADLY THE DAYS OF ME WALKING AROUND AS MY BEAUTIFUL BLUE SELF WITHOUT CAUSING A RIOT ARE STILL A LITTLE FAR AWAY.
I THINK WE SHOULD TALK.
POLICE
NY BANK
COME ON...
WHAT WAS YOUR NAME AGAIN?

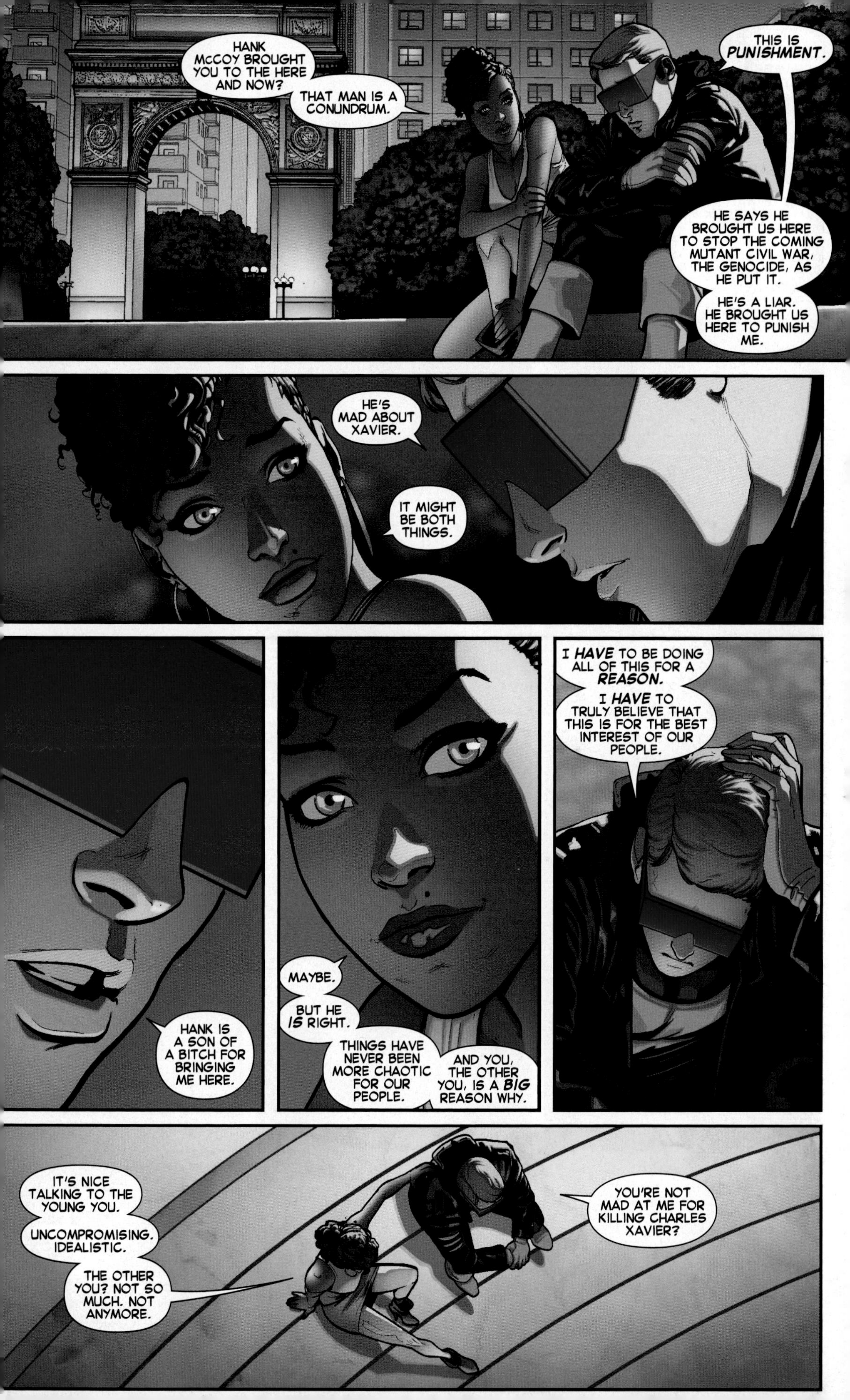
HANK McCOY BROUGHT YOU TO THE HERE AND NOW?
THAT MAN IS A CONUNDRUM.
THIS IS PUNISHMENT.
HE SAYS HE BROUGHT US HERE TO STOP THE COMING MUTANT CIVIL WAR, THE GENOCIDE, AS HE PUT IT.
HE'S A LIAR. HE BROUGHT US HERE TO PUNISH ME.
HE'S MAD ABOUT XAVIER.
IT MIGHT BE BOTH THINGS.
HANK IS A SON OF A BITCH FOR BRINGING ME HERE.
MAYBE.
BUT HE IS RIGHT.
THINGS HAVE NEVER BEEN MORE CHAOTIC FOR OUR PEOPLE.
AND YOU, THE OTHER YOU, IS A BIG REASON WHY.
I HAVE TO BE DOING ALL OF THIS FOR A REASON.
I HAVE TO TRULY BELIEVE THAT THIS IS FOR THE BEST INTEREST OF OUR PEOPLE.
IT'S NICE TALKING TO THE YOUNG YOU.
UNCOMPROMISING. IDEALISTIC.
THE OTHER YOU? NOT SO MUCH. NOT ANYMORE.
YOU'RE NOT MAD AT ME FOR KILLING CHARLES XAVIER?

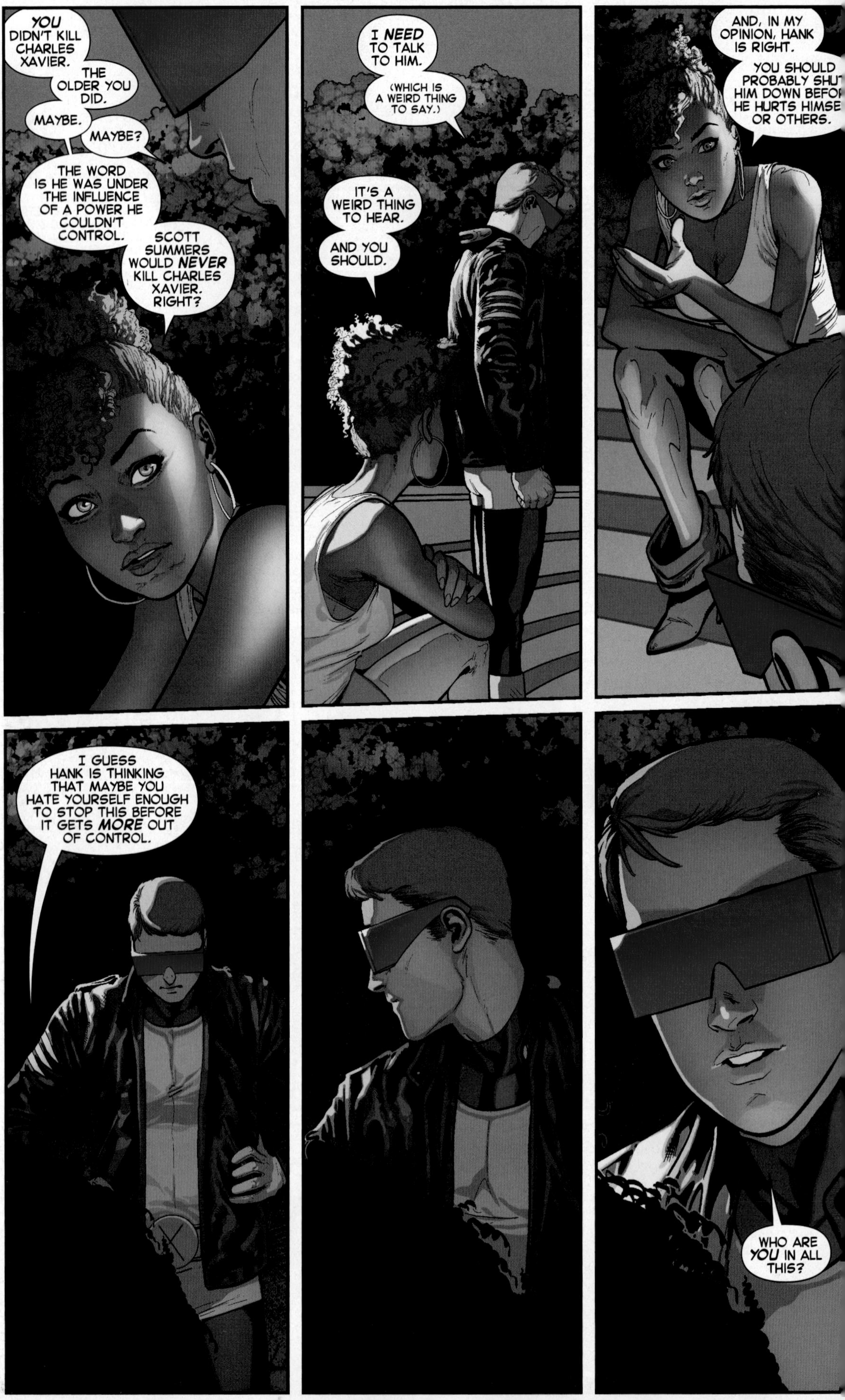
YOU DIDN'T KILL CHARLES XAVIER.
THE OLDER YOU DID.
MAYBE.
MAYBE?
THE WORD IS HE WAS UNDER THE INFLUENCE OF A POWER HE COULDN'T CONTROL.
SCOTT SUMMERS WOULD NEVER KILL CHARLES XAVIER. RIGHT?
I NEED TO TALK TO HIM.
(WHICH IS A WEIRD THING TO SAY.)
IT'S A WEIRD THING TO HEAR.
AND YOU SHOULD.
AND, IN MY OPINION, HANK IS RIGHT.
YOU SHOULD PROBABLY SHUT HIM DOWN BEFOR HE HURTS HIMSE OR OTHERS.
I GUESS HANK IS THINKING THAT MAYBE YOU HATE YOURSELF ENOUGH TO STOP THIS BEFORE IT GETS MORE OUT OF CONTROL.
WHO ARE YOU IN ALL THIS?

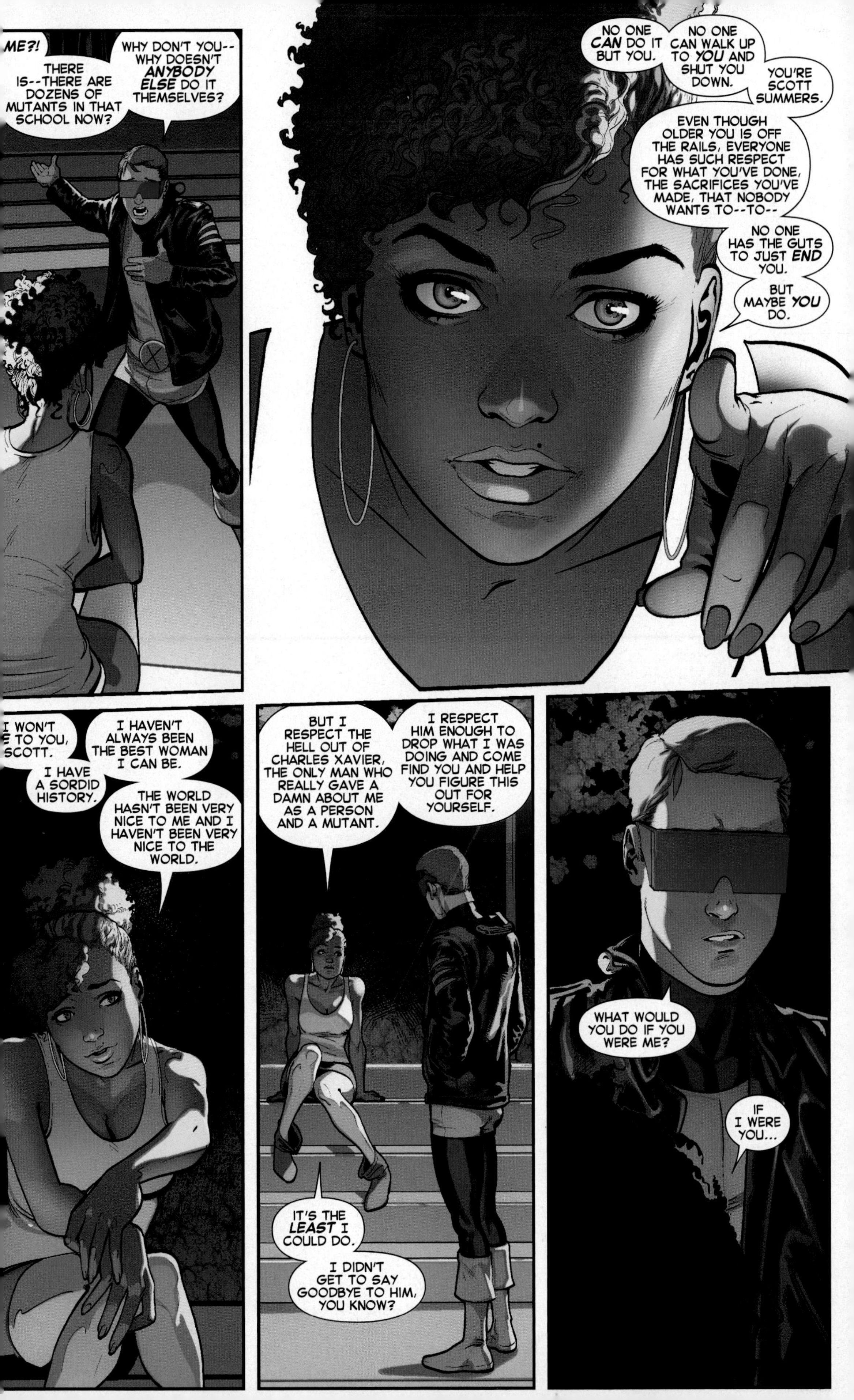
ME?!
THERE IS--THERE ARE DOZENS OF MUTANTS IN THAT SCHOOL NOW?
WHY DON'T YOU--WHY DOESN'T ANYBODY ELSE DO IT THEMSELVES?
NO ONE CAN DO IT BUT YOU.
NO ONE CAN WALK UP TO YOU AND SHUT YOU DOWN.
YOU'RE SCOTT SUMMERS.
EVEN THOUGH OLDER YOU IS OFF THE RAILS, EVERYONE HAS SUCH RESPECT FOR WHAT YOU'VE DONE, THE SACRIFICES YOU'VE MADE, THAT NOBODY WANTS TO--TO--
NO ONE HAS THE GUTS TO JUST END YOU.
BUT MAYBE YOU DO.
I WON'T TO YOU, SCOTT.
I HAVE A SORDID HISTORY.
I HAVEN'T ALWAYS BEEN THE BEST WOMAN I CAN BE.
THE WORLD HASN'T BEEN VERY NICE TO ME AND I HAVEN'T BEEN VERY NICE TO THE WORLD.
BUT I RESPECT THE HELL OUT OF CHARLES XAVIER, THE ONLY MAN WHO REALLY GAVE A DAMN ABOUT ME AS A PERSON AND A MUTANT.
I RESPECT HIM ENOUGH TO DROP WHAT I WAS DOING AND COME FIND YOU AND HELP YOU FIGURE THIS OUT FOR YOURSELF.
IT'S THE LEAST I COULD DO.
I DIDN'T GET TO SAY GOODBYE TO HIM, YOU KNOW?
WHAT WOULD YOU DO IF YOU WERE ME?
IF I WERE YOU...

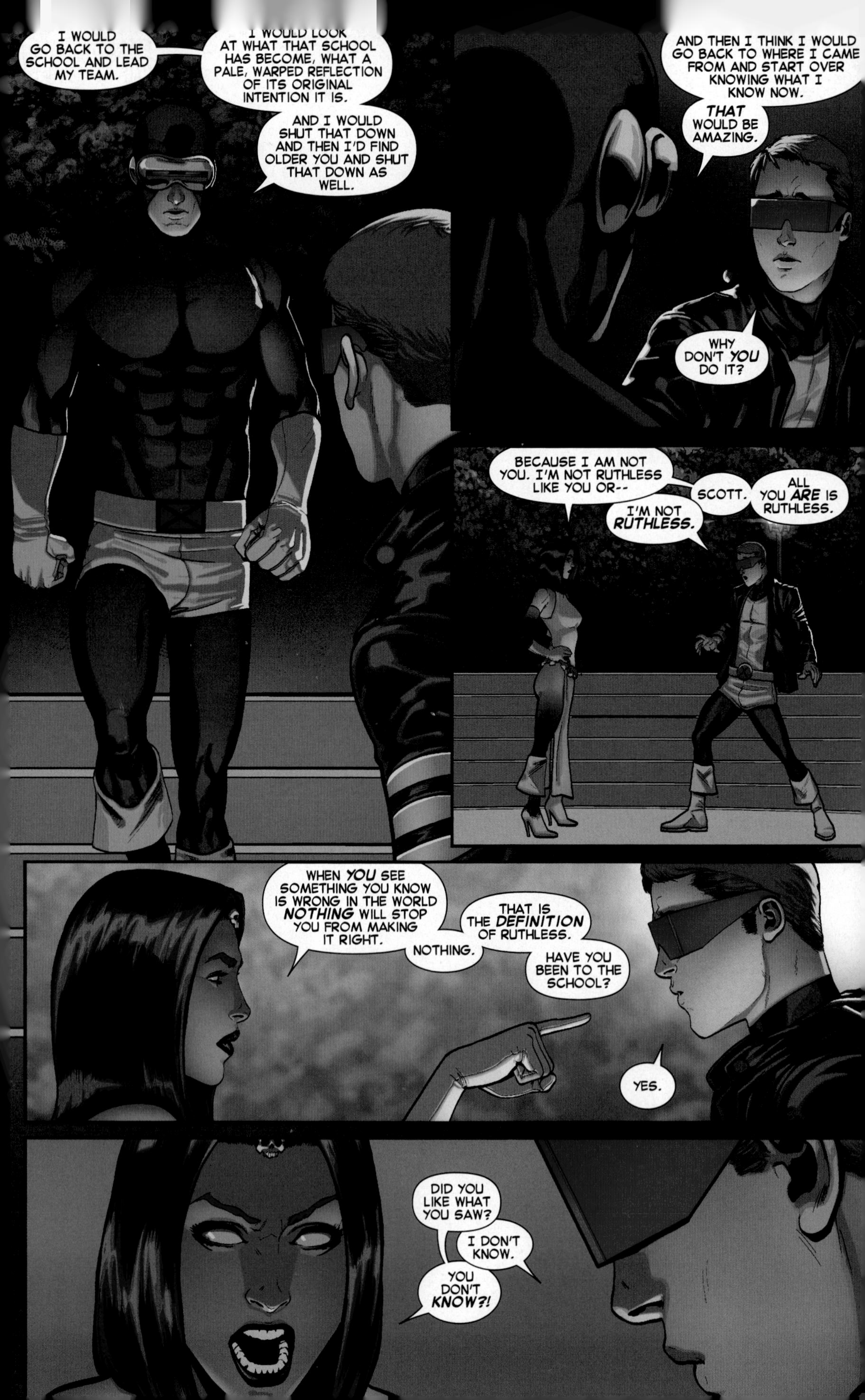
I WOULD GO BACK TO THE SCHOOL AND LEAD MY TEAM.
I WOULD LOOK AT WHAT THAT SCHOOL HAS BECOME, WHAT A PALE, WARPED REFLECTION OF ITS ORIGINAL INTENTION IT IS.
AND I WOULD SHUT THAT DOWN AND THEN I'D FIND OLDER YOU AND SHUT THAT DOWN AS WELL.
AND THEN I THINK I WOULD GO BACK TO WHERE I CAME FROM AND START OVER KNOWING WHAT I KNOW NOW.
THAT WOULD BE AMAZING.
WHY DON'T YOU DO IT?
BECAUSE I AM NOT YOU. I'M NOT RUTHLESS LIKE YOU OR--
SCOTT.
ALL YOU ARE IS RUTHLESS.
I'M NOT RUTHLESS.
WHEN YOU SEE SOMETHING YOU KNOW IS WRONG IN THE WORLD NOTHING WILL STOP YOU FROM MAKING IT RIGHT.
NOTHING.
THAT IS THE DEFINITION OF RUTHLESS.
HAVE YOU BEEN TO THE SCHOOL?
YES.
DID YOU LIKE WHAT YOU SAW?
I DON'T KNOW.
YOU DON'T KNOW?!

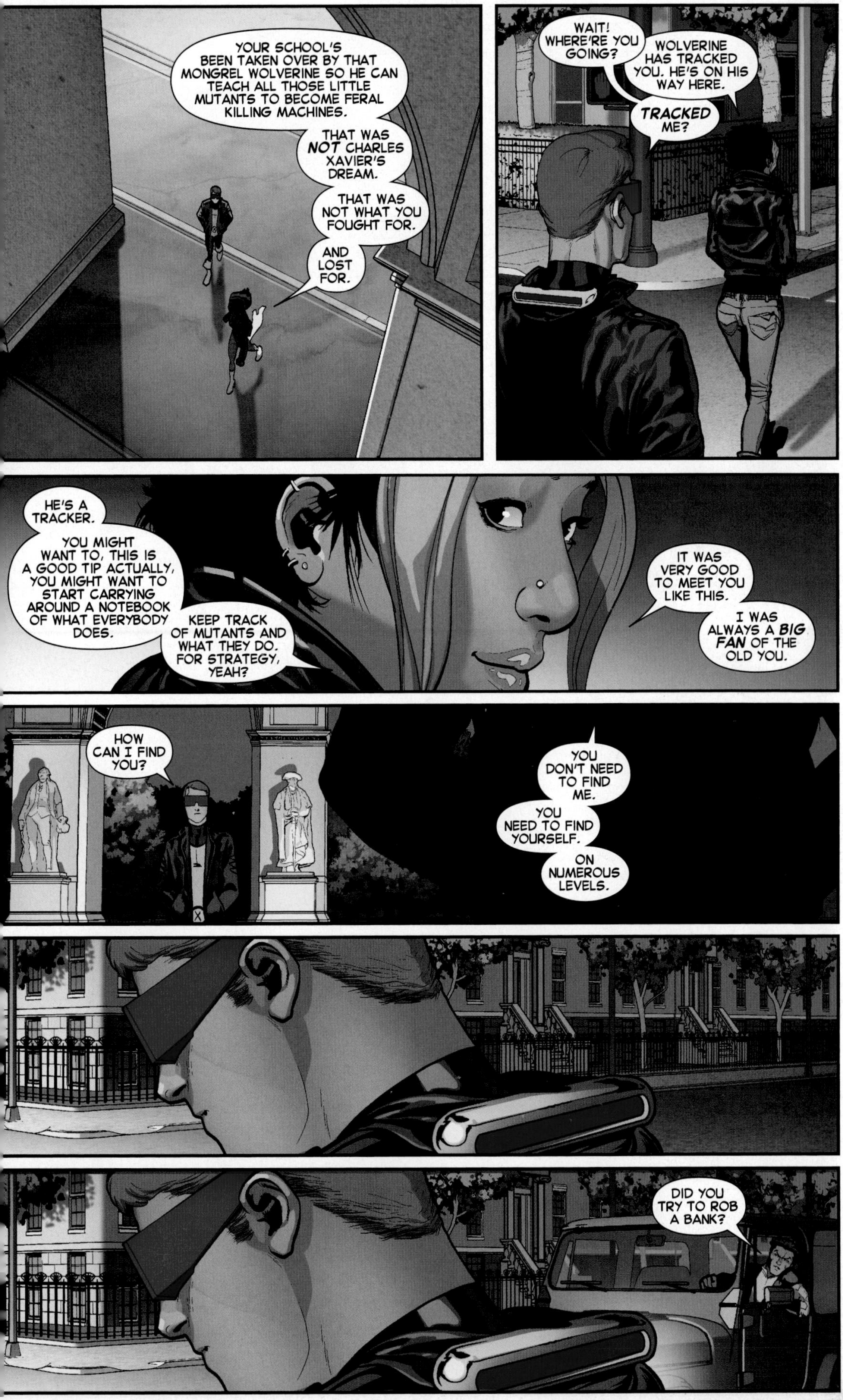
YOUR SCHOOL'S BEEN TAKEN OVER BY THAT MONGREL WOLVERINE SO HE CAN TEACH ALL THOSE LITTLE MUTANTS TO BECOME FERAL KILLING MACHINES.
THAT WAS NOT CHARLES XAVIER'S DREAM.
THAT WAS NOT WHAT YOU FOUGHT FOR.
AND LOST FOR.
WAIT! WHERE'RE YOU GOING?
WOLVERINE HAS TRACKED YOU. HE'S ON HIS WAY HERE.
TRACKED ME?
HE'S A TRACKER.
YOU MIGHT WANT TO, THIS IS A GOOD TIP ACTUALLY, YOU MIGHT WANT TO START CARRYING AROUND A NOTEBOOK OF WHAT EVERYBODY DOES.
KEEP TRACK OF MUTANTS AND WHAT THEY DO. FOR STRATEGY, YEAH?
IT WAS VERY GOOD TO MEET YOU LIKE THIS.
I WAS ALWAYS A BIG FAN OF THE OLD YOU.
HOW CAN I FIND YOU?
YOU DON'T NEED TO FIND ME.
YOU NEED TO FIND YOURSELF.
ON NUMEROUS LEVELS.
DID YOU TRY TO ROB A BANK?

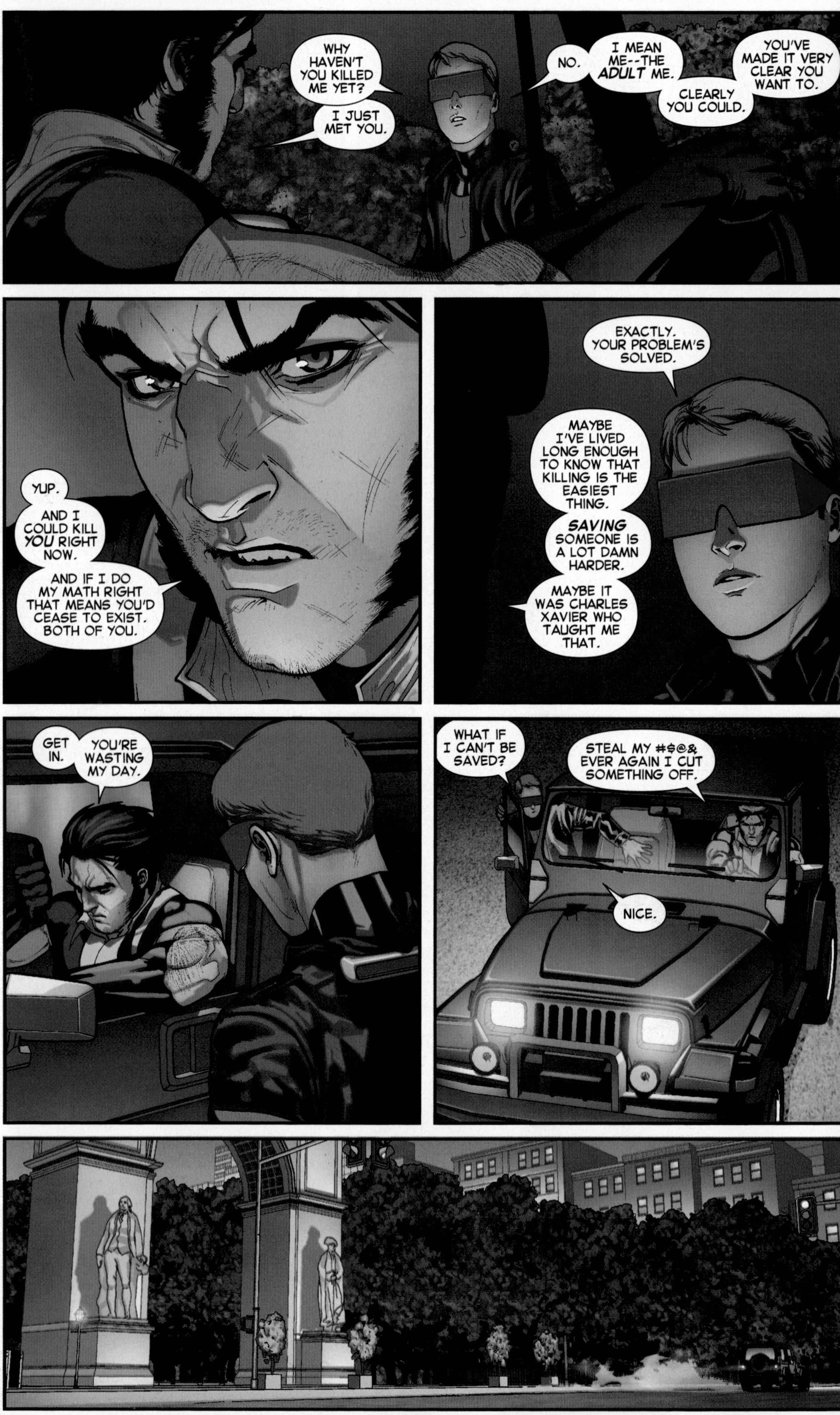
WHY HAVEN'T YOU KILLED ME YET?
I JUST MET YOU.
NO.
I MEAN ME--THE ADULT ME.
CLEARLY YOU COULD.
YOU'VE MADE IT VERY CLEAR YOU WANT TO.
YUP.
AND I COULD KILL YOU RIGHT NOW.
AND IF I DO MY MATH RIGHT THAT MEANS YOU'D CEASE TO EXIST. BOTH OF YOU.
EXACTLY. YOUR PROBLEM'S SOLVED.
MAYBE I'VE LIVED LONG ENOUGH TO KNOW THAT KILLING IS THE EASIEST THING.
SAVING SOMEONE IS A LOT DAMN HARDER.
MAYBE IT WAS CHARLES XAVIER WHO TAUGHT ME THAT.
GET IN.
YOU'RE WASTING MY DAY.
WHAT IF I CAN'T BE SAVED?
STEAL MY #$@& EVER AGAIN I CUT SOMETHING OFF.
NICE.

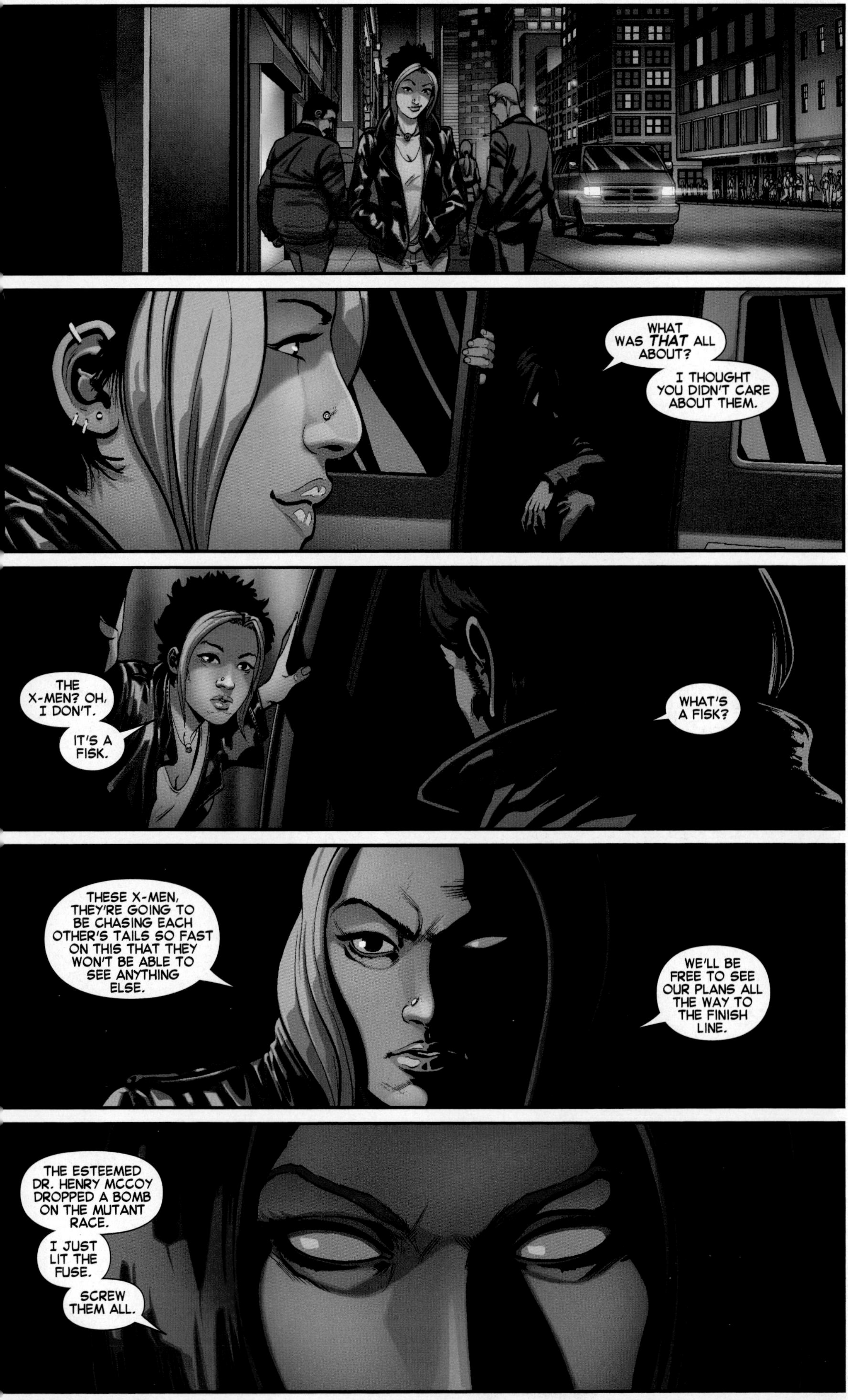
WHAT WAS *THAT* ALL ABOUT?
I THOUGHT YOU DIDN'T CARE ABOUT THEM.
THE X-MEN? OH, I DON'T.
IT'S A FISK.
WHAT'S A FISK?
THESE X-MEN, THEY'RE GOING TO BE CHASING EACH OTHER'S TAILS SO FAST ON THIS THAT THEY WON'T BE ABLE TO SEE ANYTHING ELSE.
WE'LL BE FREE TO SEE OUR PLANS ALL THE WAY TO THE FINISH LINE.
THE ESTEEMED DR. HENRY MCCOY DROPPED A BOMB ON THE MUTANT RACE.
I JUST LIT THE FUSE.
SCREW THEM ALL.

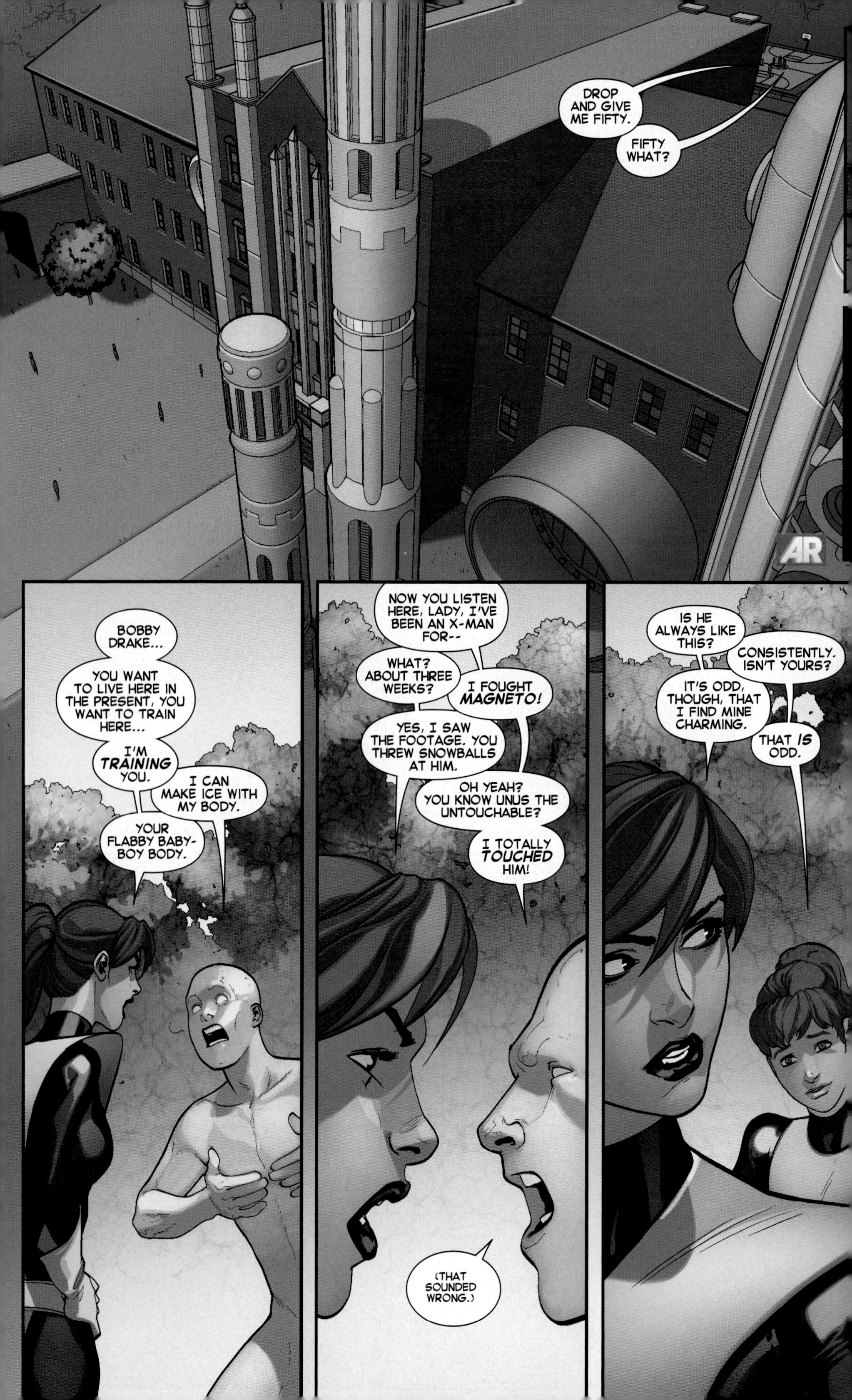
DROP AND GIVE ME FIFTY.
FIFTY WHAT?
BOBBY DRAKE...
YOU WANT TO LIVE HERE IN THE PRESENT, YOU WANT TO TRAIN HERE...
I'M *TRAINING* YOU.
I CAN MAKE ICE WITH MY BODY.
YOUR FLABBY BABY-BOY BODY.
NOW YOU LISTEN HERE, LADY, I'VE BEEN AN X-MAN FOR--
WHAT? ABOUT THREE WEEKS?
I FOUGHT *MAGNETO!*
YES, I SAW THE FOOTAGE. YOU THREW SNOWBALLS AT HIM.
OH YEAH? YOU KNOW UNUS THE UNTOUCHABLE?
I TOTALLY *TOUCHED* HIM!
(THAT SOUNDED WRONG.)
IS HE ALWAYS LIKE THIS?
CONSISTENTLY. ISN'T YOURS?
IT'S ODD, THOUGH, THAT I FIND MINE CHARMING.
THAT *IS* ODD.

TRAINING TIME.

I'M KITTY PRYDE, YOUR NEW INSTRUCTOR.

LET'S GET FIFTY PUSH-UPS IN TO WARM UP.

WARM UP?!! FIFTY PUSH-UPS IS THE *WARM UP?!*

WHERE'S WARREN AND SCOTT?

THEY'LL GET THEIRS.

TELL YOU WHAT, HOT SHOT.

YOU TAKE A SWING AT ME, RIGHT HERE, NO POWERS... CONNECT ONE...

AND I'LL NEVER BUG YOU WITH TRAINING AGAIN.

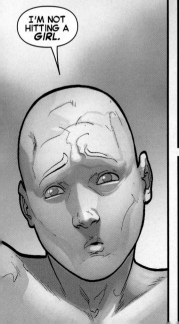

I'M NOT HITTING A *GIRL*.

I'M NOT A GIRL, I'M A *FIERCE COMPETITOR*, YOU SEXIST TWIT.

DON'T CALL ME A--

I KNEW HANK HERE WAS THE SMART ONE... I DIDN'T REALIZE YOU WERE ACTUALLY THE DUMB ONE.

DON'T. LISTEN, HEY. DON'T CALL ME--

DROP AND GIVE ME FIFTY OR SHOW ME YOU CAN FIGHT LIKE A MAN, ICE BOY.

DON'T CALL ME--

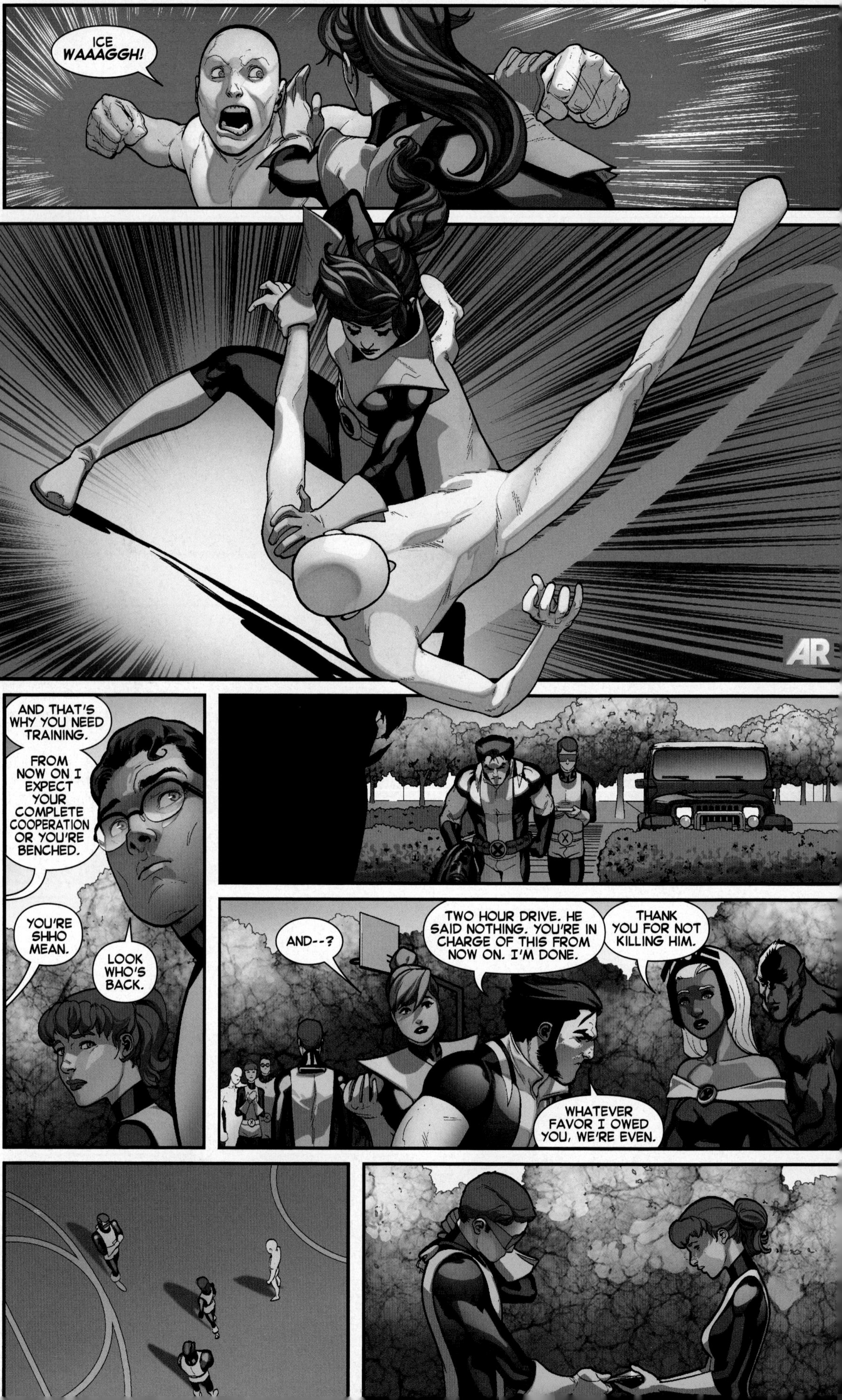
ICE
WAAAGGH!
AND THAT'S WHY YOU NEED TRAINING.
FROM NOW ON I EXPECT YOUR COMPLETE COOPERATION OR YOU'RE BENCHED.
YOU'RE SHHO MEAN.
LOOK WHO'S BACK.
AND--?
TWO HOUR DRIVE. HE SAID NOTHING. YOU'RE IN CHARGE OF THIS FROM NOW ON. I'M DONE.
THANK YOU FOR NOT KILLING HIM.
WHATEVER FAVOR I OWED YOU, WE'RE EVEN.

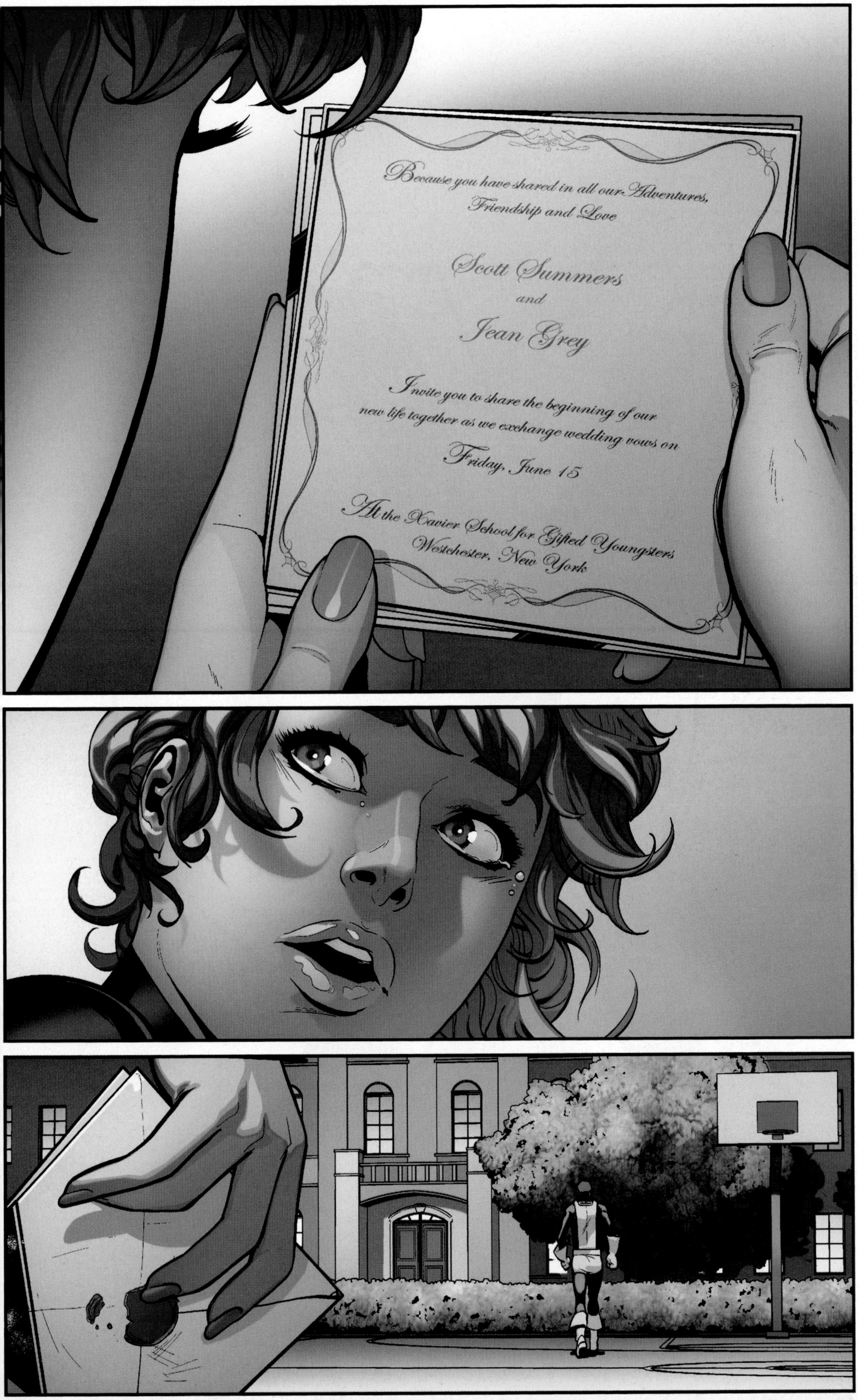
Because you have shared in all our Adventures, Friendship and Love
Scott Summers
and
Jean Grey
Invite you to share the beginning of our new life together as we exchange wedding vows on
Friday, June 15
At the Xavier School for Gifted Youngsters
Westchester, New York

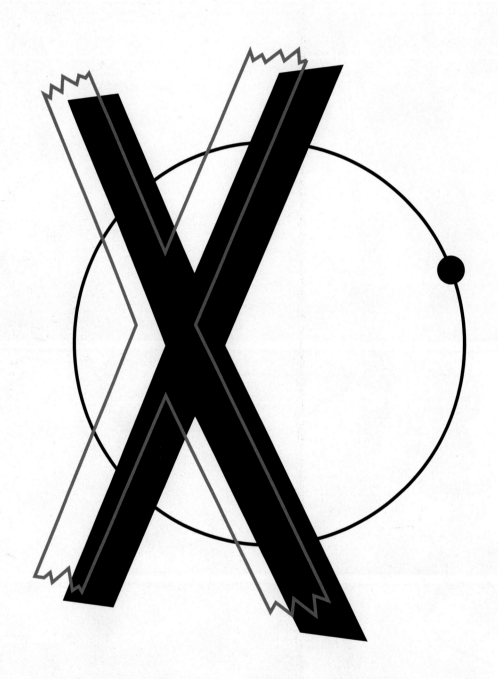

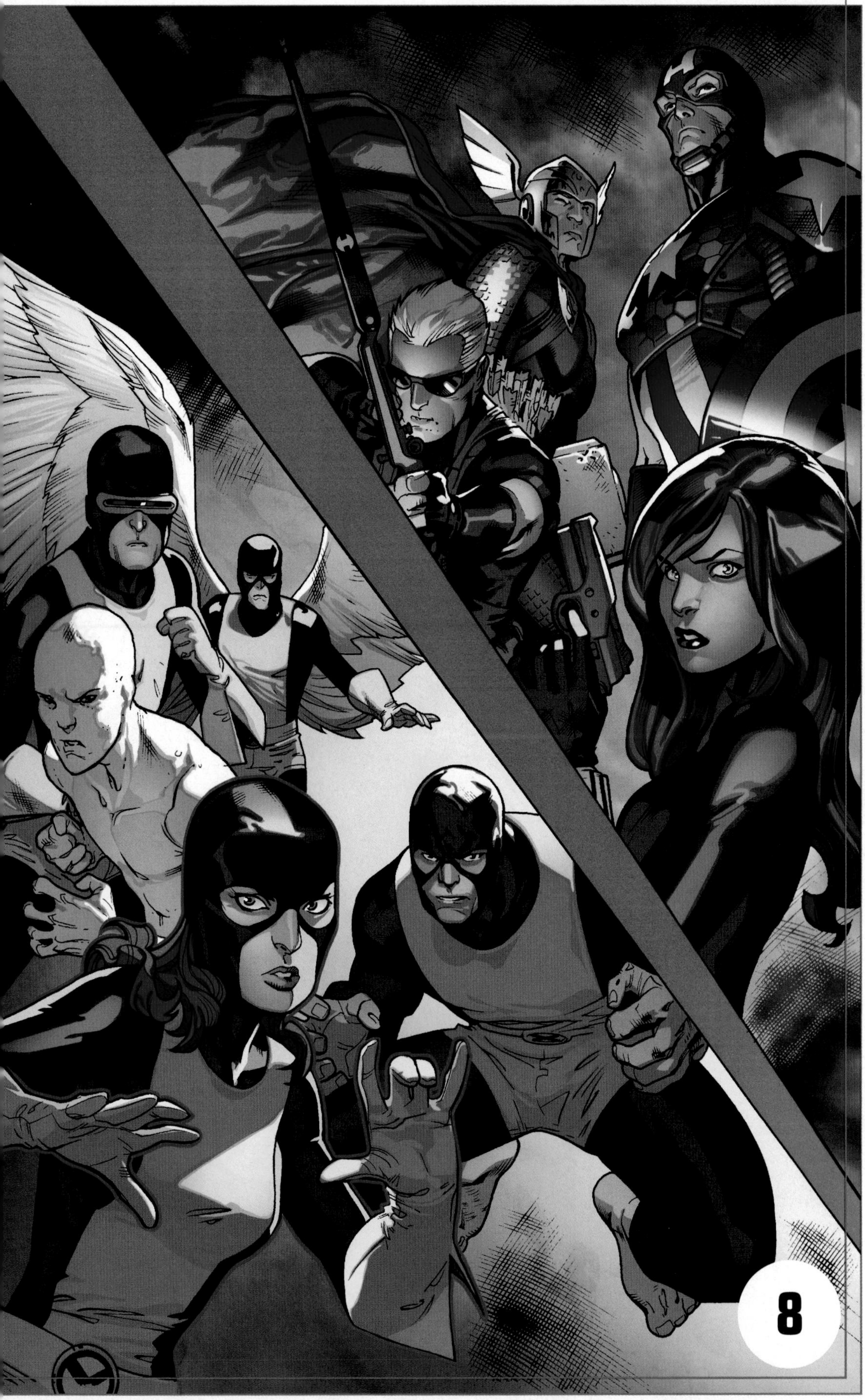

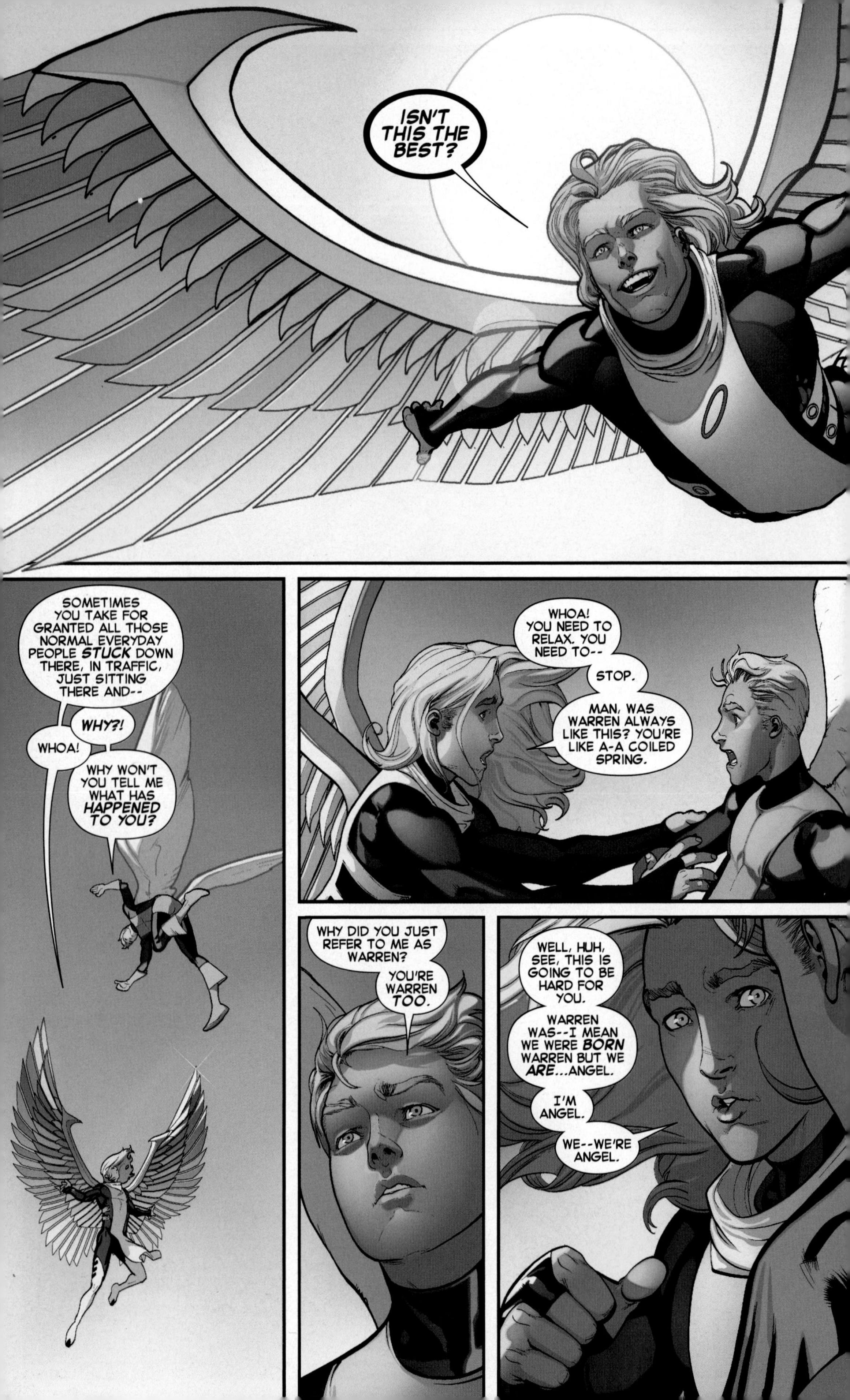
ISN'T THIS THE BEST?
SOMETIMES YOU TAKE FOR GRANTED ALL THOSE NORMAL EVERYDAY PEOPLE STUCK DOWN THERE, IN TRAFFIC, JUST SITTING THERE AND--
WHY?!
WHOA!
WHY WON'T YOU TELL ME WHAT HAS HAPPENED TO YOU?
WHOA! YOU NEED TO RELAX. YOU NEED TO--
STOP.
MAN, WAS WARREN ALWAYS LIKE THIS? YOU'RE LIKE A-A COILED SPRING.
WHY DID YOU JUST REFER TO ME AS WARREN?
YOU'RE WARREN TOO.
WELL, HUH, SEE, THIS IS GOING TO BE HARD FOR YOU.
WARREN WAS--I MEAN WE WERE BORN WARREN BUT WE ARE...ANGEL.
I'M ANGEL.
WE--WE'RE ANGEL.

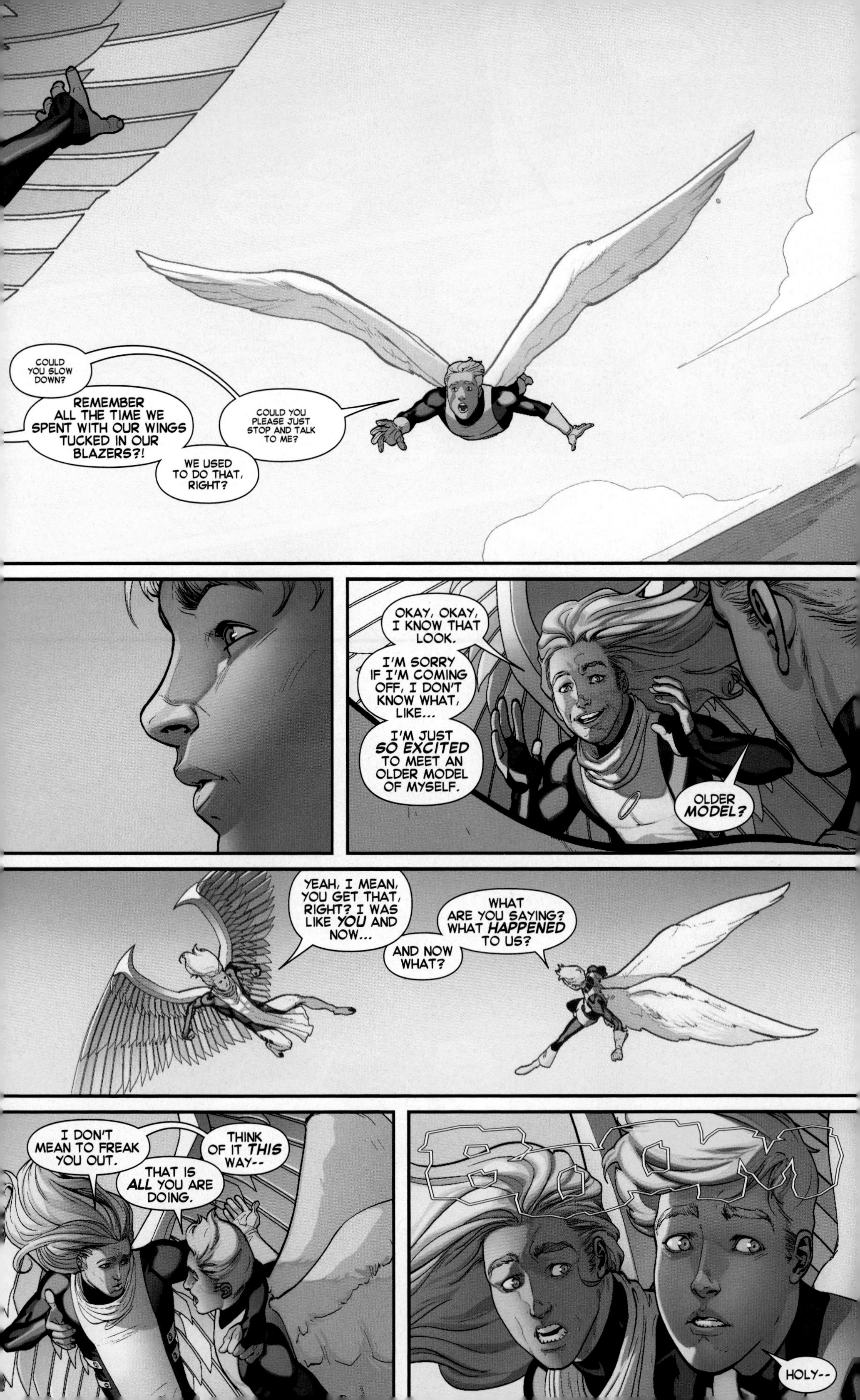
COULD YOU SLOW DOWN?
REMEMBER ALL THE TIME WE SPENT WITH OUR WINGS TUCKED IN OUR BLAZERS?!
WE USED TO DO THAT, RIGHT?
COULD YOU PLEASE JUST STOP AND TALK TO ME?
OKAY, OKAY, I KNOW THAT LOOK.
I'M SORRY IF I'M COMING OFF, I DON'T KNOW WHAT, LIKE...
I'M JUST SO EXCITED TO MEET AN OLDER MODEL OF MYSELF.
OLDER MODEL?
YEAH, I MEAN, YOU GET THAT, RIGHT? I WAS LIKE YOU AND NOW...
AND NOW WHAT?
WHAT ARE YOU SAYING? WHAT HAPPENED TO US?
I DON'T MEAN TO FREAK YOU OUT.
THAT IS ALL YOU ARE DOING.
THINK OF IT THIS WAY--
HOLY--

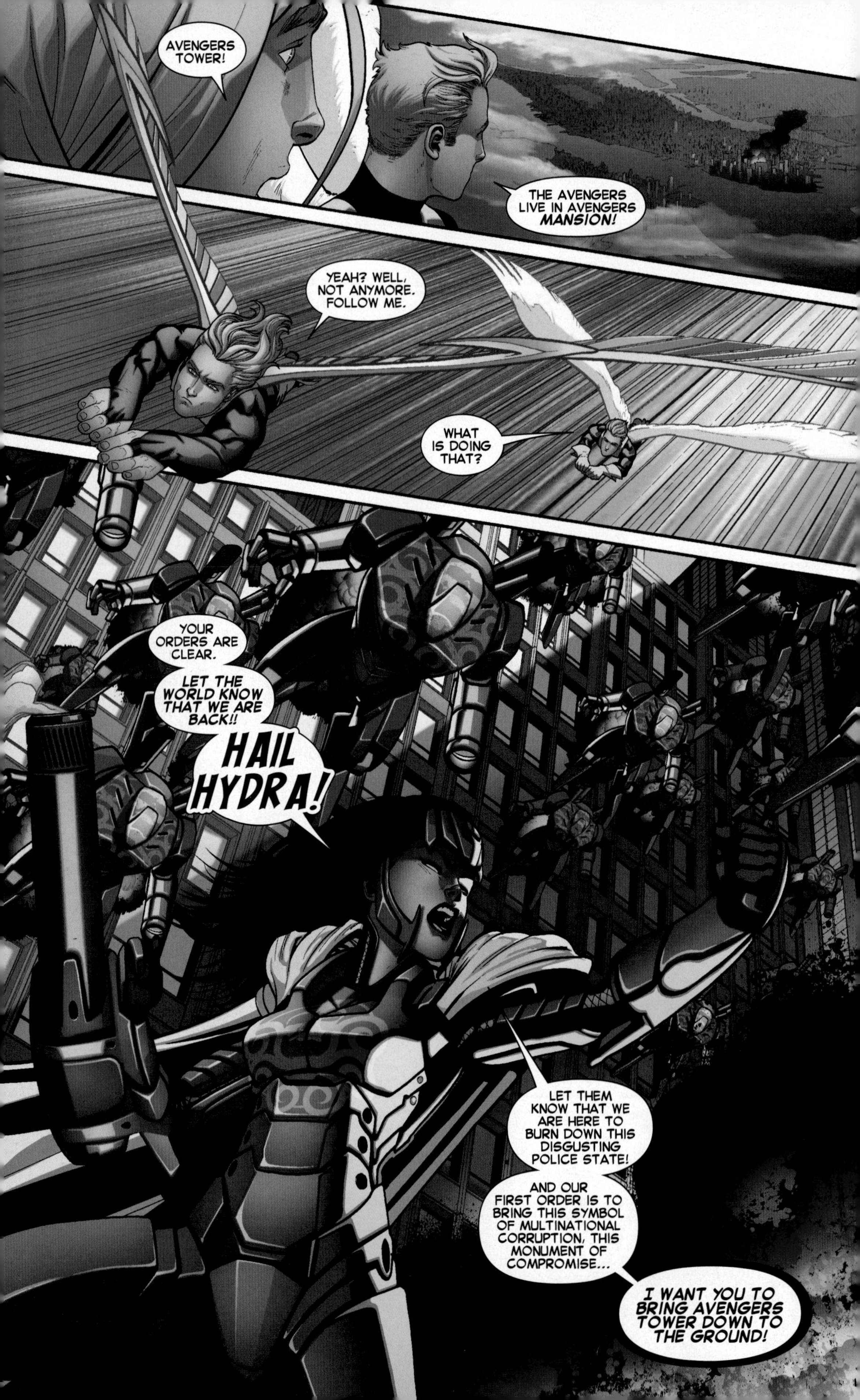
AVENGERS TOWER!
THE AVENGERS LIVE IN AVENGERS MANSION!
YEAH? WELL, NOT ANYMORE. FOLLOW ME.
WHAT IS DOING THAT?
YOUR ORDERS ARE CLEAR.
LET THE WORLD KNOW THAT WE ARE BACK!!
HAIL HYDRA!
LET THEM KNOW THAT WE ARE HERE TO BURN DOWN THIS DISGUSTING POLICE STATE!
AND OUR FIRST ORDER IS TO BRING THIS SYMBOL OF MULTINATIONAL CORRUPTION, THIS MONUMENT OF COMPROMISE...
I WANT YOU TO BRING AVENGERS TOWER DOWN TO THE GROUND!

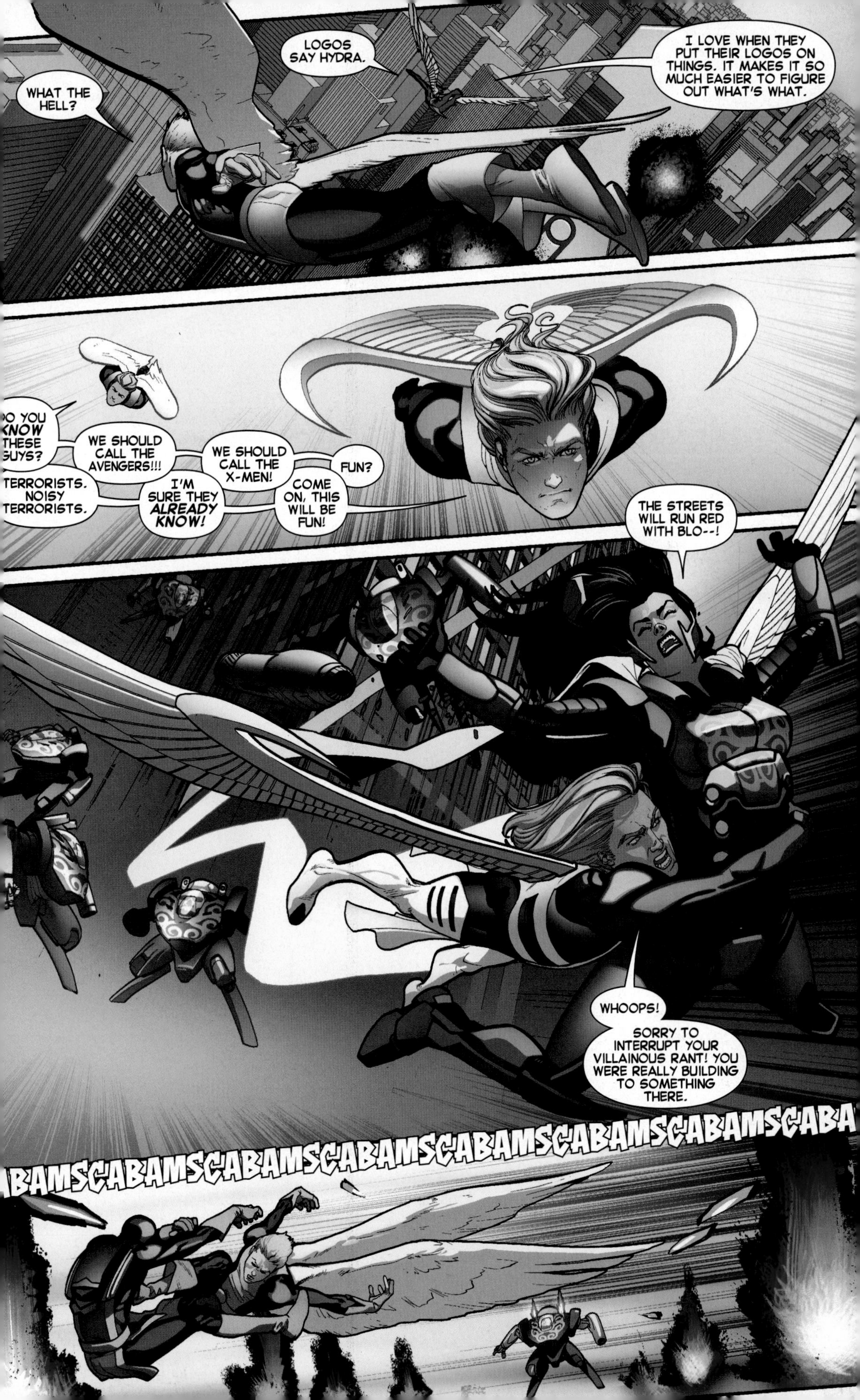

WHAT THE HELL?
LOGOS SAY HYDRA.
I LOVE WHEN THEY PUT THEIR LOGOS ON THINGS. IT MAKES IT SO MUCH EASIER TO FIGURE OUT WHAT'S WHAT.
O YOU *KNOW* THESE GUYS?
TERRORISTS. NOISY TERRORISTS.
WE SHOULD CALL THE AVENGERS!!!
I'M SURE THEY *ALREADY KNOW!*
WE SHOULD CALL THE X-MEN!
COME ON, THIS WILL BE FUN!
FUN?
THE STREETS WILL RUN RED WITH BLO--!
WHOOPS!
SORRY TO INTERRUPT YOUR VILLAINOUS RANT! YOU WERE REALLY BUILDING TO SOMETHING THERE.
BAMSCABAMSCABAMSCABAMSCABAMSCABAMSCABAMSCABA

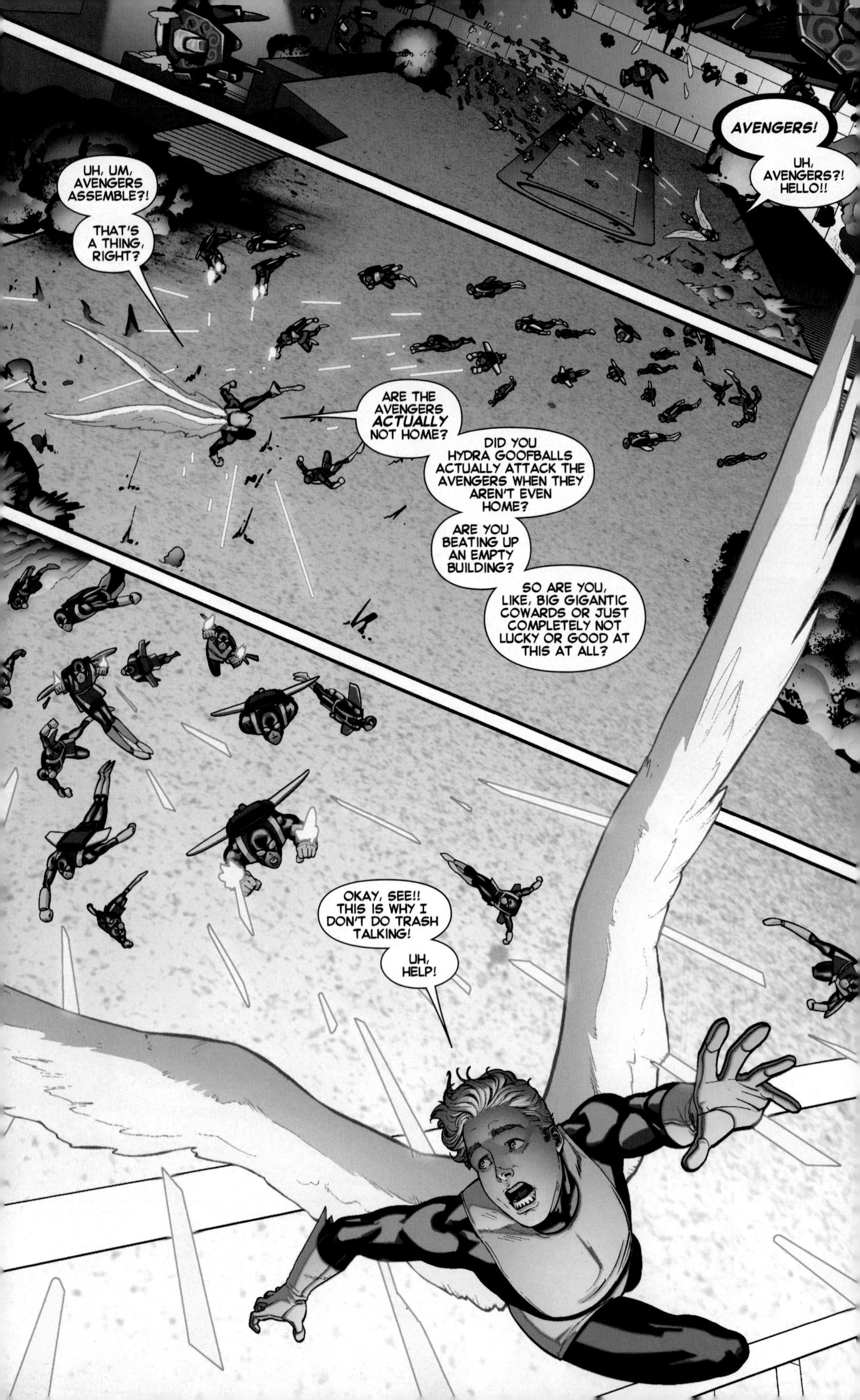
AVENGERS!
UH, AVENGERS?! HELLO!!
UH, UM, AVENGERS ASSEMBLE?!
THAT'S A THING, RIGHT?
ARE THE AVENGERS ACTUALLY NOT HOME?
DID YOU HYDRA GOOFBALLS ACTUALLY ATTACK THE AVENGERS WHEN THEY AREN'T EVEN HOME?
ARE YOU BEATING UP AN EMPTY BUILDING?
SO ARE YOU, LIKE, BIG GIGANTIC COWARDS OR JUST COMPLETELY NOT LUCKY OR GOOD AT THIS AT ALL?
OKAY, SEE!! THIS IS WHY I DON'T DO TRASH TALKING!
UH, HELP!

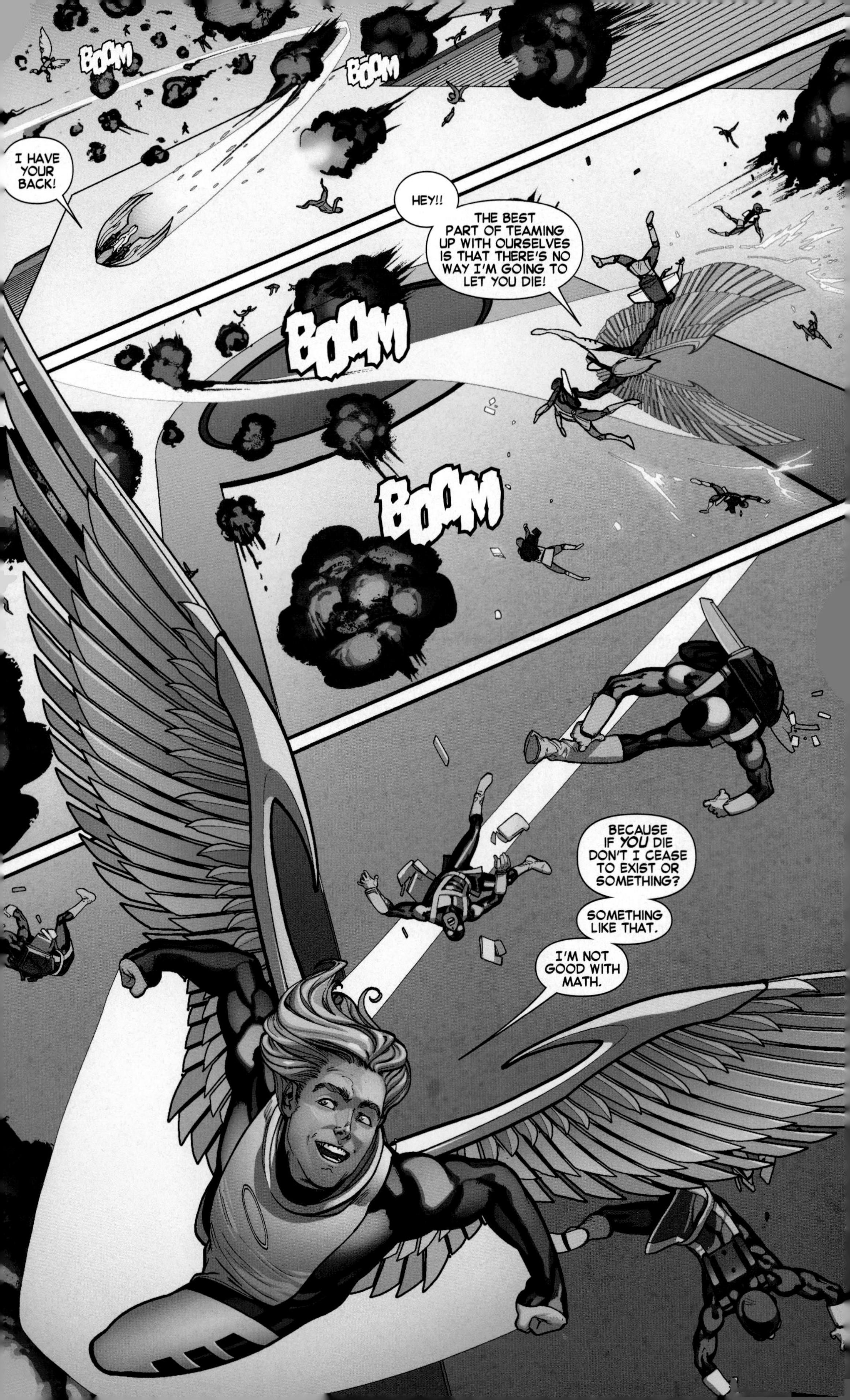
BOOM
BOOM
I HAVE YOUR BACK!
HEY!!
THE BEST PART OF TEAMING UP WITH OURSELVES IS THAT THERE'S NO WAY I'M GOING TO LET YOU DIE!
BOOM
BOOM
BECAUSE IF *YOU* DIE DON'T I CEASE TO EXIST OR SOMETHING?
SOMETHING LIKE THAT.
I'M NOT GOOD WITH MATH.

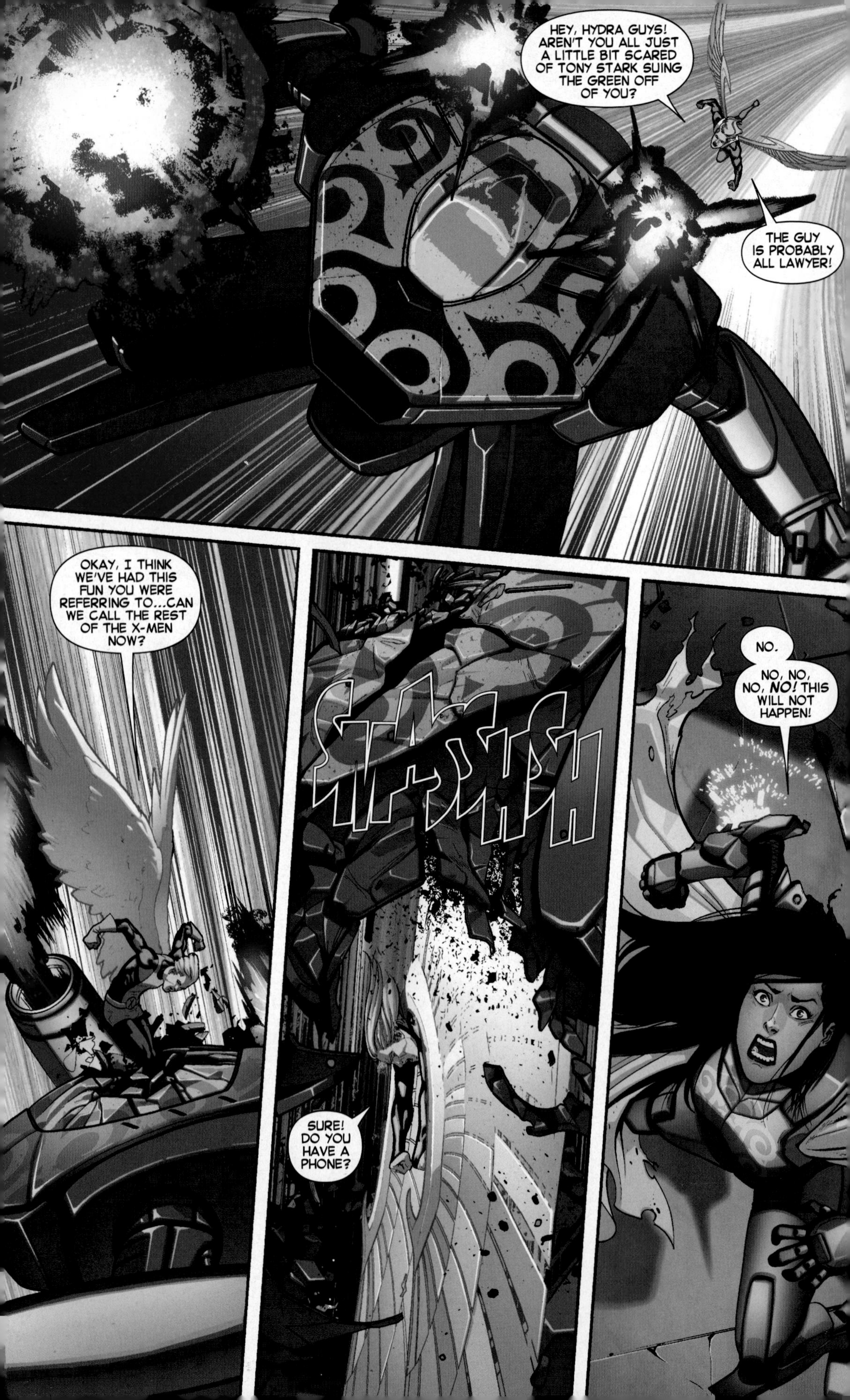
HEY, HYDRA GUYS! AREN'T YOU ALL JUST A LITTLE BIT SCARED OF TONY STARK SUING THE GREEN OFF OF YOU?
THE GUY IS PROBABLY ALL LAWYER!
OKAY, I THINK WE'VE HAD THIS FUN YOU WERE REFERRING TO...CAN WE CALL THE REST OF THE X-MEN NOW?
SSHHH
SURE! DO YOU HAVE A PHONE?
NO.
NO, NO, NO, NO! THIS WILL NOT HAPPEN!

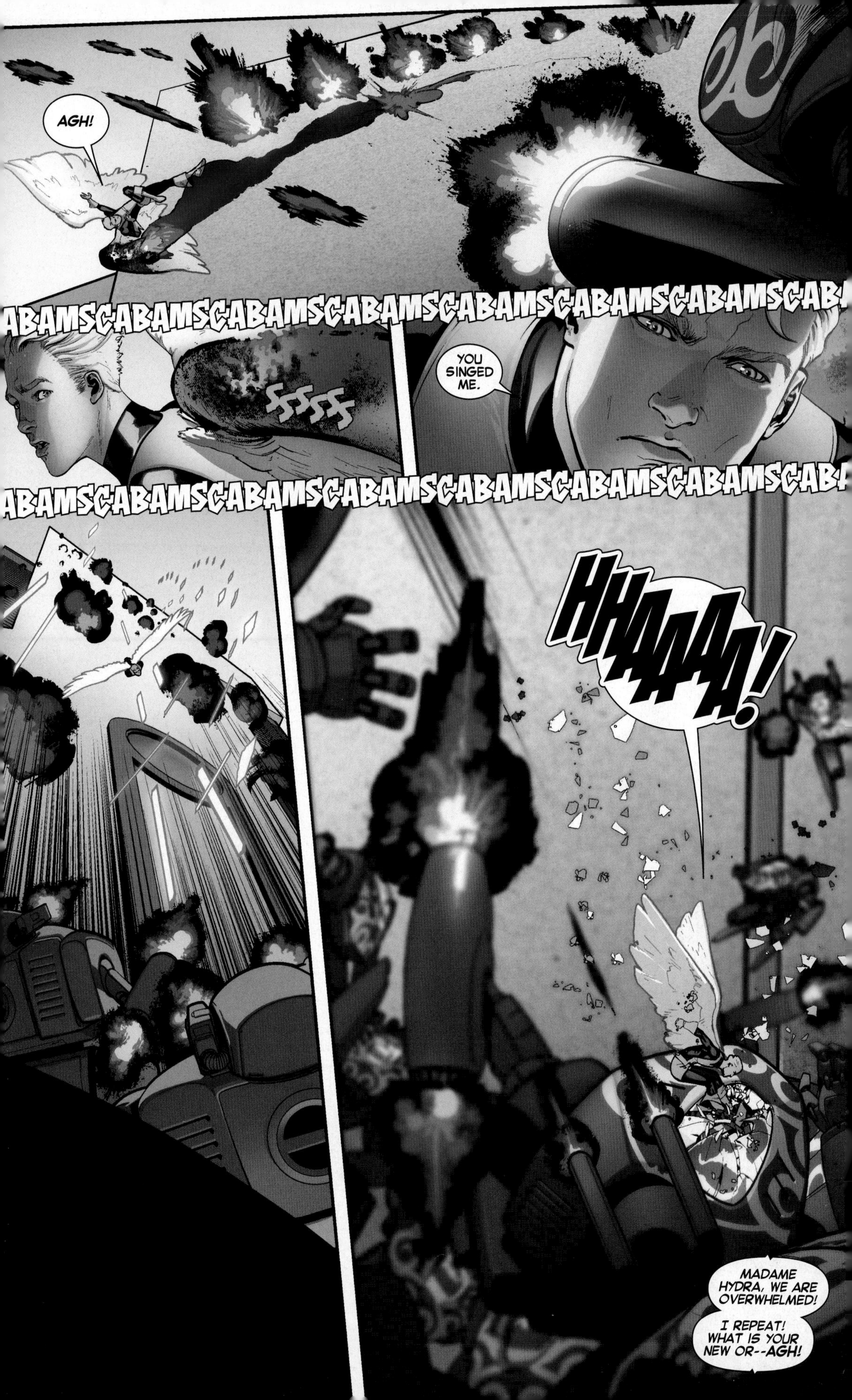
AGH!
ABAMSCABAMSCABAMSCABAMSCABAMSCABAMSCAB
SSSSS
YOU SINGED ME.
ABAMSCABAMSCABAMSCABAMSCABAMSCABAMSCAB
HHAAAAA!
MADAME HYDRA, WE ARE OVERWHELMED!
I REPEAT! WHAT IS YOUR NEW OR--AGH!

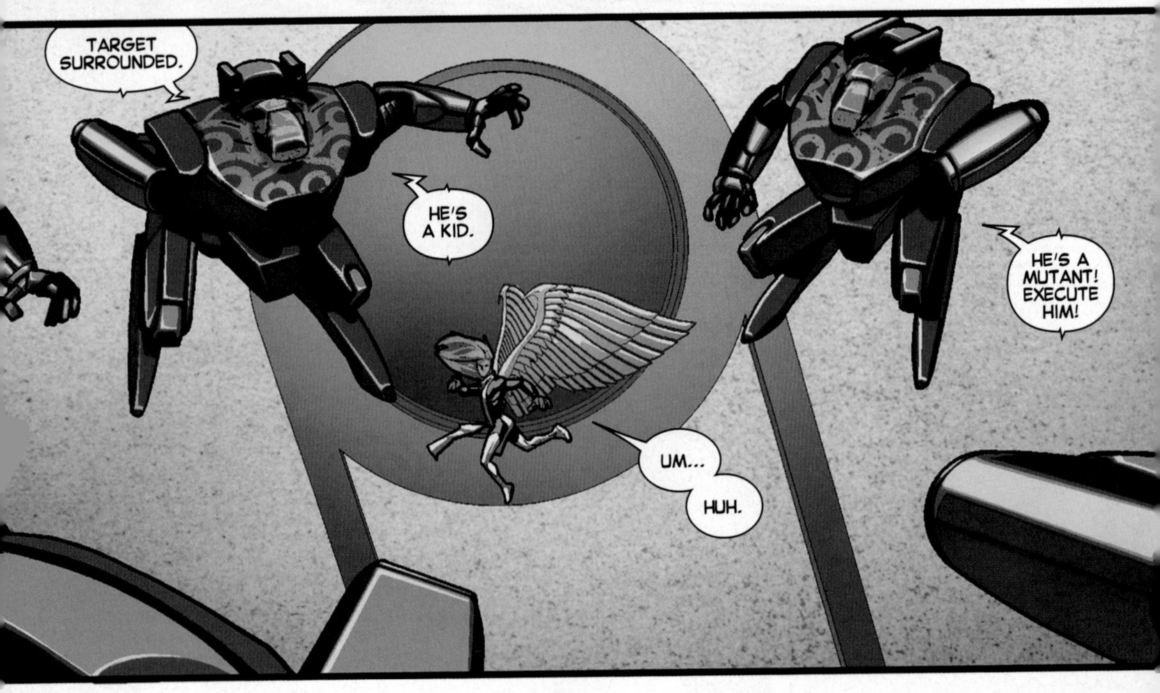
TARGET SURROUNDED.
HE'S A KID.
HE'S A MUTANT! EXECUTE HIM!
UM...
HUH.

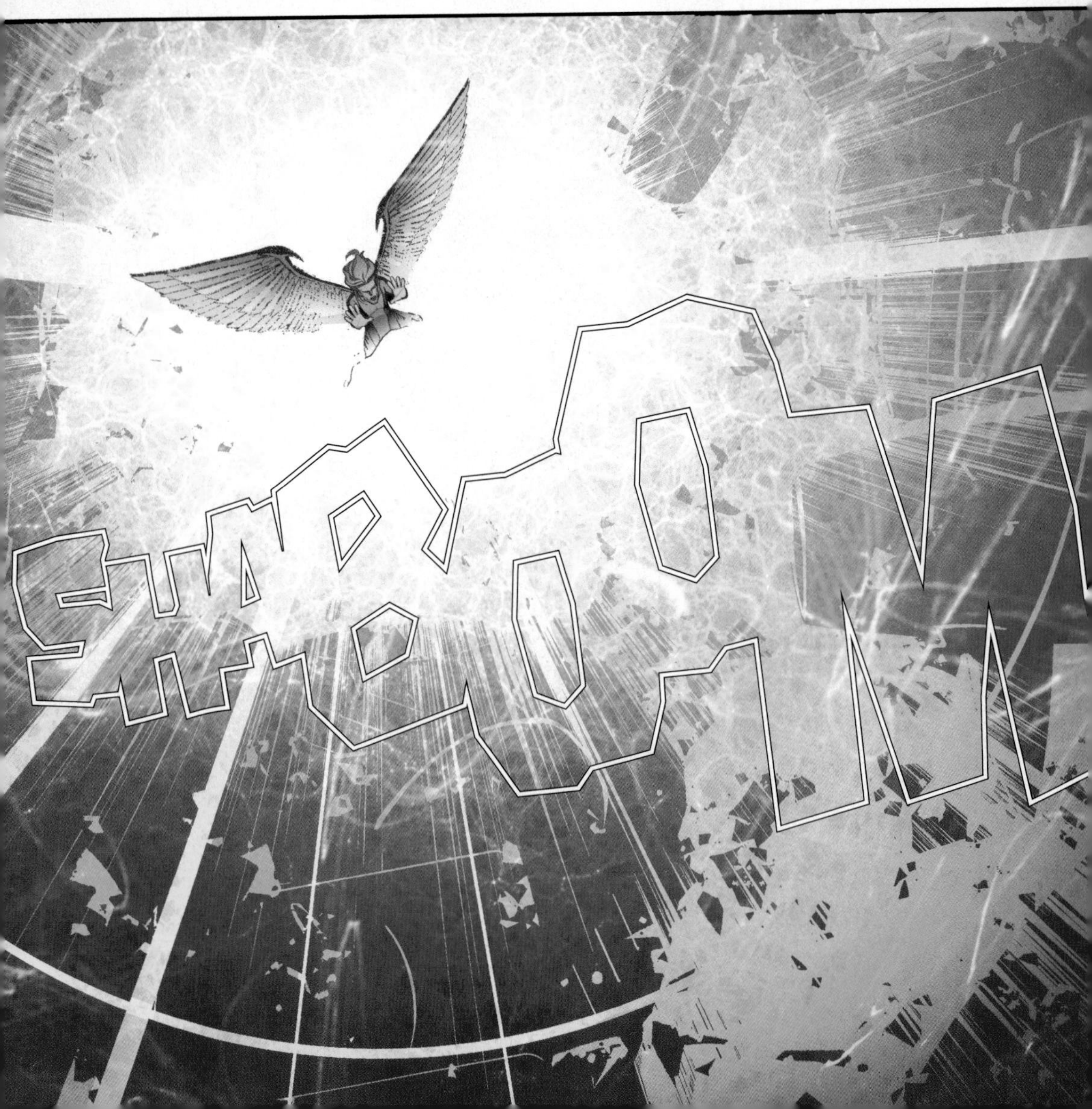

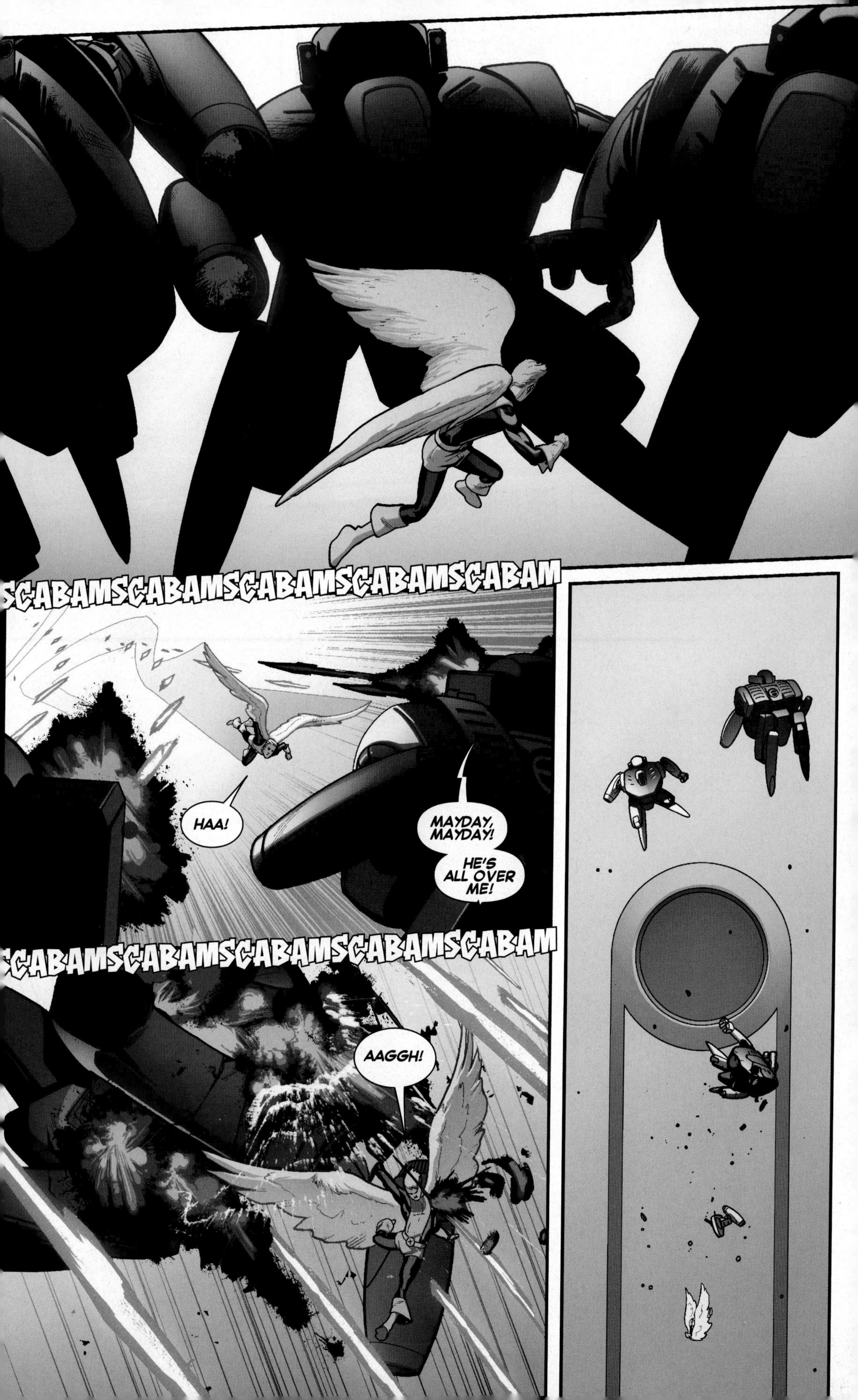
SCABAMSCABAMSCABAMSCABAMSCABAM
HAA!
MAYDAY, MAYDAY!
HE'S ALL OVER ME!
SCABAMSCABAMSCABAMSCABAMSCABAM
AAGGH!

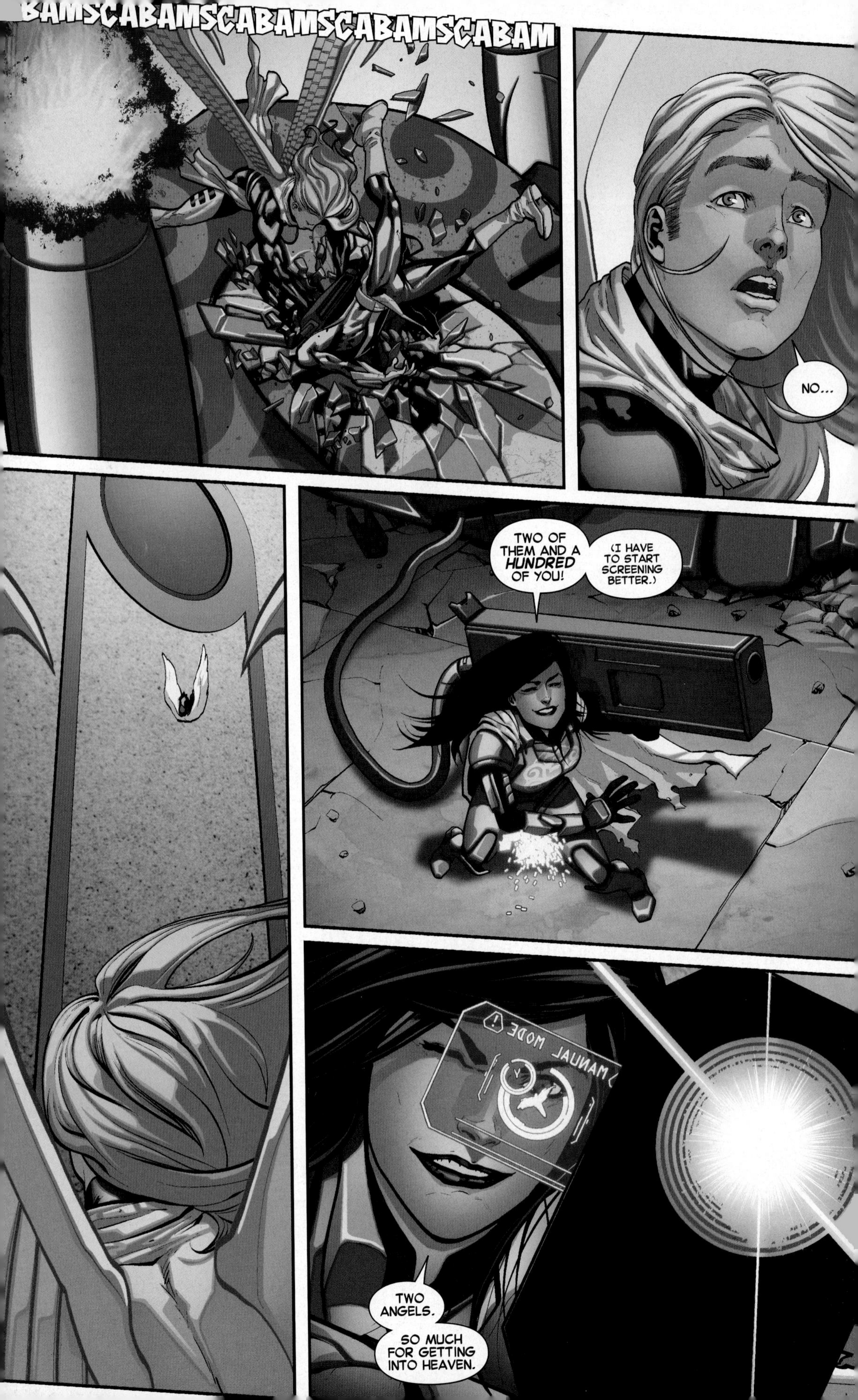
BAMSCABAMSCABAMSCABAMSCABAM
NO...
TWO OF THEM AND A *HUNDRED* OF YOU!
(I HAVE TO START SCREENING BETTER.)
MANUAL MODE
TWO ANGELS.
SO MUCH FOR GETTING INTO HEAVEN.

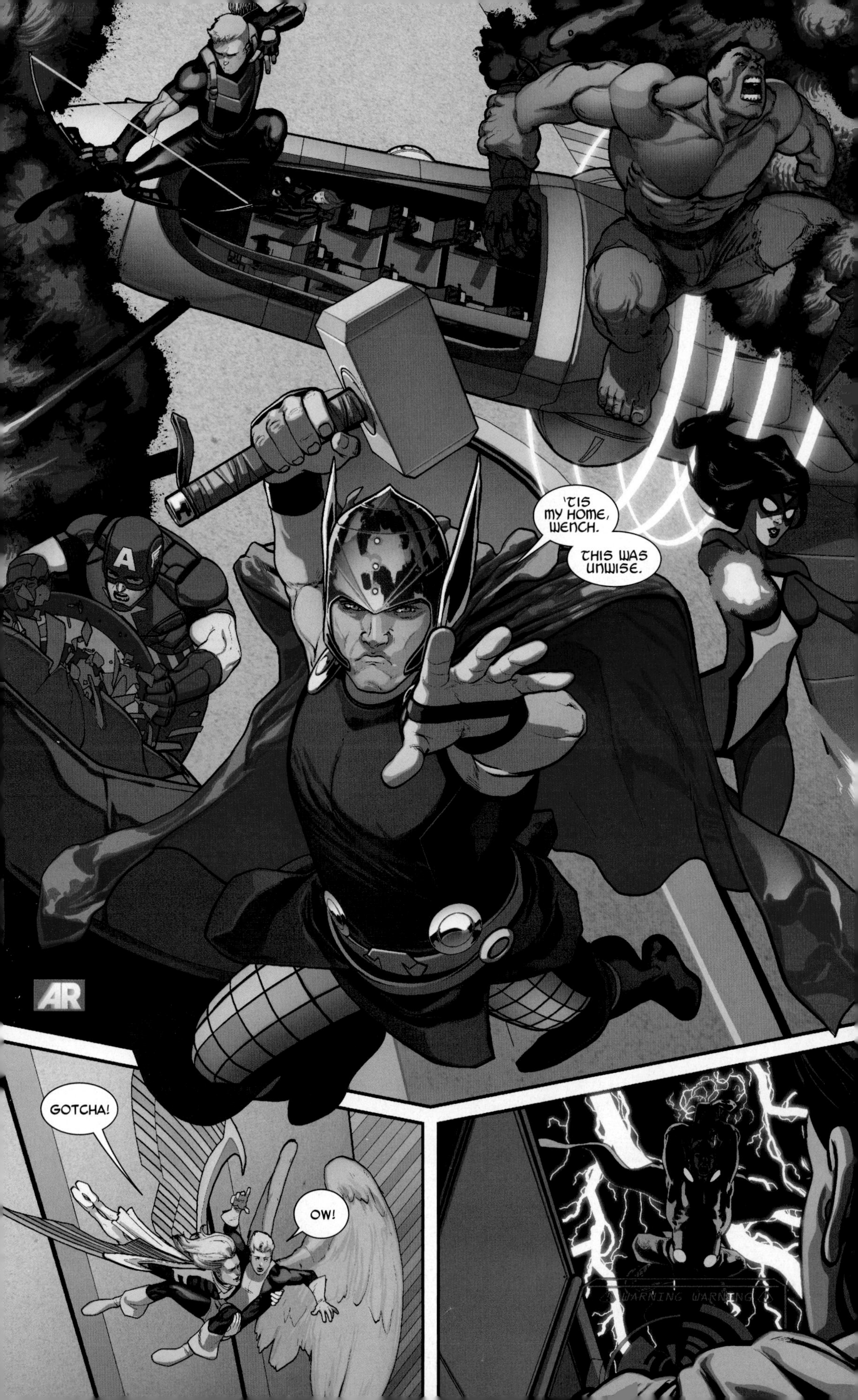
'TIS MY HOME, WENCH.
THIS WAS UNWISE.
GOTCHA!
OW!
WARNING WARNING

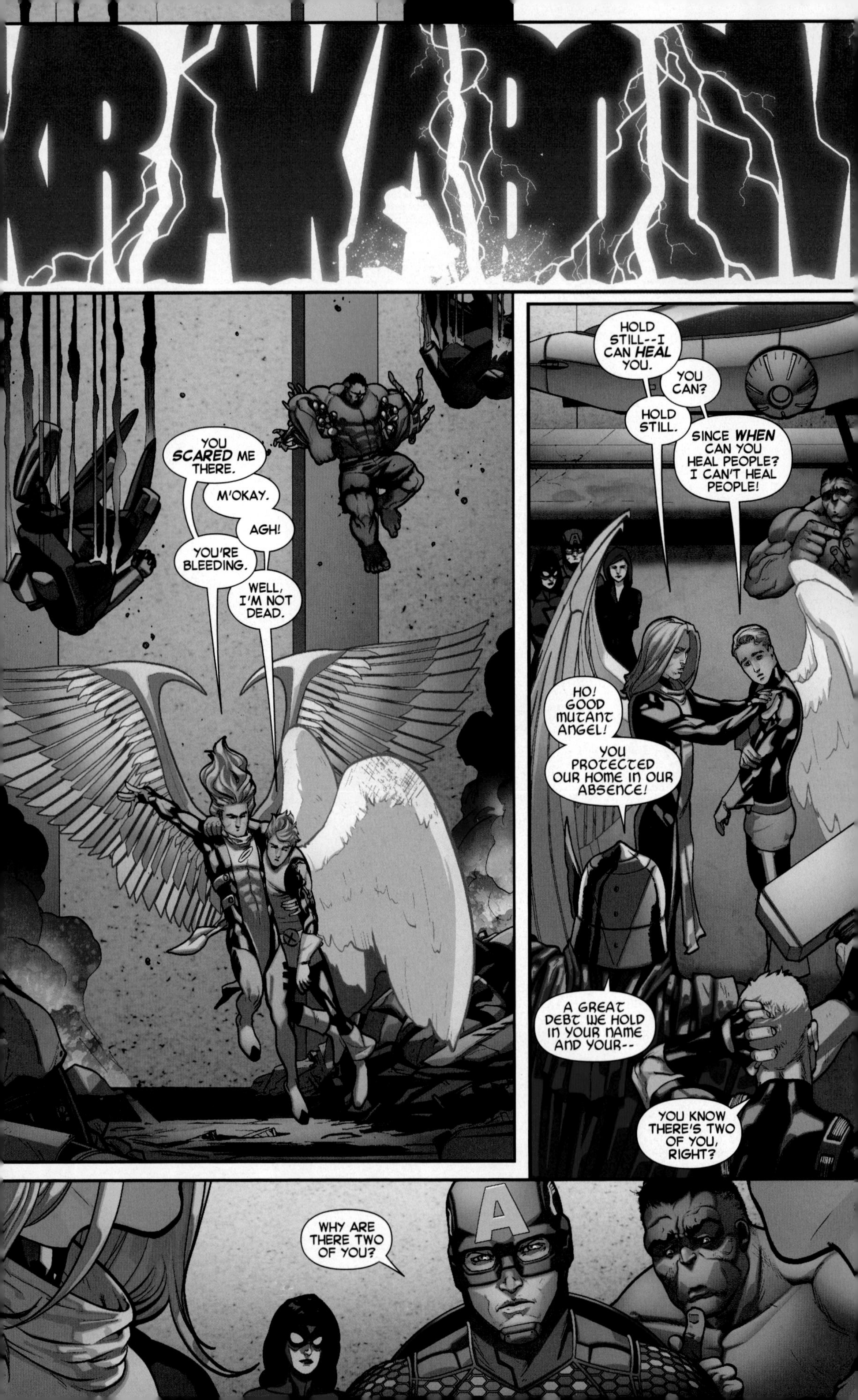
YOU SCARED ME THERE.
M'OKAY.
AGH!
YOU'RE BLEEDING.
WELL, I'M NOT DEAD.
HOLD STILL--I CAN HEAL YOU.
YOU CAN?
HOLD STILL.
SINCE WHEN CAN YOU HEAL PEOPLE? I CAN'T HEAL PEOPLE!
HO! GOOD MUTANT ANGEL!
YOU PROTECTED OUR HOME IN OUR ABSENCE!
A GREAT DEBT WE HOLD IN YOUR NAME AND YOUR--
YOU KNOW THERE'S TWO OF YOU, RIGHT?
WHY ARE THERE TWO OF YOU?

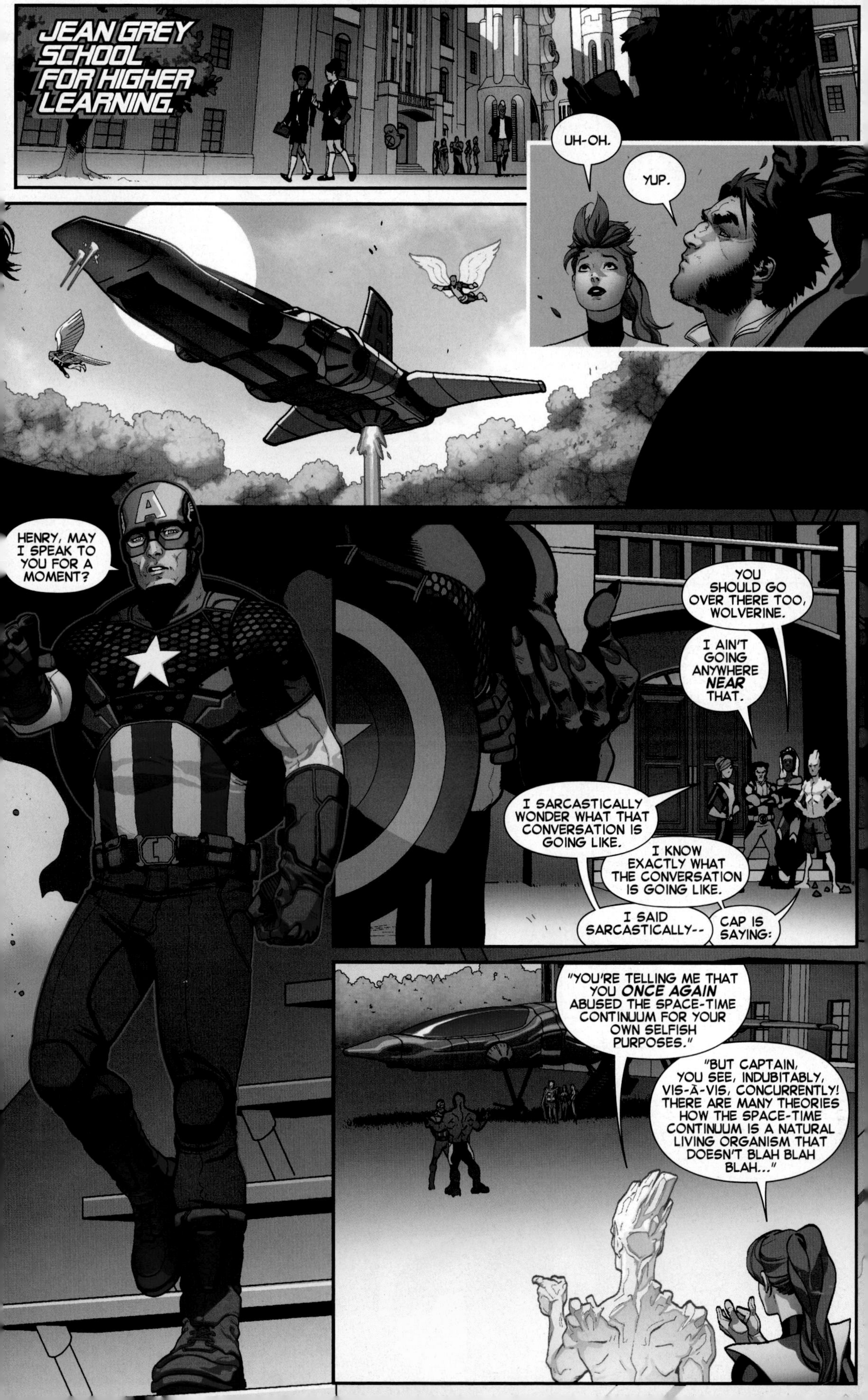
JEAN GREY SCHOOL FOR HIGHER LEARNING.
UH-OH.
YUP.
HENRY, MAY I SPEAK TO YOU FOR A MOMENT?
YOU SHOULD GO OVER THERE TOO, WOLVERINE.
I AIN'T GOING ANYWHERE NEAR THAT.
I SARCASTICALLY WONDER WHAT THAT CONVERSATION IS GOING LIKE.
I KNOW EXACTLY WHAT THE CONVERSATION IS GOING LIKE.
I SAID SARCASTICALLY--
CAP IS SAYING:
"YOU'RE TELLING ME THAT YOU ONCE AGAIN ABUSED THE SPACE-TIME CONTINUUM FOR YOUR OWN SELFISH PURPOSES."
"BUT CAPTAIN, YOU SEE, INDUBITABLY, VIS-À-VIS, CONCURRENTLY! THERE ARE MANY THEORIES HOW THE SPACE-TIME CONTINUUM IS A NATURAL LIVING ORGANISM THAT DOESN'T BLAH BLAH BLAH..."

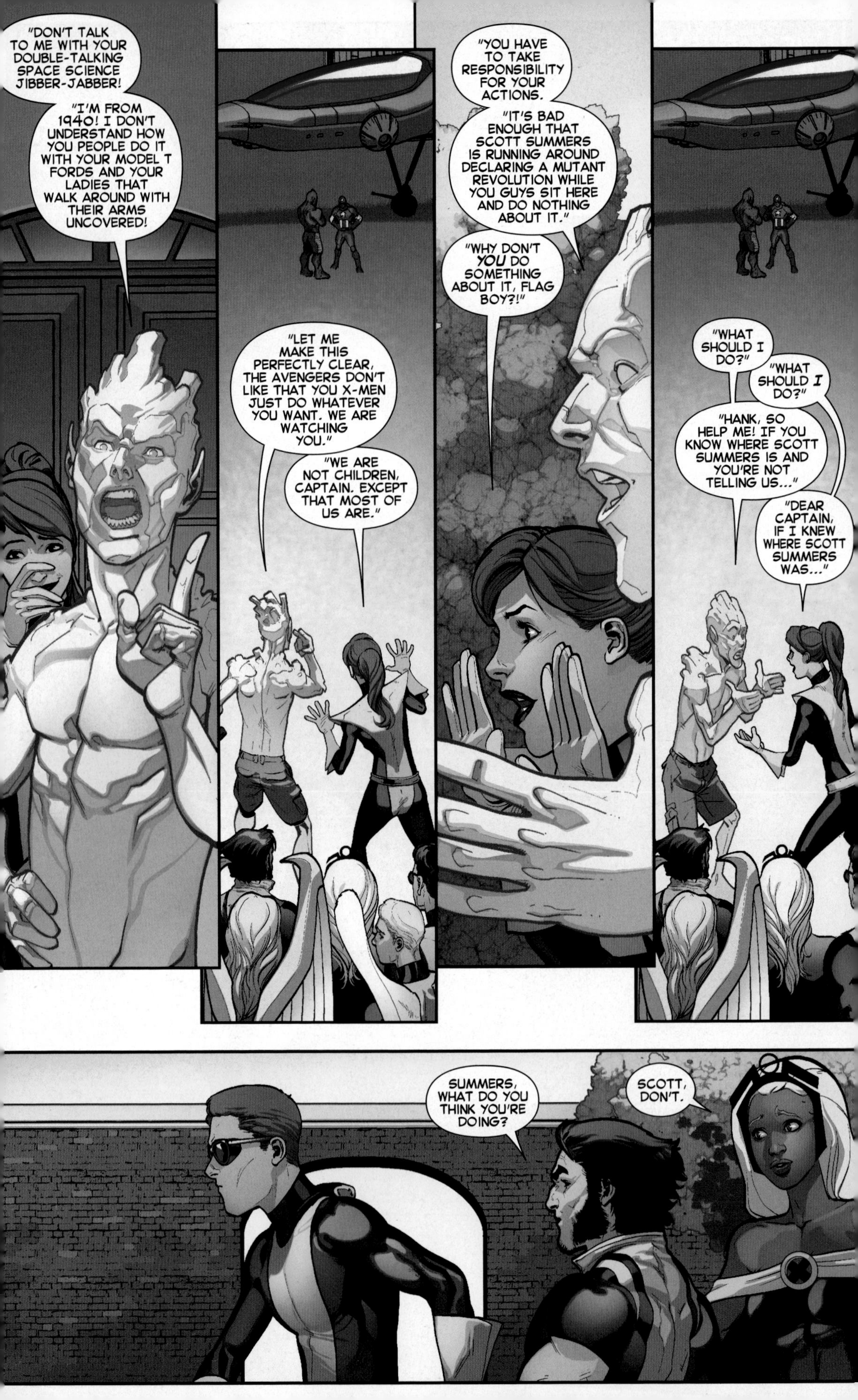
"DON'T TALK TO ME WITH YOUR DOUBLE-TALKING SPACE SCIENCE JIBBER-JABBER!
"I'M FROM 1940! I DON'T UNDERSTAND HOW YOU PEOPLE DO IT WITH YOUR MODEL T FORDS AND YOUR LADIES THAT WALK AROUND WITH THEIR ARMS UNCOVERED!
"LET ME MAKE THIS PERFECTLY CLEAR, THE AVENGERS DON'T LIKE THAT YOU X-MEN JUST DO WHATEVER YOU WANT. WE ARE WATCHING YOU."
"WE ARE NOT CHILDREN, CAPTAIN. EXCEPT THAT MOST OF US ARE."
"YOU HAVE TO TAKE RESPONSIBILITY FOR YOUR ACTIONS.
"IT'S BAD ENOUGH THAT SCOTT SUMMERS IS RUNNING AROUND DECLARING A MUTANT REVOLUTION WHILE YOU GUYS SIT HERE AND DO NOTHING ABOUT IT."
"WHY DON'T YOU DO SOMETHING ABOUT IT, FLAG BOY?!"
"WHAT SHOULD I DO?"
"WHAT SHOULD I DO?"
"HANK, SO HELP ME! IF YOU KNOW WHERE SCOTT SUMMERS IS AND YOU'RE NOT TELLING US..."
"DEAR CAPTAIN, IF I KNEW WHERE SCOTT SUMMERS WAS..."
SUMMERS, WHAT DO YOU THINK YOU'RE DOING?
SCOTT, DON'T.

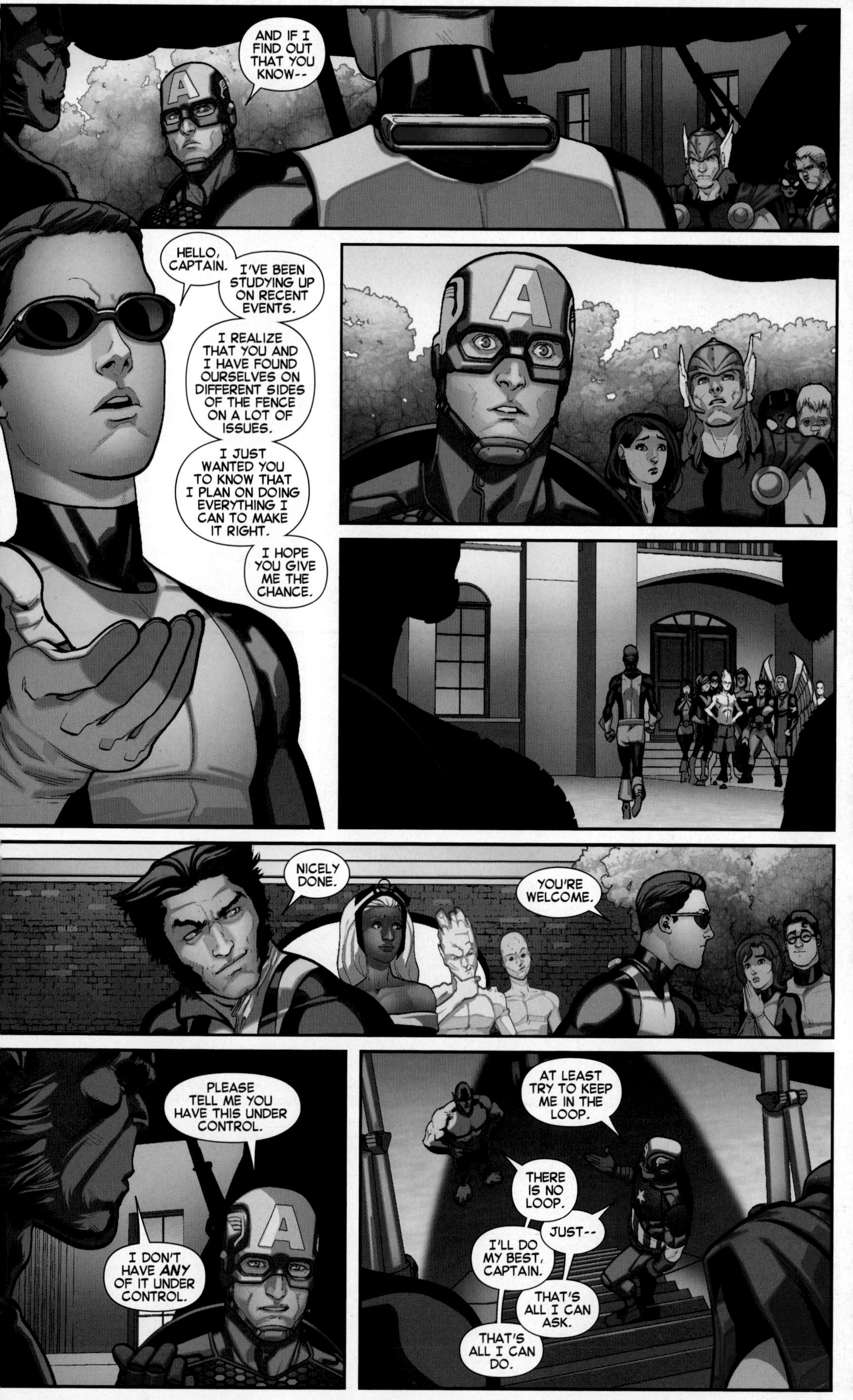

AND IF I FIND OUT THAT YOU KNOW--
HELLO, CAPTAIN.
I'VE BEEN STUDYING UP ON RECENT EVENTS.
I REALIZE THAT YOU AND I HAVE FOUND OURSELVES ON DIFFERENT SIDES OF THE FENCE ON A LOT OF ISSUES.
I JUST WANTED YOU TO KNOW THAT I PLAN ON DOING EVERYTHING I CAN TO MAKE IT RIGHT.
I HOPE YOU GIVE ME THE CHANCE.
NICELY DONE.
YOU'RE WELCOME.
PLEASE TELL ME YOU HAVE THIS UNDER CONTROL.
I DON'T HAVE ANY OF IT UNDER CONTROL.
AT LEAST TRY TO KEEP ME IN THE LOOP.
THERE IS NO LOOP.
JUST--
I'LL DO MY BEST, CAPTAIN.
THAT'S ALL I CAN ASK.
THAT'S ALL I CAN DO.

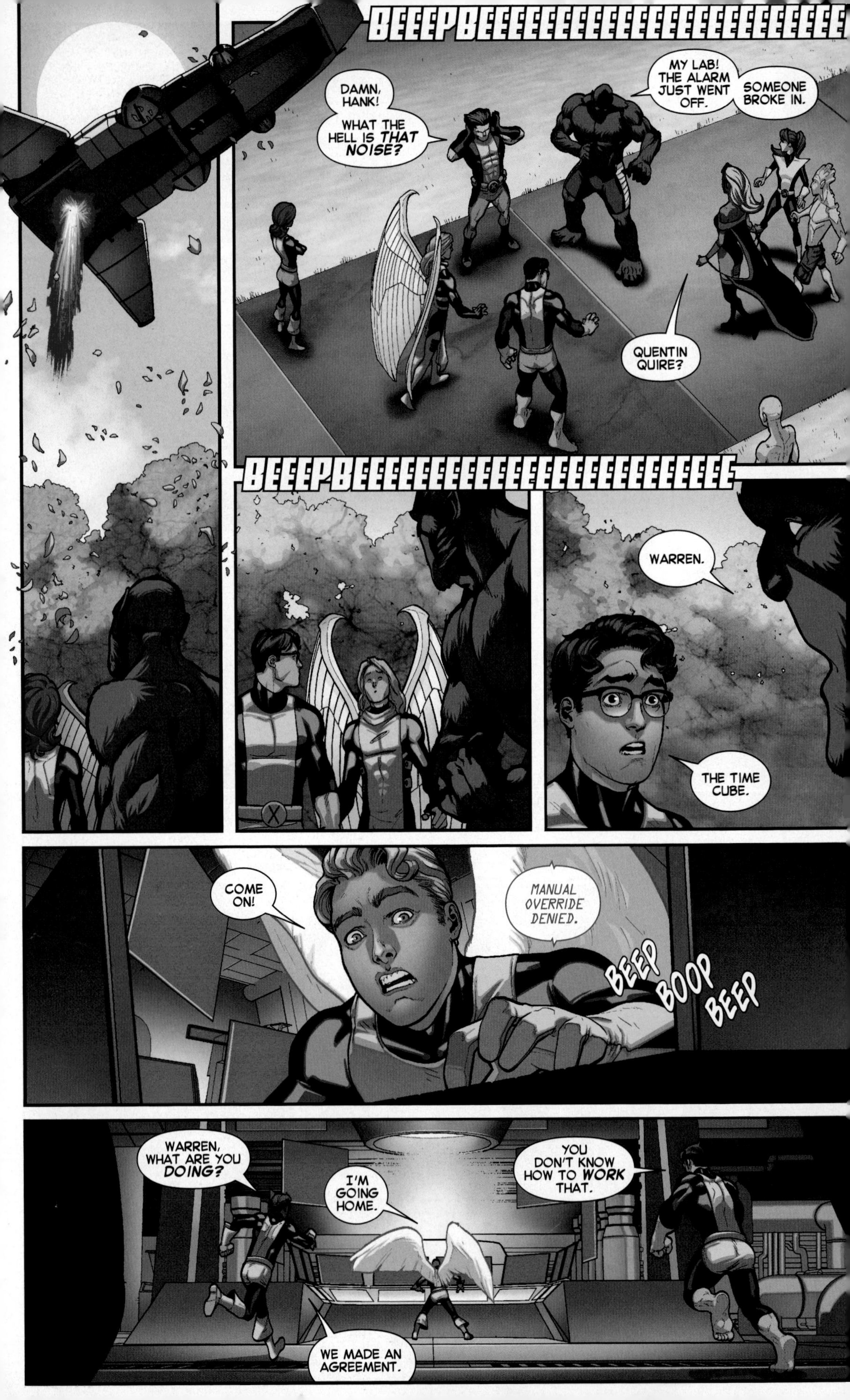
BEEEPBEEEEEEEEEEEEEEEEEEEEEEEEE
DAMN, HANK!
WHAT THE HELL IS THAT NOISE?
MY LAB! THE ALARM JUST WENT OFF.
SOMEONE BROKE IN.
QUENTIN QUIRE?
BEEEPBEEEEEEEEEEEEEEEEEEEEEEEE
WARREN.
THE TIME CUBE.
COME ON!
MANUAL OVERRIDE DENIED.
BEEP BOOP BEEP
WARREN, WHAT ARE YOU DOING?
I'M GOING HOME.
YOU DON'T KNOW HOW TO WORK THAT.
WE MADE AN AGREEMENT.

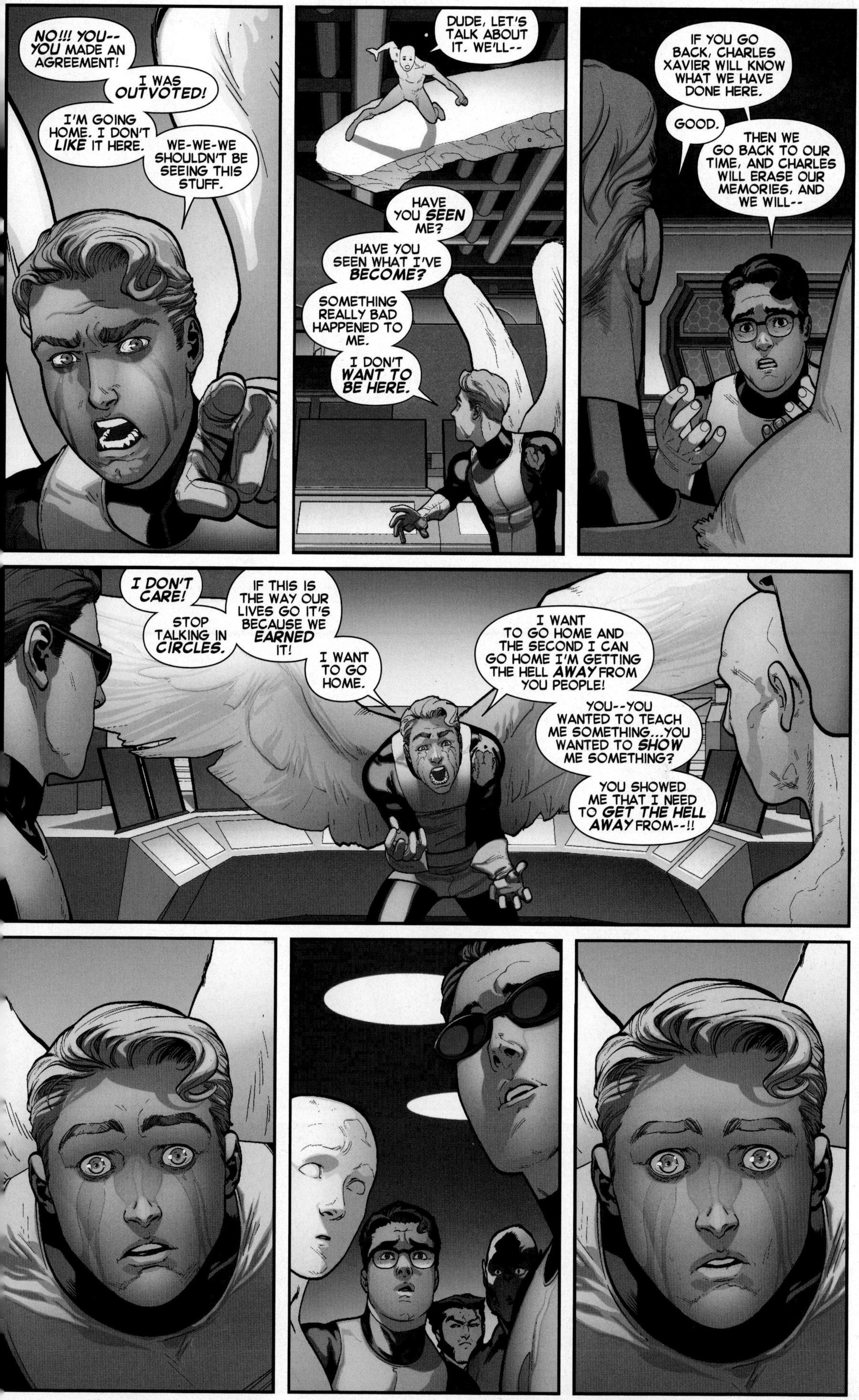
NO!!! YOU-- YOU MADE AN AGREEMENT!
I WAS OUTVOTED!
I'M GOING HOME. I DON'T LIKE IT HERE.
WE-WE-WE SHOULDN'T BE SEEING THIS STUFF.
DUDE, LET'S TALK ABOUT IT. WE'LL--
HAVE YOU SEEN ME?
HAVE YOU SEEN WHAT I'VE BECOME?
SOMETHING REALLY BAD HAPPENED TO ME.
I DON'T WANT TO BE HERE.
IF YOU GO BACK, CHARLES XAVIER WILL KNOW WHAT WE HAVE DONE HERE.
GOOD.
THEN WE GO BACK TO OUR TIME, AND CHARLES WILL ERASE OUR MEMORIES, AND WE WILL--
I DON'T CARE!
STOP TALKING IN CIRCLES.
IF THIS IS THE WAY OUR LIVES GO IT'S BECAUSE WE EARNED IT!
I WANT TO GO HOME.
I WANT TO GO HOME AND THE SECOND I CAN GO HOME I'M GETTING THE HELL AWAY FROM YOU PEOPLE!
YOU--YOU WANTED TO TEACH ME SOMETHING...YOU WANTED TO SHOW ME SOMETHING?
YOU SHOWED ME THAT I NEED TO GET THE HELL AWAY FROM--!!

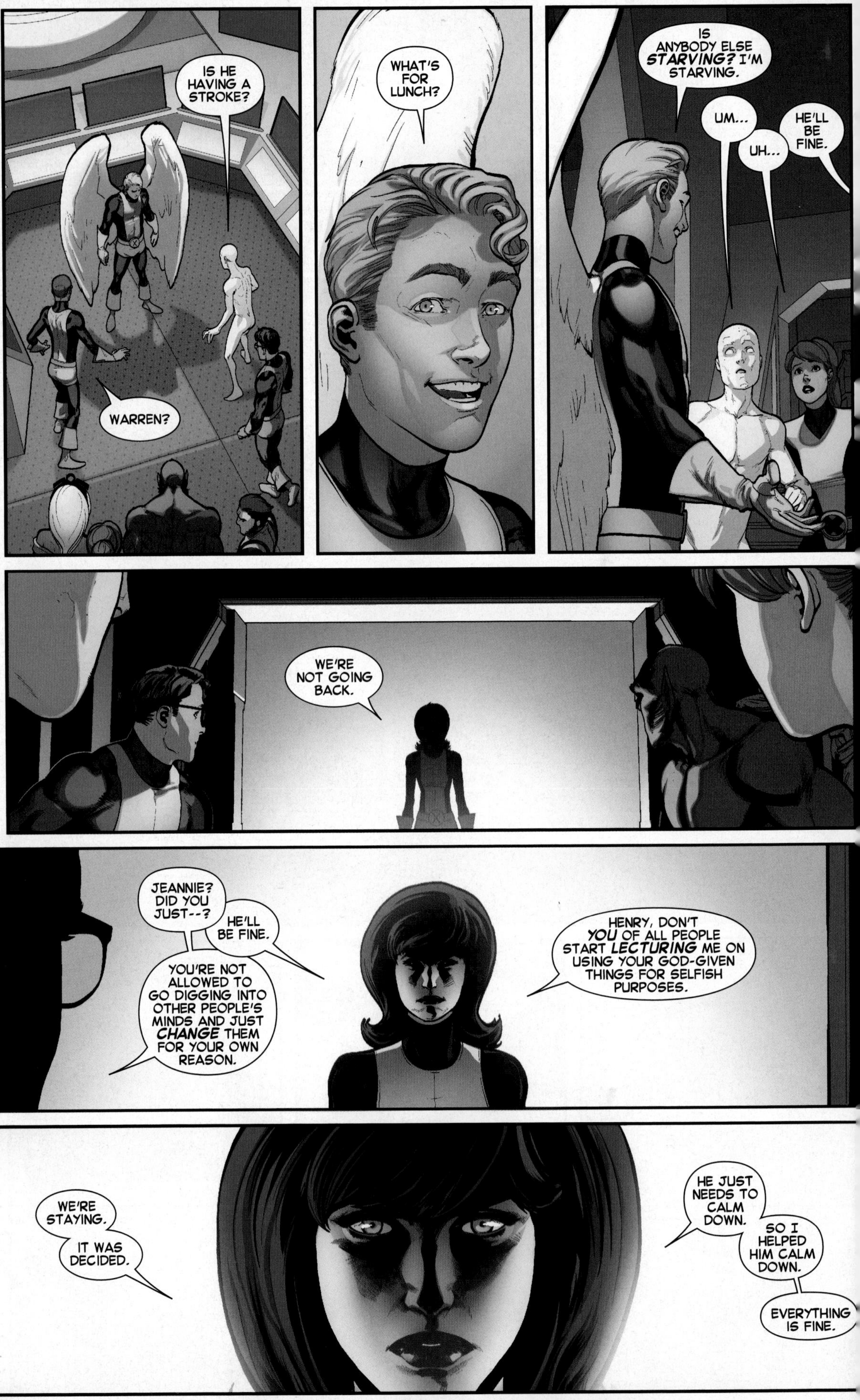
IS HE HAVING A STROKE?
WARREN?
WHAT'S FOR LUNCH?
IS ANYBODY ELSE STARVING? I'M STARVING.
UM...
UH...
HE'LL BE FINE.
WE'RE NOT GOING BACK.
JEANNIE? DID YOU JUST--?
YOU'RE NOT ALLOWED TO GO DIGGING INTO OTHER PEOPLE'S MINDS AND JUST CHANGE THEM FOR YOUR OWN REASON.
HE'LL BE FINE.
HENRY, DON'T YOU OF ALL PEOPLE START LECTURING ME ON USING YOUR GOD-GIVEN THINGS FOR SELFISH PURPOSES.
WE'RE STAYING.
IT WAS DECIDED.
HE JUST NEEDS TO CALM DOWN.
SO I HELPED HIM CALM DOWN.
EVERYTHING IS FINE.

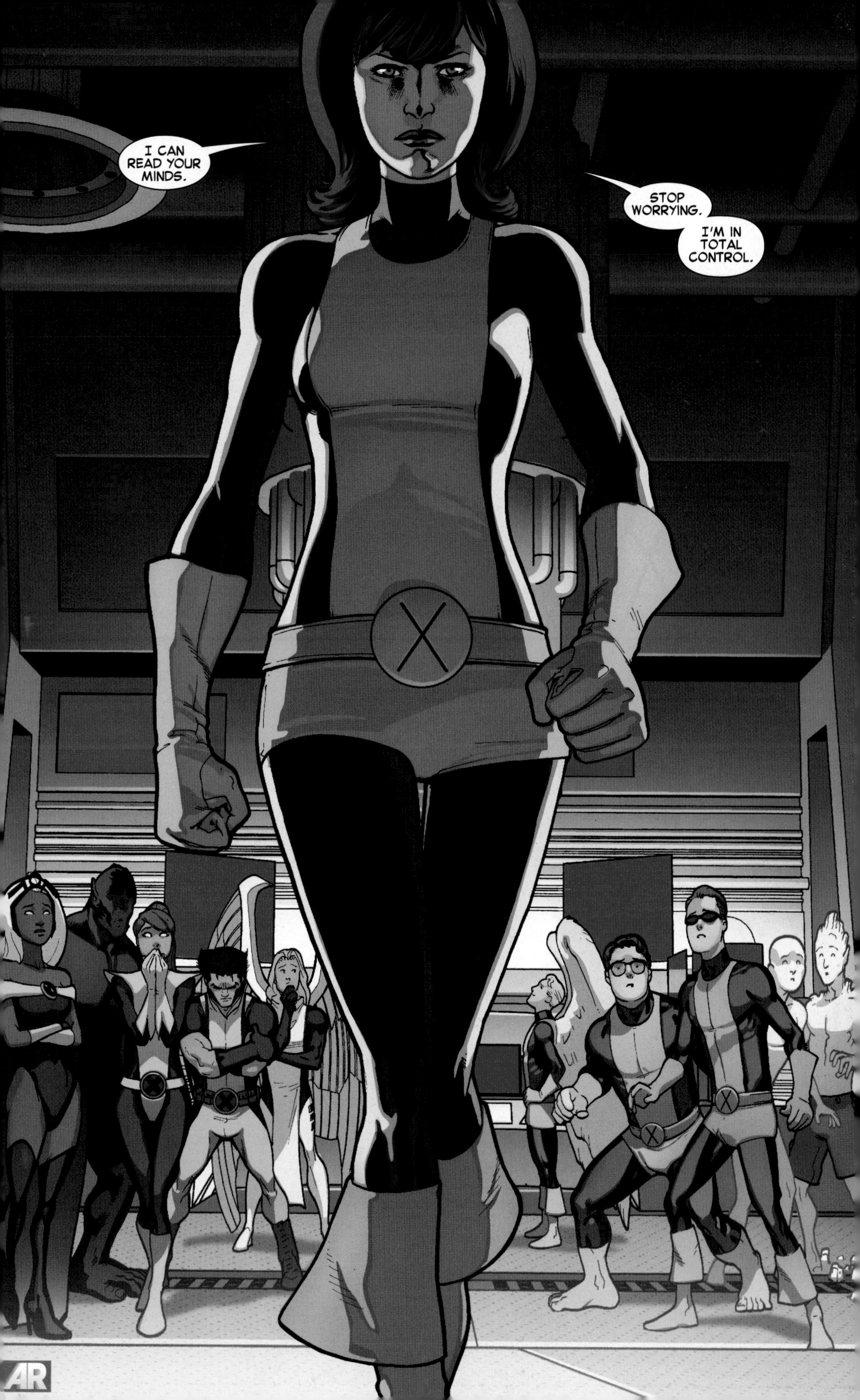
I CAN READ YOUR MINDS.
STOP WORRYING.
I'M IN TOTAL CONTROL.

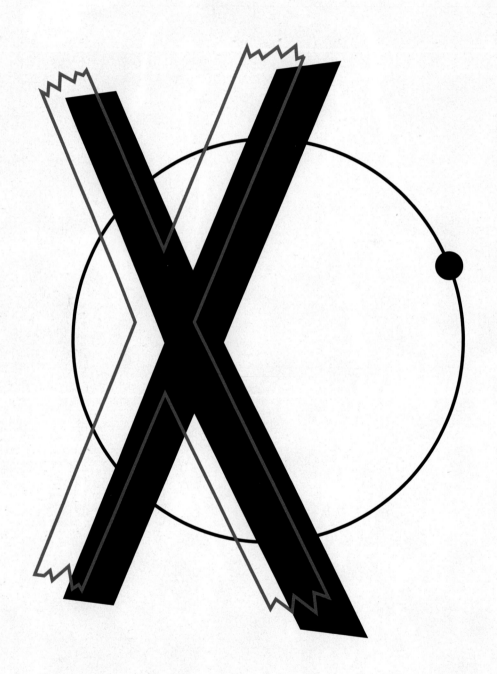

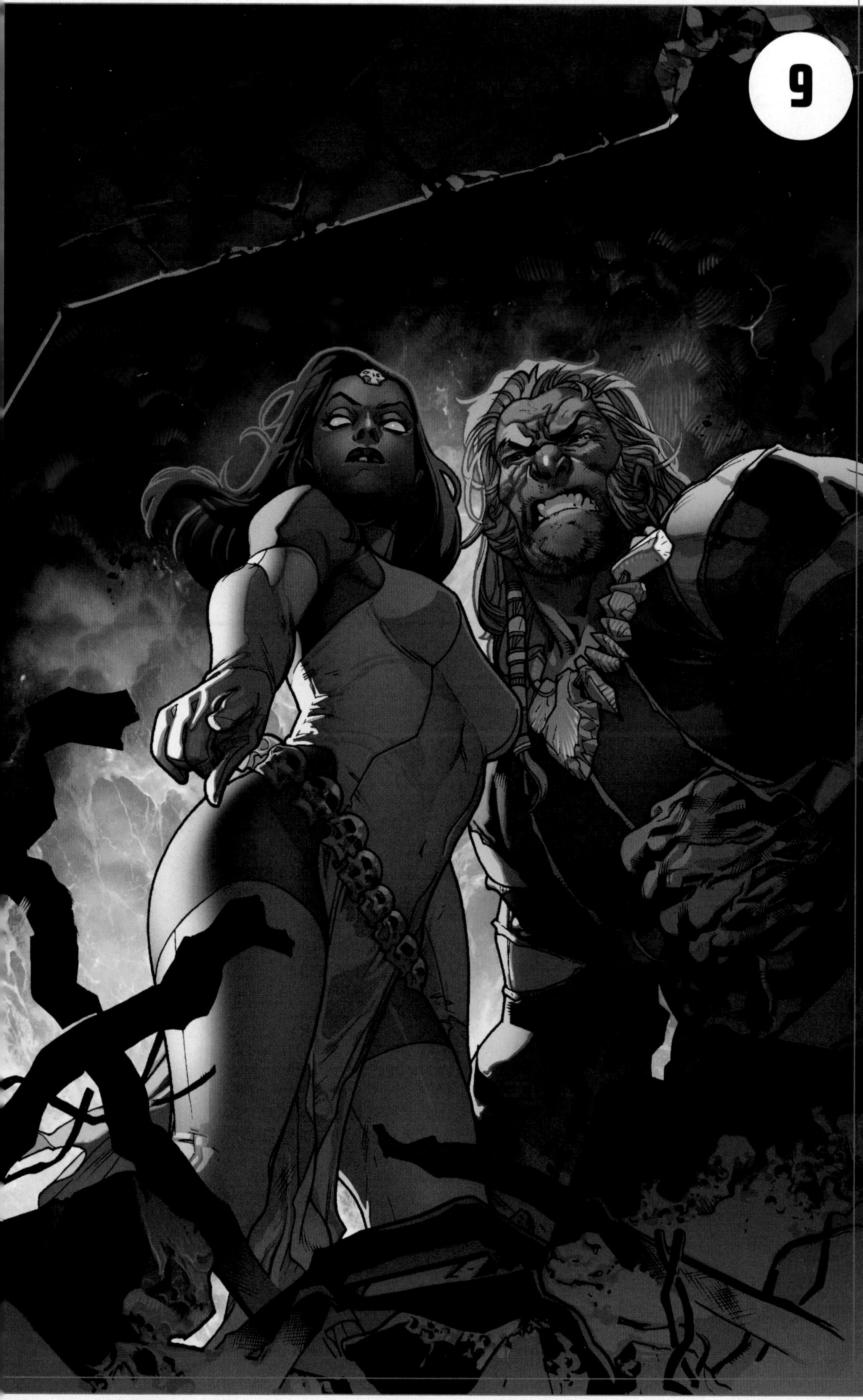
9

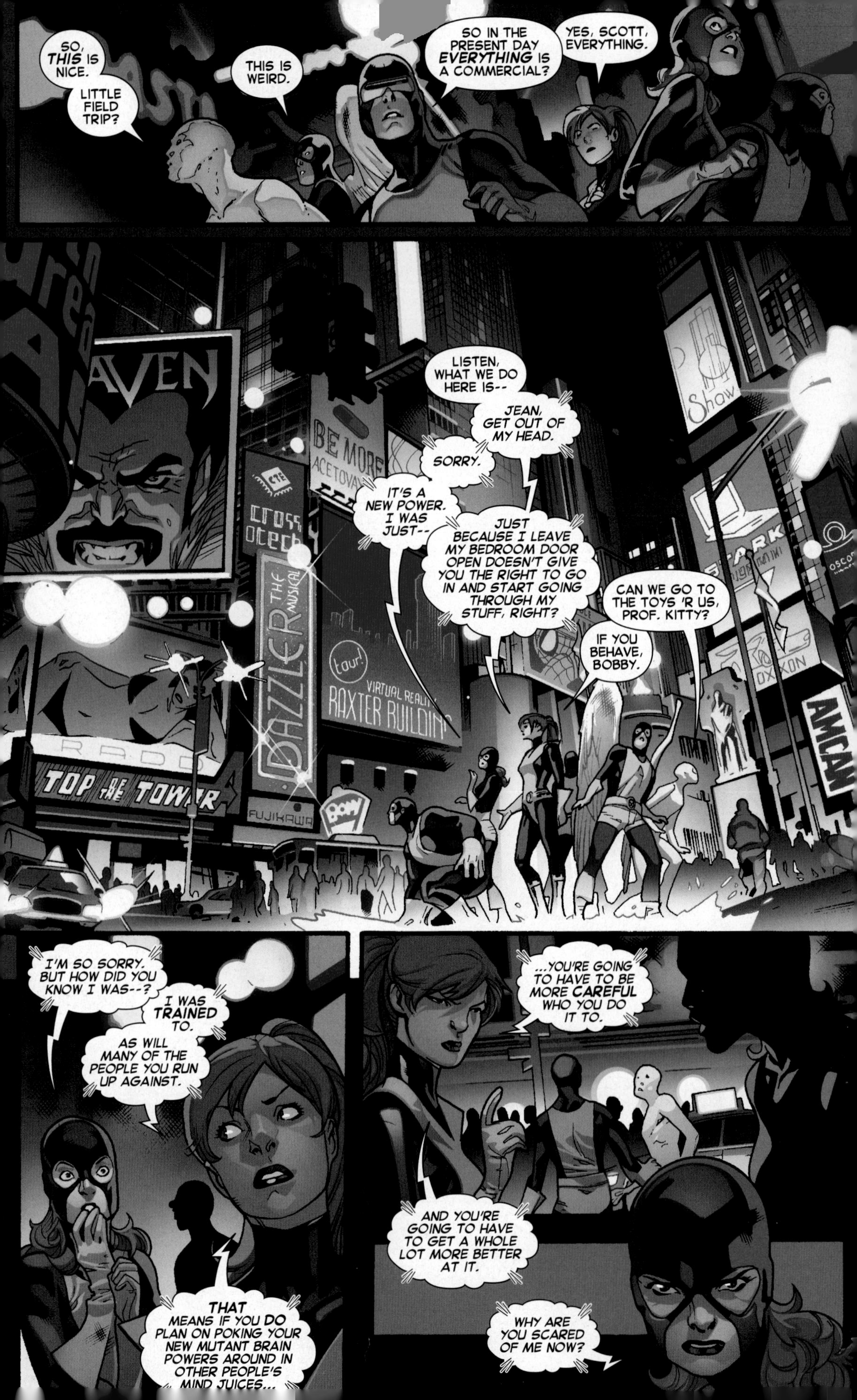
SO, THIS IS NICE.
LITTLE FIELD TRIP?
THIS IS WEIRD.
SO IN THE PRESENT DAY EVERYTHING IS A COMMERCIAL?
YES, SCOTT, EVERYTHING.
LISTEN, WHAT WE DO HERE IS--
JEAN, GET OUT OF MY HEAD.
SORRY.
IT'S A NEW POWER. I WAS JUST--
JUST BECAUSE I LEAVE MY BEDROOM DOOR OPEN DOESN'T GIVE YOU THE RIGHT TO GO IN AND START GOING THROUGH MY STUFF, RIGHT?
CAN WE GO TO THE TOYS 'R US, PROF. KITTY?
IF YOU BEHAVE, BOBBY.
BE MORE
DAZZLER THE MUSICAL
VIRTUAL REALITY BAXTER BUILDING
TOP OF THE TOWER
FUJIKAWA
STARK
AMCAN
I'M SO SORRY. BUT HOW DID YOU KNOW I WAS--?
I WAS TRAINED TO.
AS WILL MANY OF THE PEOPLE YOU RUN UP AGAINST.
THAT MEANS IF YOU DO PLAN ON POKING YOUR NEW MUTANT BRAIN POWERS AROUND IN OTHER PEOPLE'S MIND JUICES...
...YOU'RE GOING TO HAVE TO BE MORE CAREFUL WHO YOU DO IT TO.
AND YOU'RE GOING TO HAVE TO GET A WHOLE LOT MORE BETTER AT IT.
WHY ARE YOU SCARED OF ME NOW?

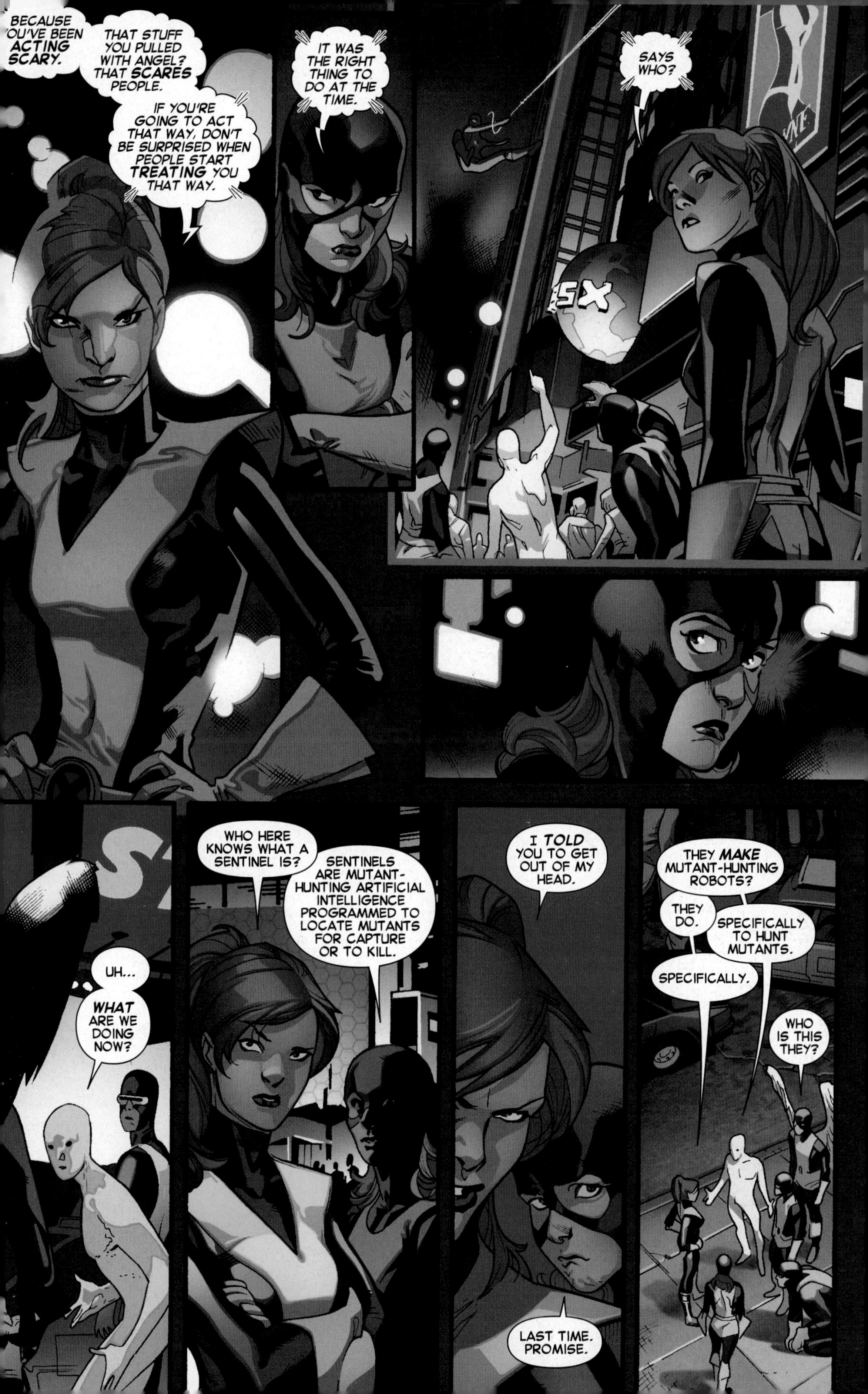
BECAUSE YOU'VE BEEN ACTING SCARY.
THAT STUFF YOU PULLED WITH ANGEL? THAT SCARES PEOPLE.
IF YOU'RE GOING TO ACT THAT WAY, DON'T BE SURPRISED WHEN PEOPLE START TREATING YOU THAT WAY.
IT WAS THE RIGHT THING TO DO AT THE TIME.
SAYS WHO?
UH...
WHAT ARE WE DOING NOW?
WHO HERE KNOWS WHAT A SENTINEL IS?
SENTINELS ARE MUTANT-HUNTING ARTIFICIAL INTELLIGENCE PROGRAMMED TO LOCATE MUTANTS FOR CAPTURE OR TO KILL.
I TOLD YOU TO GET OUT OF MY HEAD.
LAST TIME. PROMISE.
THEY MAKE MUTANT-HUNTING ROBOTS?
THEY DO.
SPECIFICALLY TO HUNT MUTANTS.
SPECIFICALLY.
WHO IS THIS THEY?

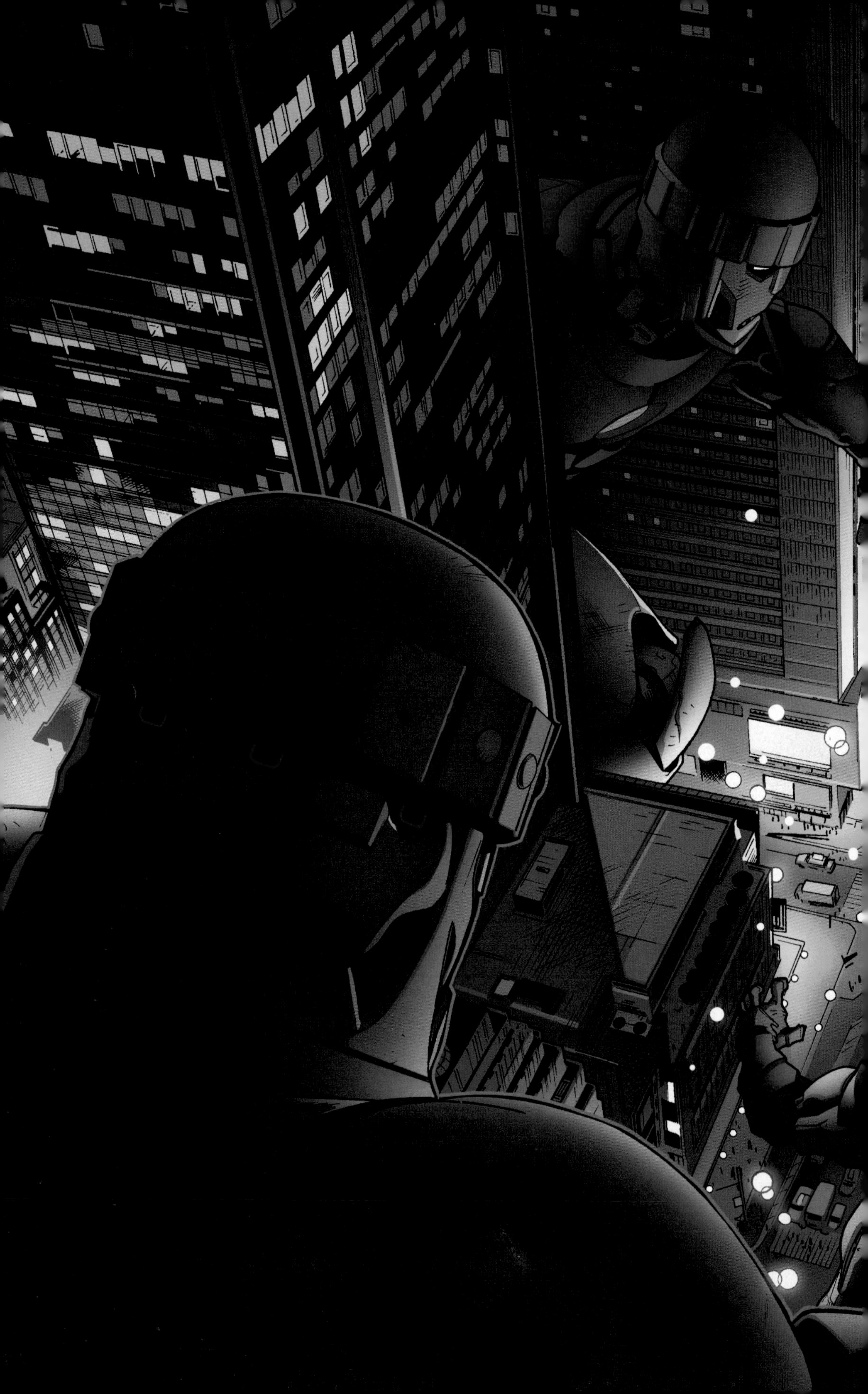

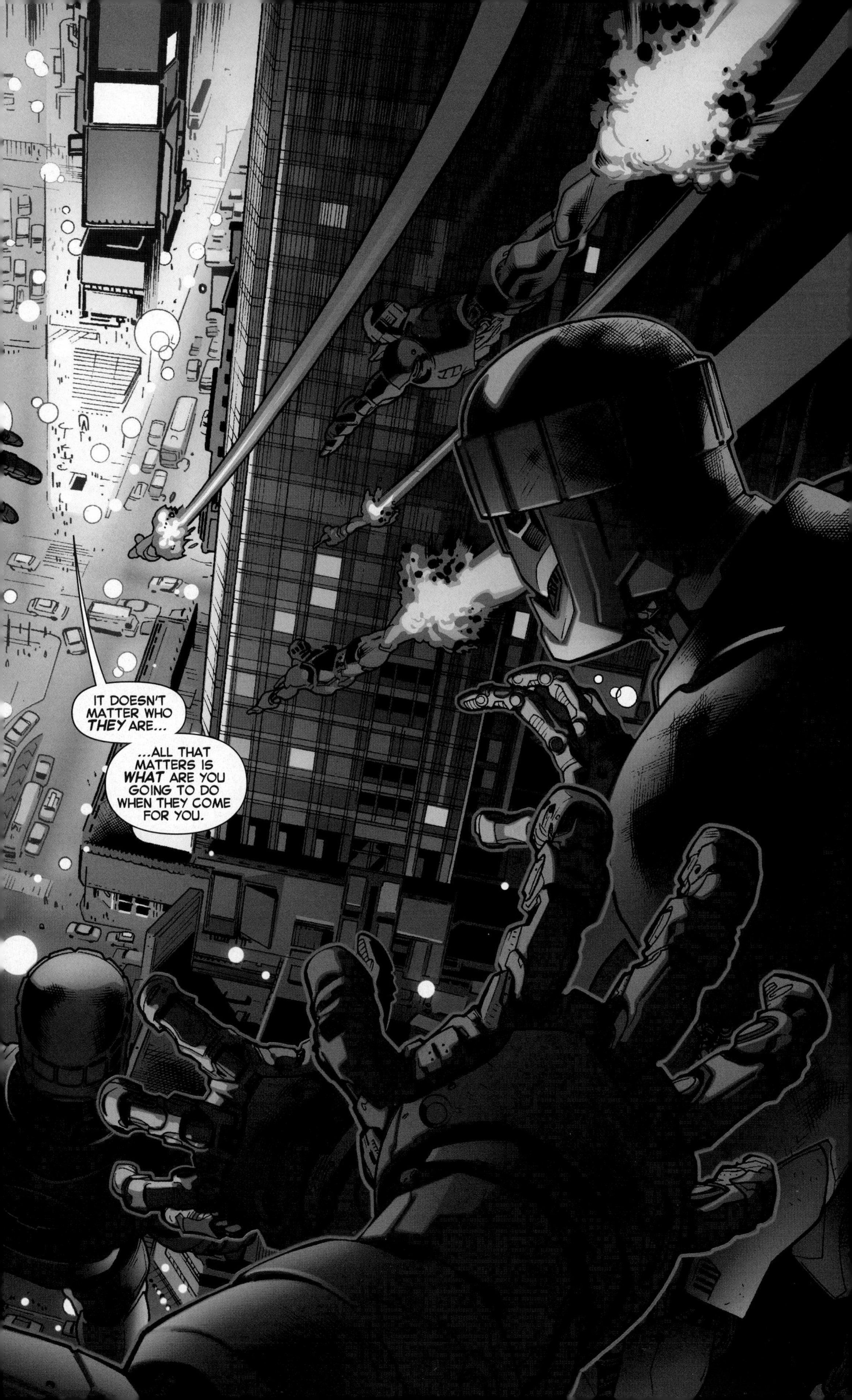
IT DOESN'T MATTER WHO THEY ARE...
...ALL THAT MATTERS IS WHAT ARE YOU GOING TO DO WHEN THEY COME FOR YOU.

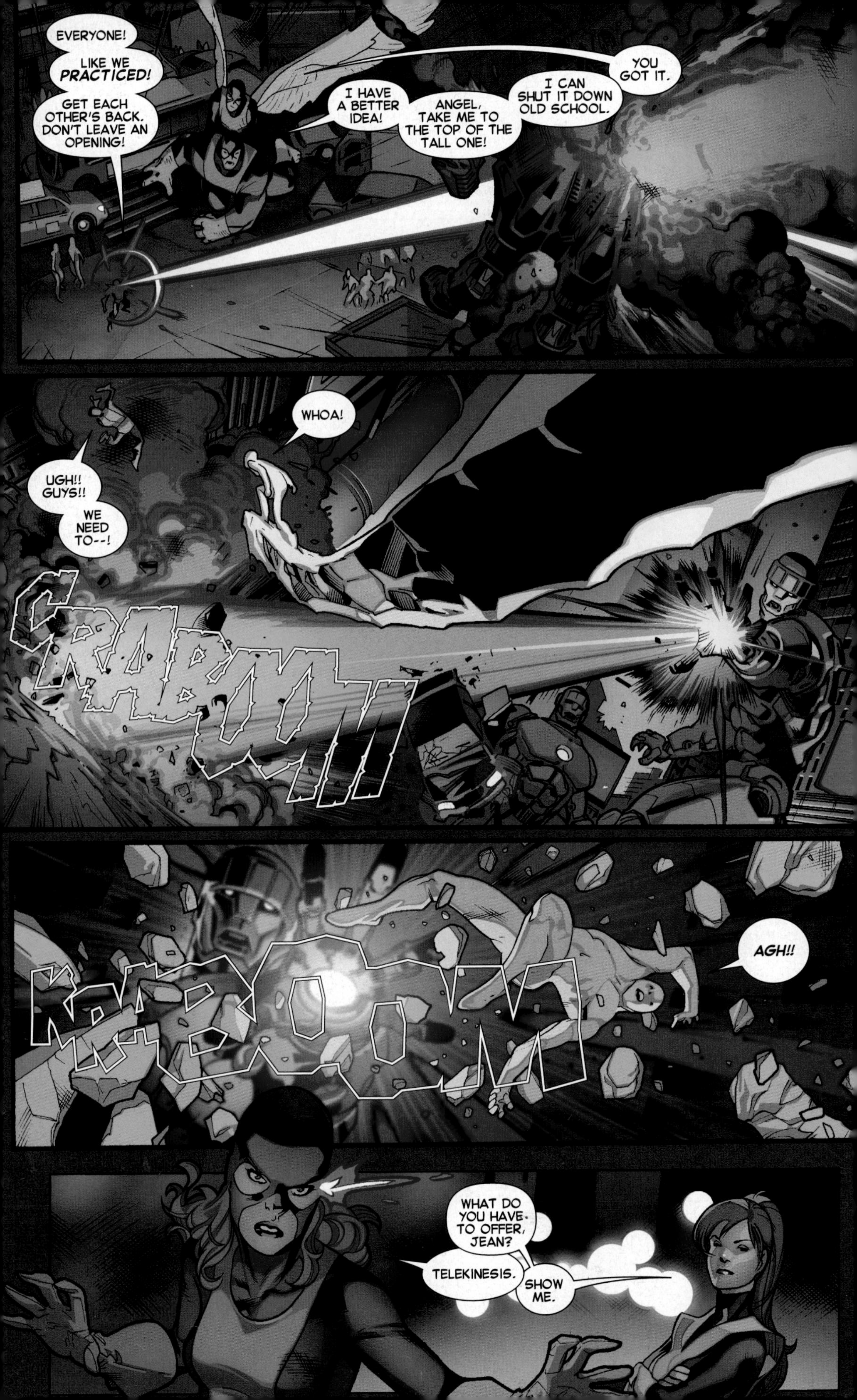
EVERYONE!
LIKE WE *PRACTICED!*
GET EACH OTHER'S BACK. DON'T LEAVE AN OPENING!
I HAVE A BETTER IDEA!
ANGEL, TAKE ME TO THE TOP OF THE TALL ONE!
I CAN SHUT IT DOWN OLD SCHOOL.
YOU GOT IT.
UGH!! GUYS!!
WE NEED TO--!
WHOA!
KRABOOM
KRABOOOM
AGH!!
WHAT DO YOU HAVE TO OFFER, JEAN?
TELEKINESIS.
SHOW ME.

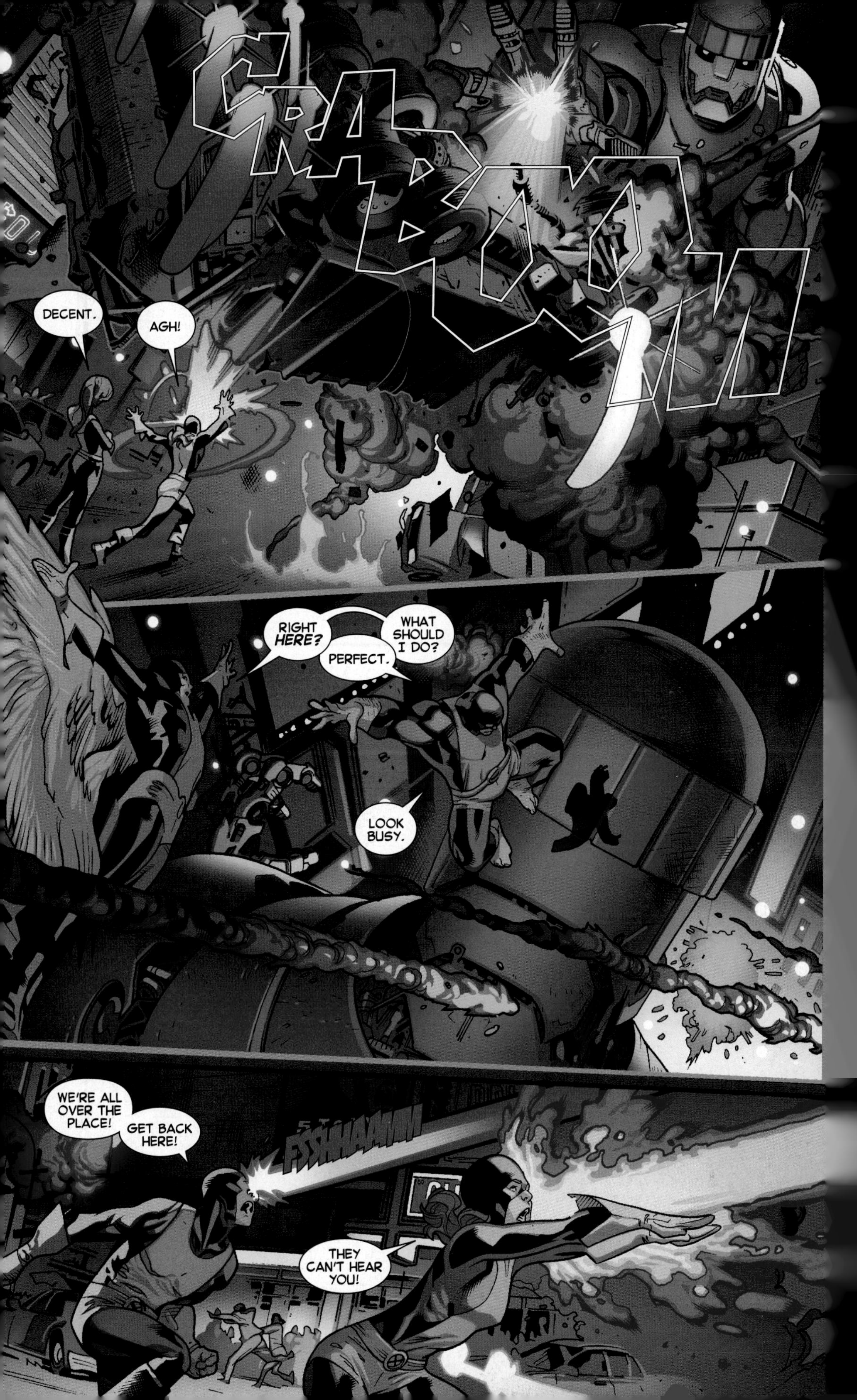

CRA-BOOM
DECENT.
AGH!
RIGHT HERE?
WHAT SHOULD I DO?
PERFECT.
LOOK BUSY.
WE'RE ALL OVER THE PLACE!
GET BACK HERE!
FSSHHAAAMM
THEY CAN'T HEAR YOU!

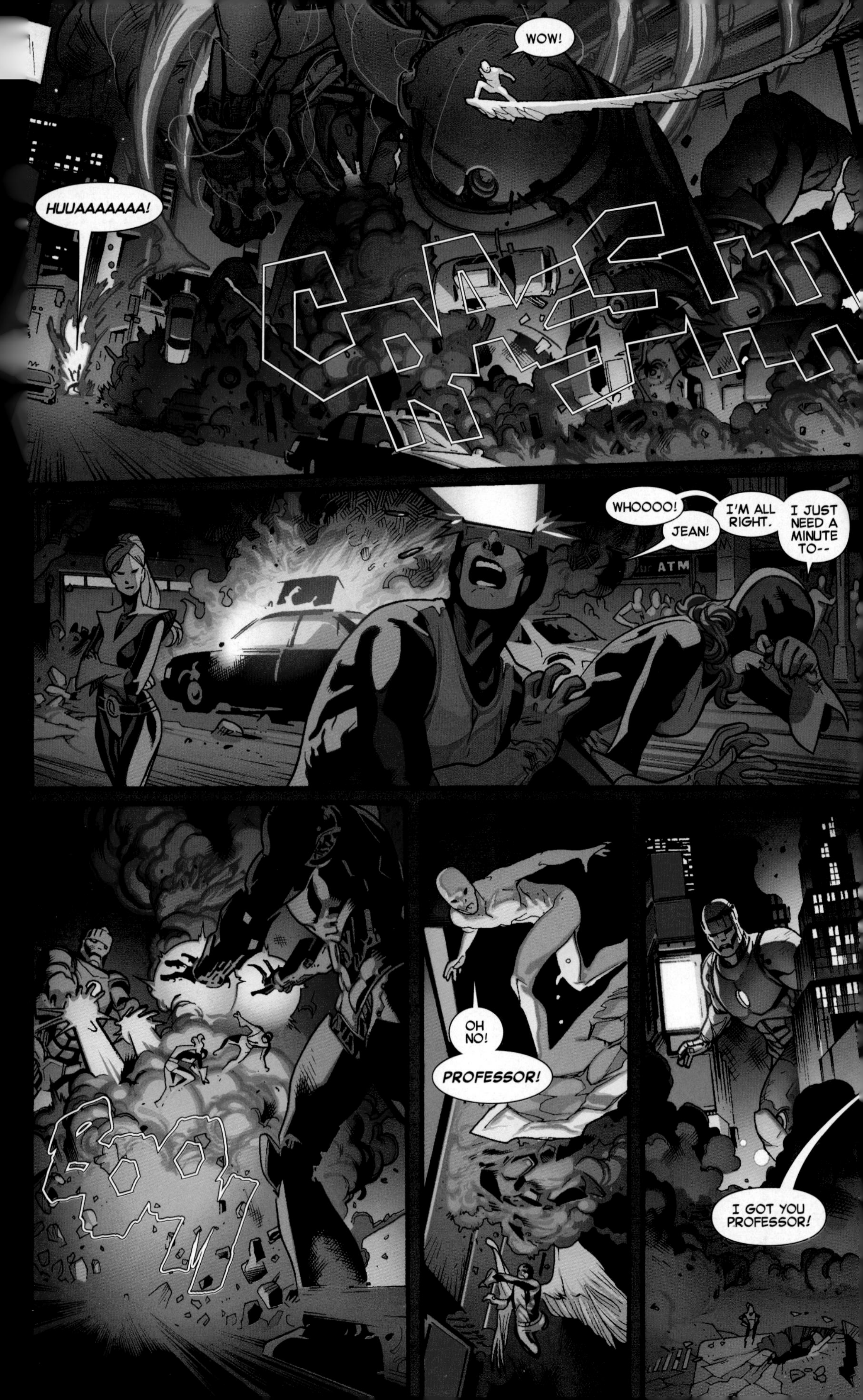
WOW!
HUUAAAAAAA!
CRASH
WHOOOO!
JEAN!
I'M ALL RIGHT.
I JUST NEED A MINUTE TO--
ATM
OH NO!
PROFESSOR!
I GOT YOU PROFESSOR!

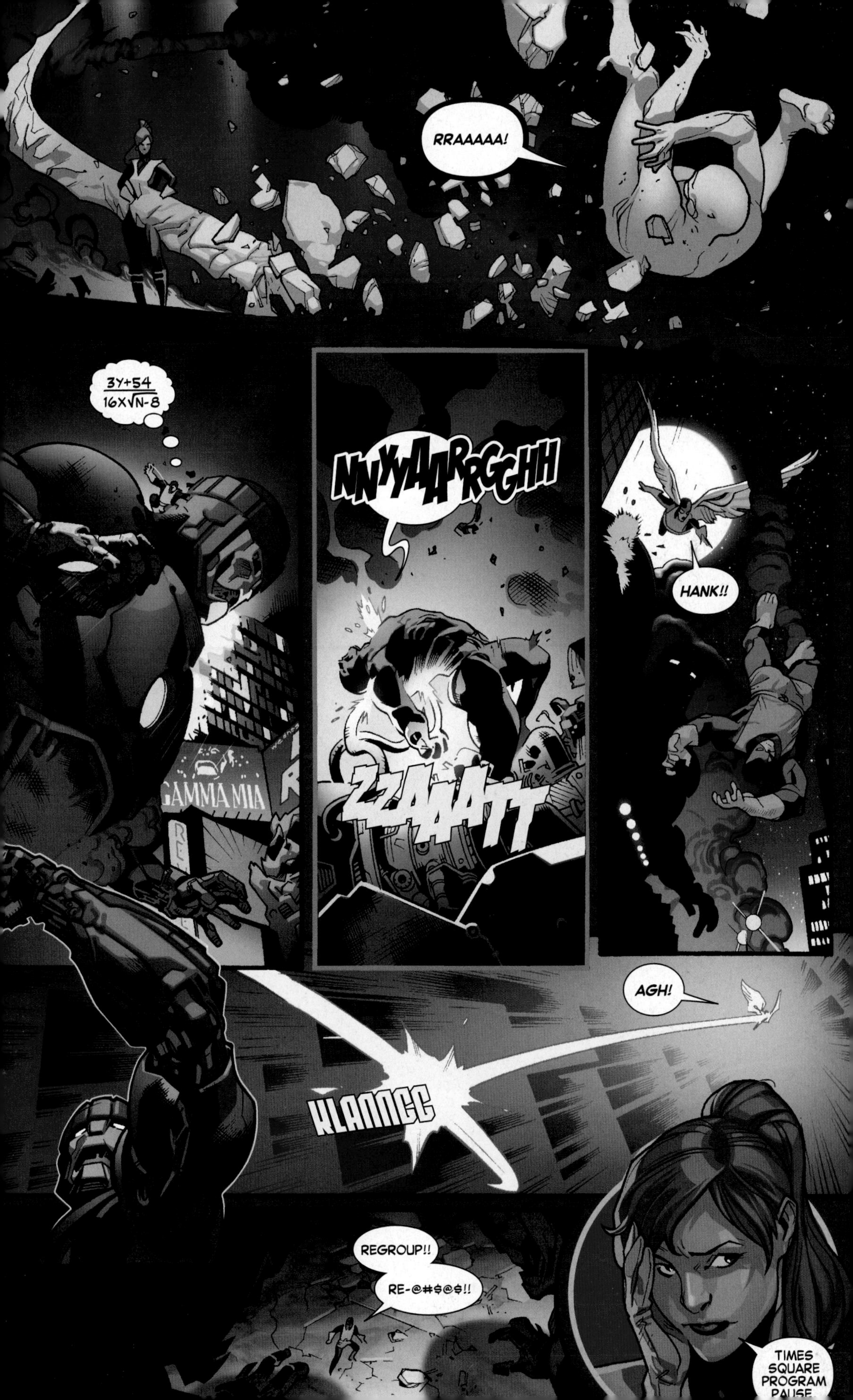
RRAAAAA!
3Y+54 / 16X√N-8
NNYYAARRGGHH
ZZAAATT
HANK!!
GAMMA MIA
AGH!
KLANNGG
REGROUP!!
RE-@#$@$!!
TIMES SQUARE PROGRAM PAUSE

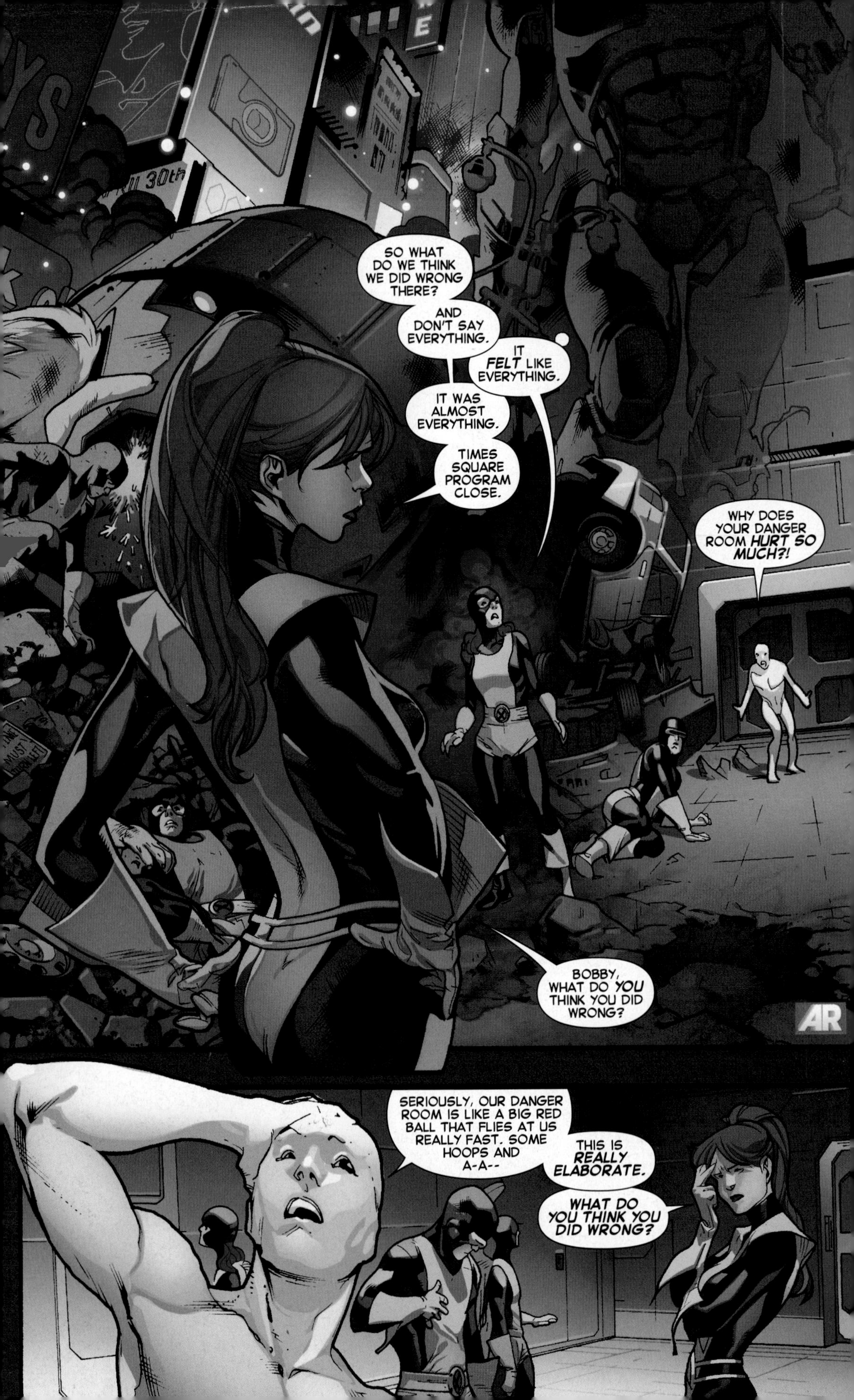
SO WHAT DO WE THINK WE DID WRONG THERE?
AND DON'T SAY EVERYTHING.
IT FELT LIKE EVERYTHING.
IT WAS ALMOST EVERYTHING.
TIMES SQUARE PROGRAM CLOSE.
WHY DOES YOUR DANGER ROOM HURT SO MUCH?!
BOBBY, WHAT DO YOU THINK YOU DID WRONG?
AR
SERIOUSLY, OUR DANGER ROOM IS LIKE A BIG RED BALL THAT FLIES AT US REALLY FAST. SOME HOOPS AND A-A--
THIS IS REALLY ELABORATE.
WHAT DO YOU THINK YOU DID WRONG?

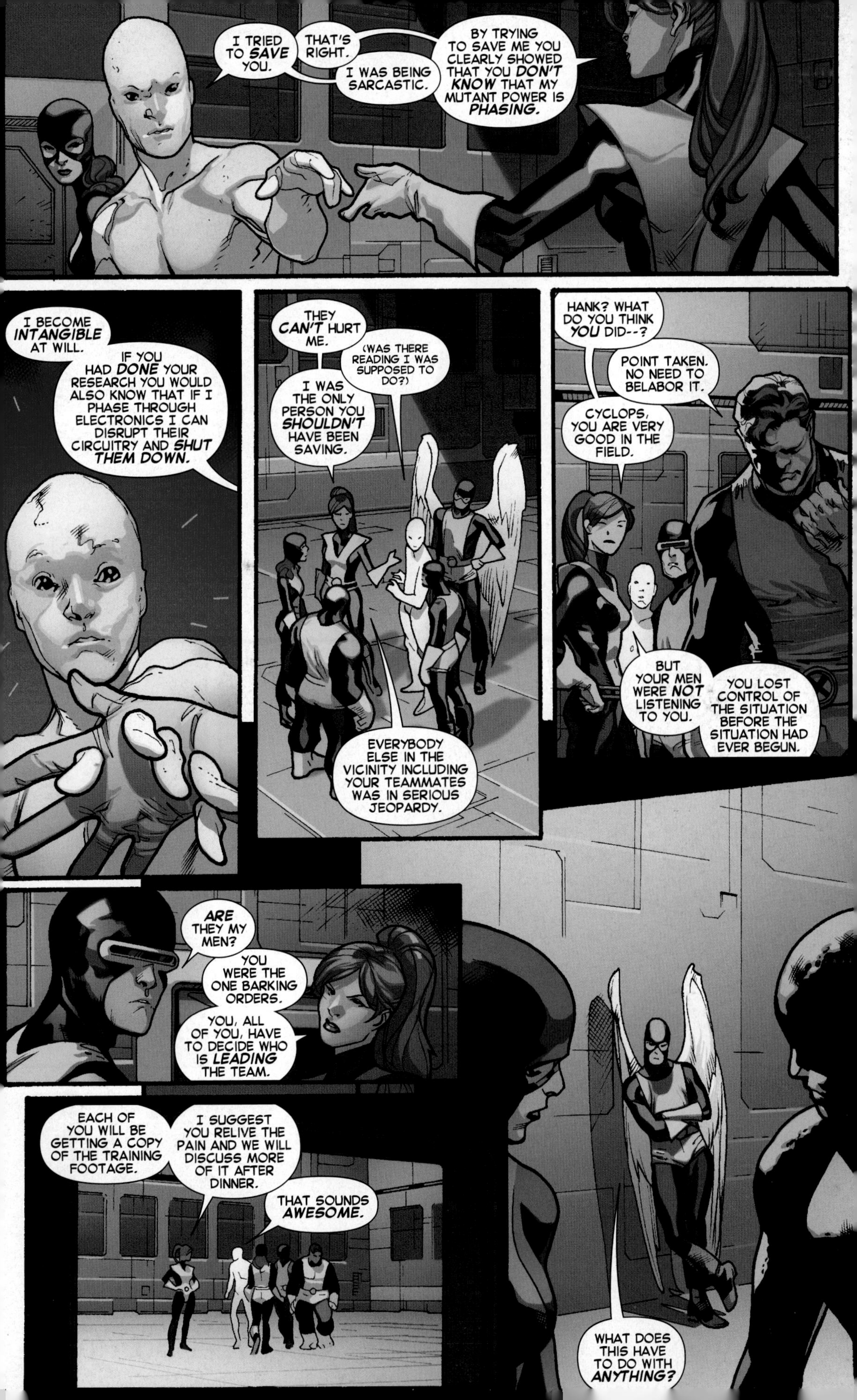
I TRIED TO SAVE YOU.
THAT'S RIGHT.
I WAS BEING SARCASTIC.
BY TRYING TO SAVE ME YOU CLEARLY SHOWED THAT YOU DON'T KNOW THAT MY MUTANT POWER IS PHASING.
I BECOME INTANGIBLE AT WILL.
IF YOU HAD DONE YOUR RESEARCH YOU WOULD ALSO KNOW THAT IF I PHASE THROUGH ELECTRONICS I CAN DISRUPT THEIR CIRCUITRY AND SHUT THEM DOWN.
THEY CAN'T HURT ME.
(WAS THERE READING I WAS SUPPOSED TO DO?)
I WAS THE ONLY PERSON YOU SHOULDN'T HAVE BEEN SAVING.
EVERYBODY ELSE IN THE VICINITY INCLUDING YOUR TEAMMATES WAS IN SERIOUS JEOPARDY.
HANK? WHAT DO YOU THINK YOU DID--?
POINT TAKEN. NO NEED TO BELABOR IT.
CYCLOPS, YOU ARE VERY GOOD IN THE FIELD.
BUT YOUR MEN WERE NOT LISTENING TO YOU.
YOU LOST CONTROL OF THE SITUATION BEFORE THE SITUATION HAD EVER BEGUN.
ARE THEY MY MEN?
YOU WERE THE ONE BARKING ORDERS.
YOU, ALL OF YOU, HAVE TO DECIDE WHO IS LEADING THE TEAM.
EACH OF YOU WILL BE GETTING A COPY OF THE TRAINING FOOTAGE.
I SUGGEST YOU RELIVE THE PAIN AND WE WILL DISCUSS MORE OF IT AFTER DINNER.
THAT SOUNDS AWESOME.
WHAT DOES THIS HAVE TO DO WITH ANYTHING?

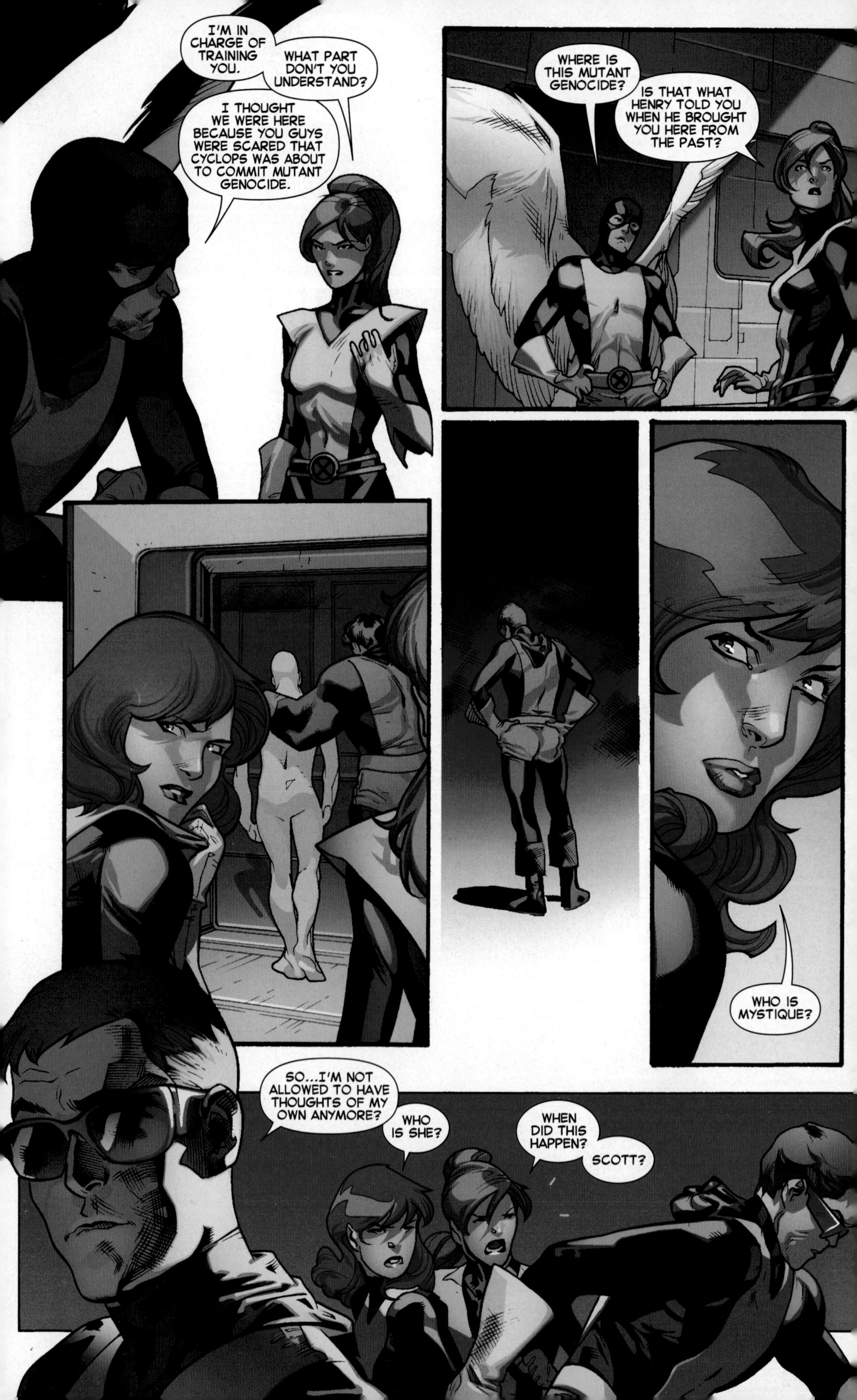

I'M IN CHARGE OF TRAINING YOU.
WHAT PART DON'T YOU UNDERSTAND?
I THOUGHT WE WERE HERE BECAUSE YOU GUYS WERE SCARED THAT CYCLOPS WAS ABOUT TO COMMIT MUTANT GENOCIDE.
WHERE IS THIS MUTANT GENOCIDE?
IS THAT WHAT HENRY TOLD YOU WHEN HE BROUGHT YOU HERE FROM THE PAST?
WHO IS MYSTIQUE?
SO...I'M NOT ALLOWED TO HAVE THOUGHTS OF MY OWN ANYMORE?
WHO IS SHE?
WHEN DID THIS HAPPEN?
SCOTT?

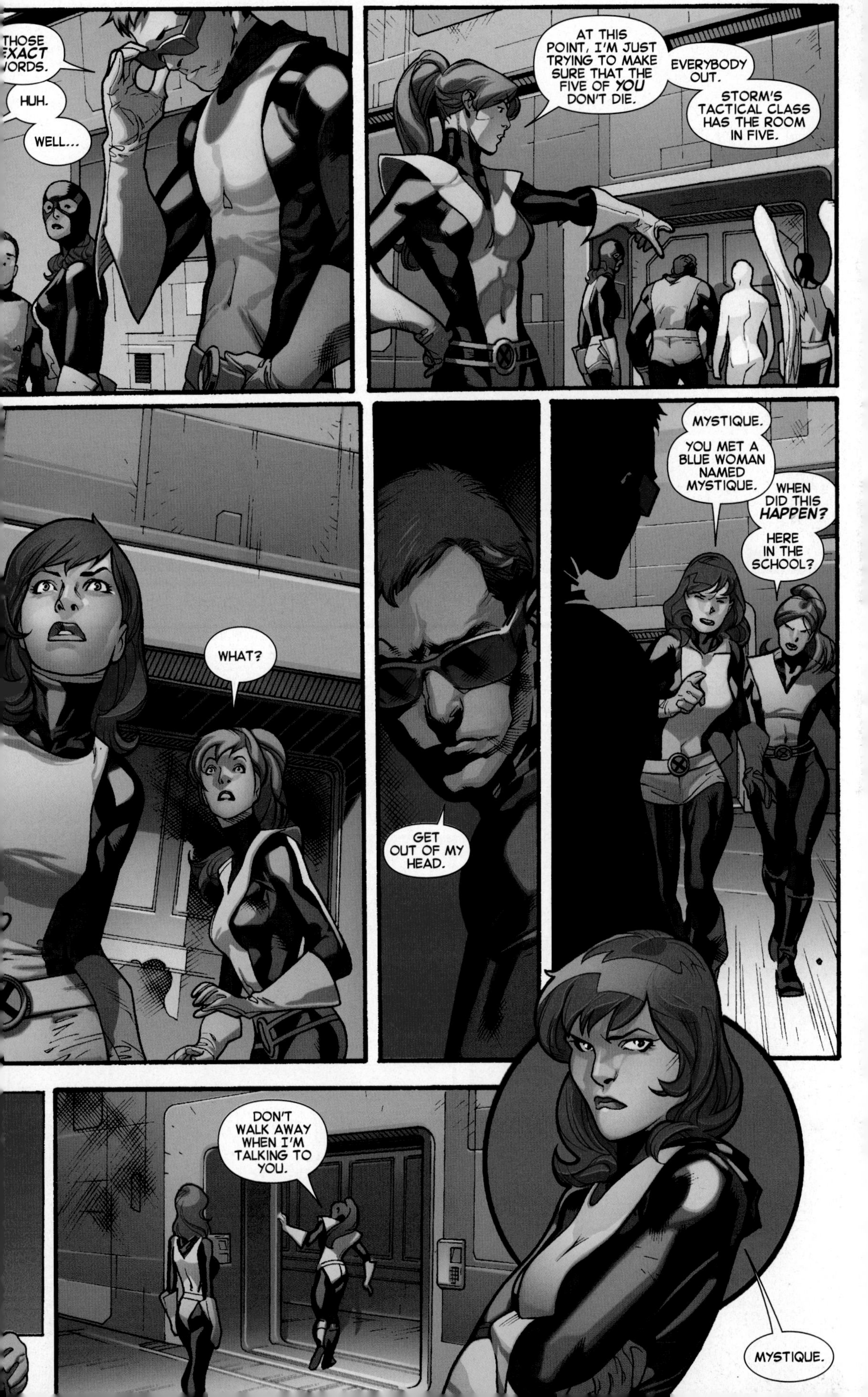
THOSE EXACT WORDS.
HUH.
WELL...
AT THIS POINT, I'M JUST TRYING TO MAKE SURE THAT THE FIVE OF YOU DON'T DIE.
EVERYBODY OUT.
STORM'S TACTICAL CLASS HAS THE ROOM IN FIVE.
WHAT?
GET OUT OF MY HEAD.
MYSTIQUE.
YOU MET A BLUE WOMAN NAMED MYSTIQUE.
WHEN DID THIS HAPPEN?
HERE IN THE SCHOOL?
DON'T WALK AWAY WHEN I'M TALKING TO YOU.
MYSTIQUE.

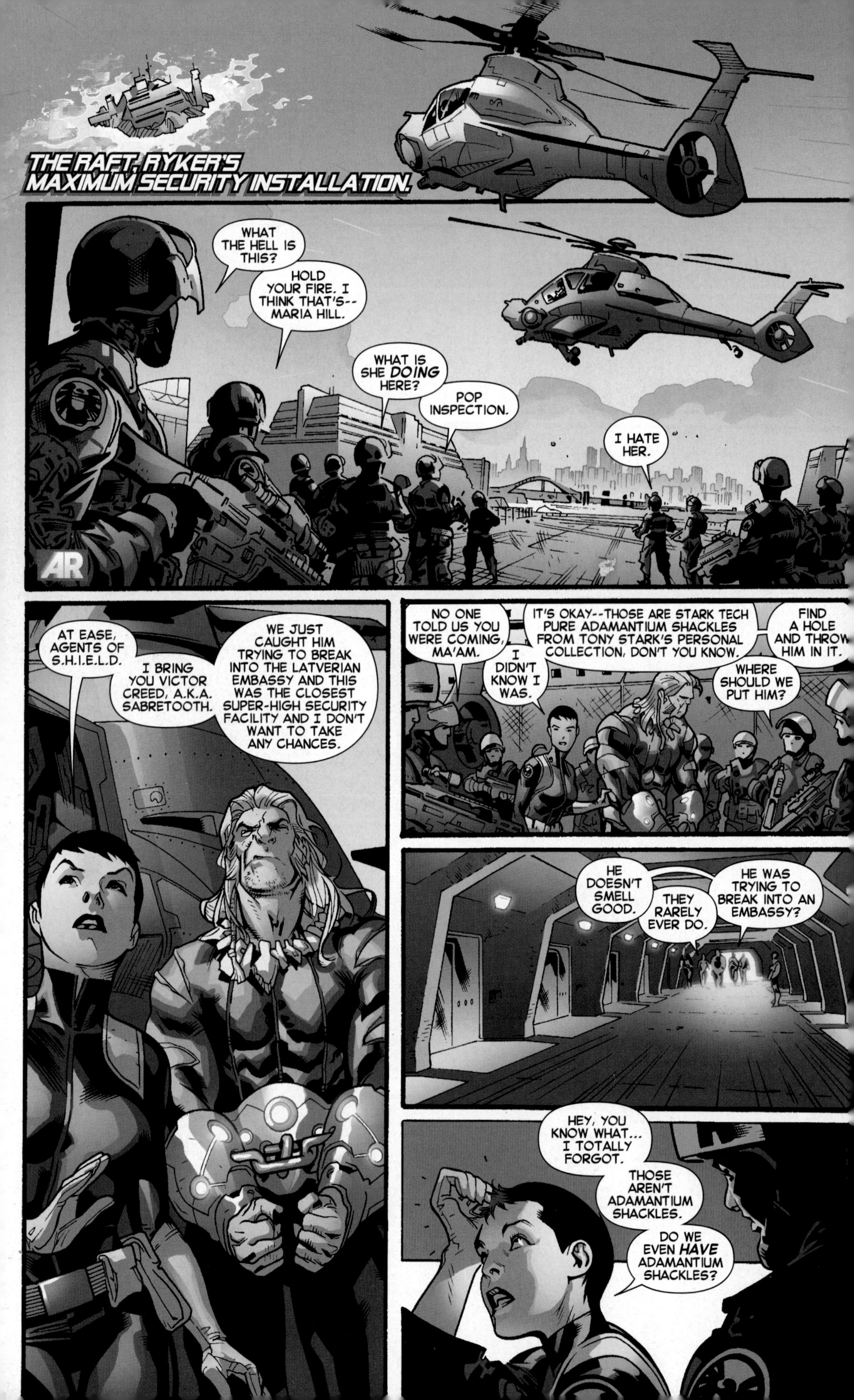
THE RAFT, RYKER'S MAXIMUM SECURITY INSTALLATION.
WHAT THE HELL IS THIS?
HOLD YOUR FIRE. I THINK THAT'S-- MARIA HILL.
WHAT IS SHE DOING HERE?
POP INSPECTION.
I HATE HER.
AT EASE, AGENTS OF S.H.I.E.L.D.
I BRING YOU VICTOR CREED, A.K.A. SABRETOOTH.
WE JUST CAUGHT HIM TRYING TO BREAK INTO THE LATVERIAN EMBASSY AND THIS WAS THE CLOSEST SUPER-HIGH SECURITY FACILITY AND I DON'T WANT TO TAKE ANY CHANCES.
NO ONE TOLD US YOU WERE COMING, MA'AM.
I DIDN'T KNOW I WAS.
IT'S OKAY--THOSE ARE STARK TECH PURE ADAMANTIUM SHACKLES FROM TONY STARK'S PERSONAL COLLECTION, DON'T YOU KNOW.
WHERE SHOULD WE PUT HIM?
FIND A HOLE AND THROW HIM IN IT.
HE DOESN'T SMELL GOOD.
THEY RARELY EVER DO.
HE WAS TRYING TO BREAK INTO AN EMBASSY?
HEY, YOU KNOW WHAT... I TOTALLY FORGOT.
THOSE AREN'T ADAMANTIUM SHACKLES.
DO WE EVEN HAVE ADAMANTIUM SHACKLES?

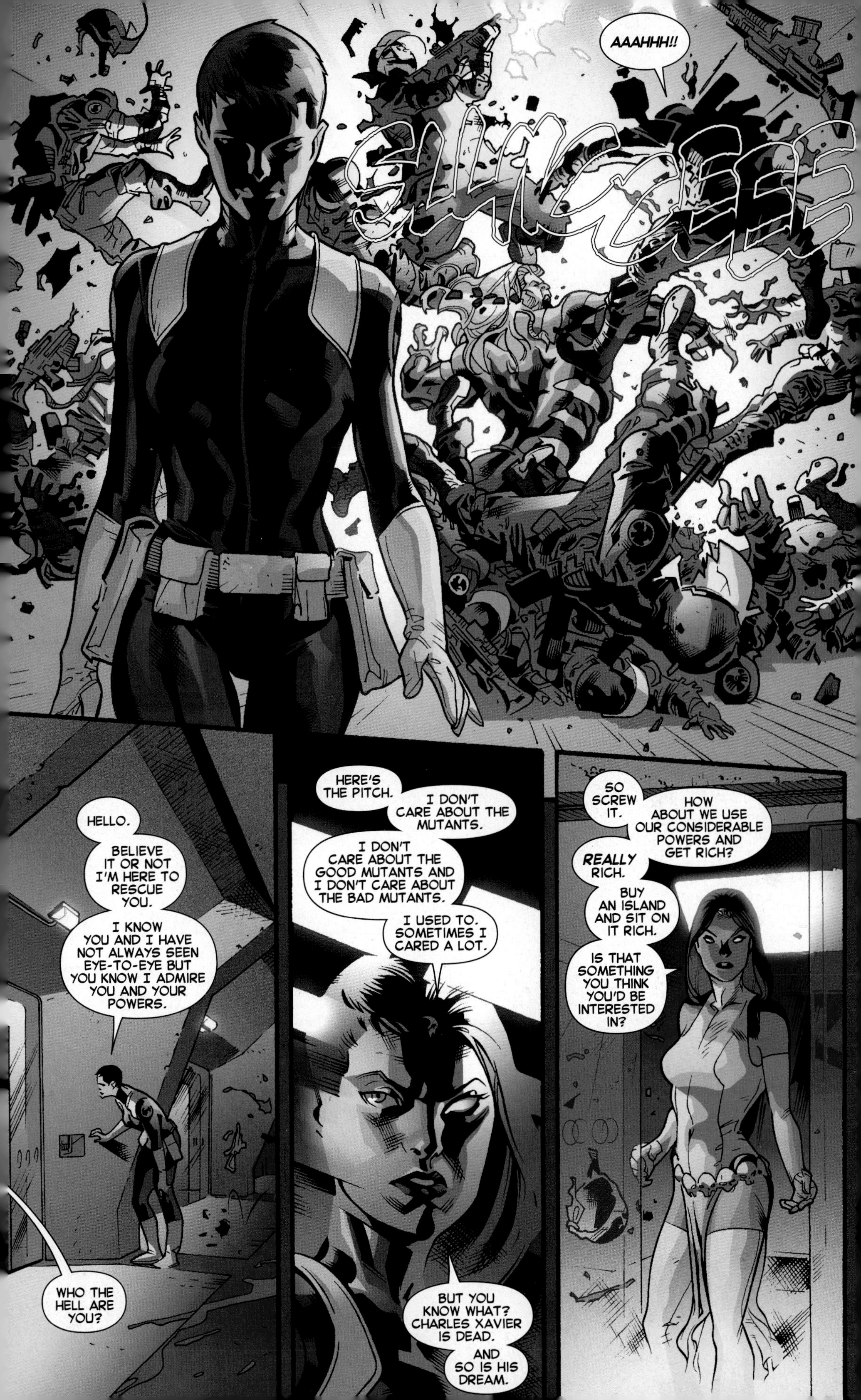
AAAHHH!!
HELLO.
BELIEVE IT OR NOT I'M HERE TO RESCUE YOU.
I KNOW YOU AND I HAVE NOT ALWAYS SEEN EYE-TO-EYE BUT YOU KNOW I ADMIRE YOU AND YOUR POWERS.
WHO THE HELL ARE YOU?
HERE'S THE PITCH.
I DON'T CARE ABOUT THE MUTANTS.
I DON'T CARE ABOUT THE GOOD MUTANTS AND I DON'T CARE ABOUT THE BAD MUTANTS.
I USED TO. SOMETIMES I CARED A LOT.
BUT YOU KNOW WHAT? CHARLES XAVIER IS DEAD.
AND SO IS HIS DREAM.
SO SCREW IT.
HOW ABOUT WE USE OUR CONSIDERABLE POWERS AND GET RICH?
REALLY RICH.
BUY AN ISLAND AND SIT ON IT RICH.
IS THAT SOMETHING YOU THINK YOU'D BE INTERESTED IN?

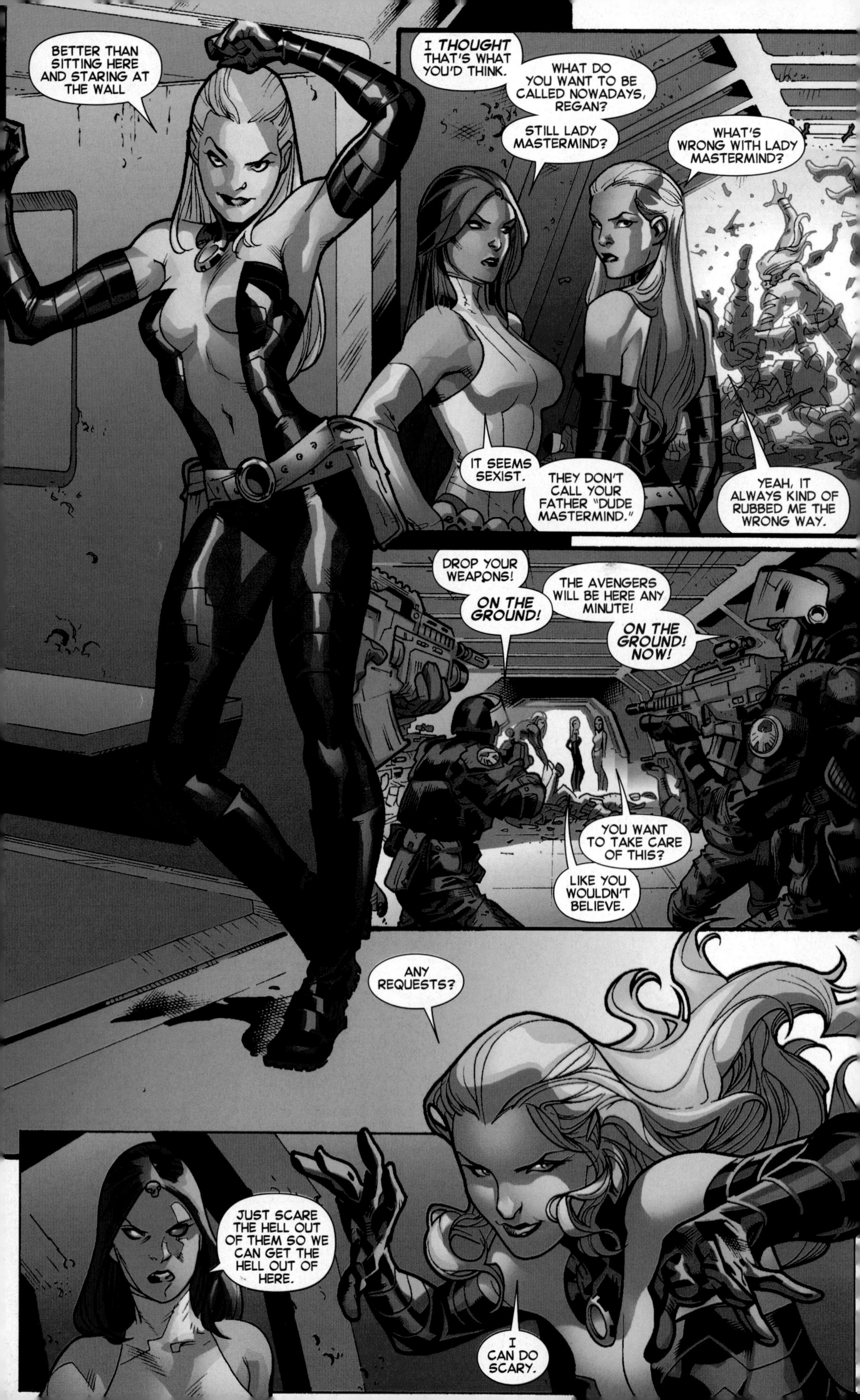
BETTER THAN SITTING HERE AND STARING AT THE WALL
I THOUGHT THAT'S WHAT YOU'D THINK.
WHAT DO YOU WANT TO BE CALLED NOWADAYS, REGAN?
STILL LADY MASTERMIND?
WHAT'S WRONG WITH LADY MASTERMIND?
IT SEEMS SEXIST.
THEY DON'T CALL YOUR FATHER "DUDE MASTERMIND."
YEAH, IT ALWAYS KIND OF RUBBED ME THE WRONG WAY.
DROP YOUR WEAPONS!
ON THE GROUND!
THE AVENGERS WILL BE HERE ANY MINUTE!
ON THE GROUND! NOW!
YOU WANT TO TAKE CARE OF THIS?
LIKE YOU WOULDN'T BELIEVE.
ANY REQUESTS?
JUST SCARE THE HELL OUT OF THEM SO WE CAN GET THE HELL OUT OF HERE.
I CAN DO SCARY.

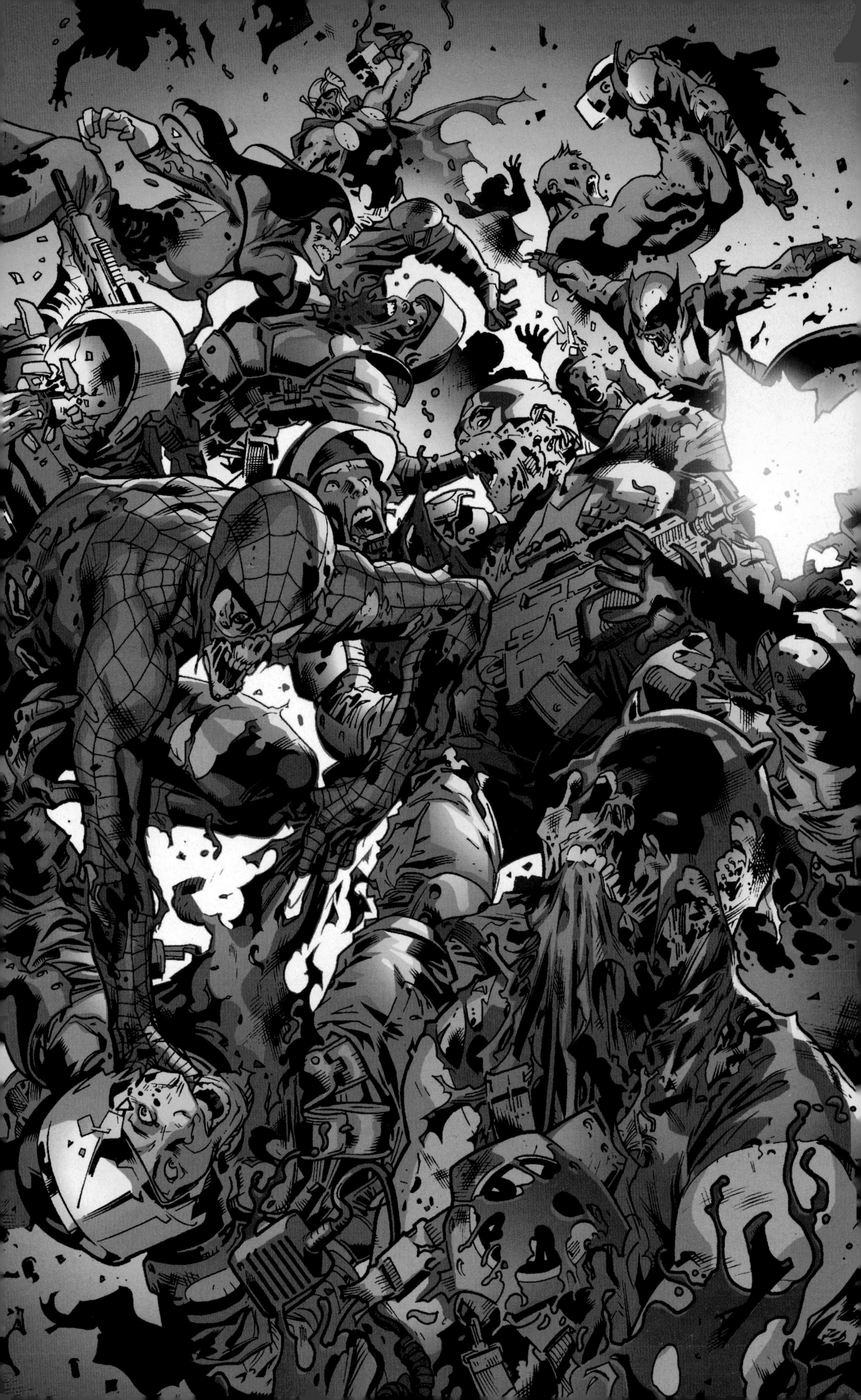

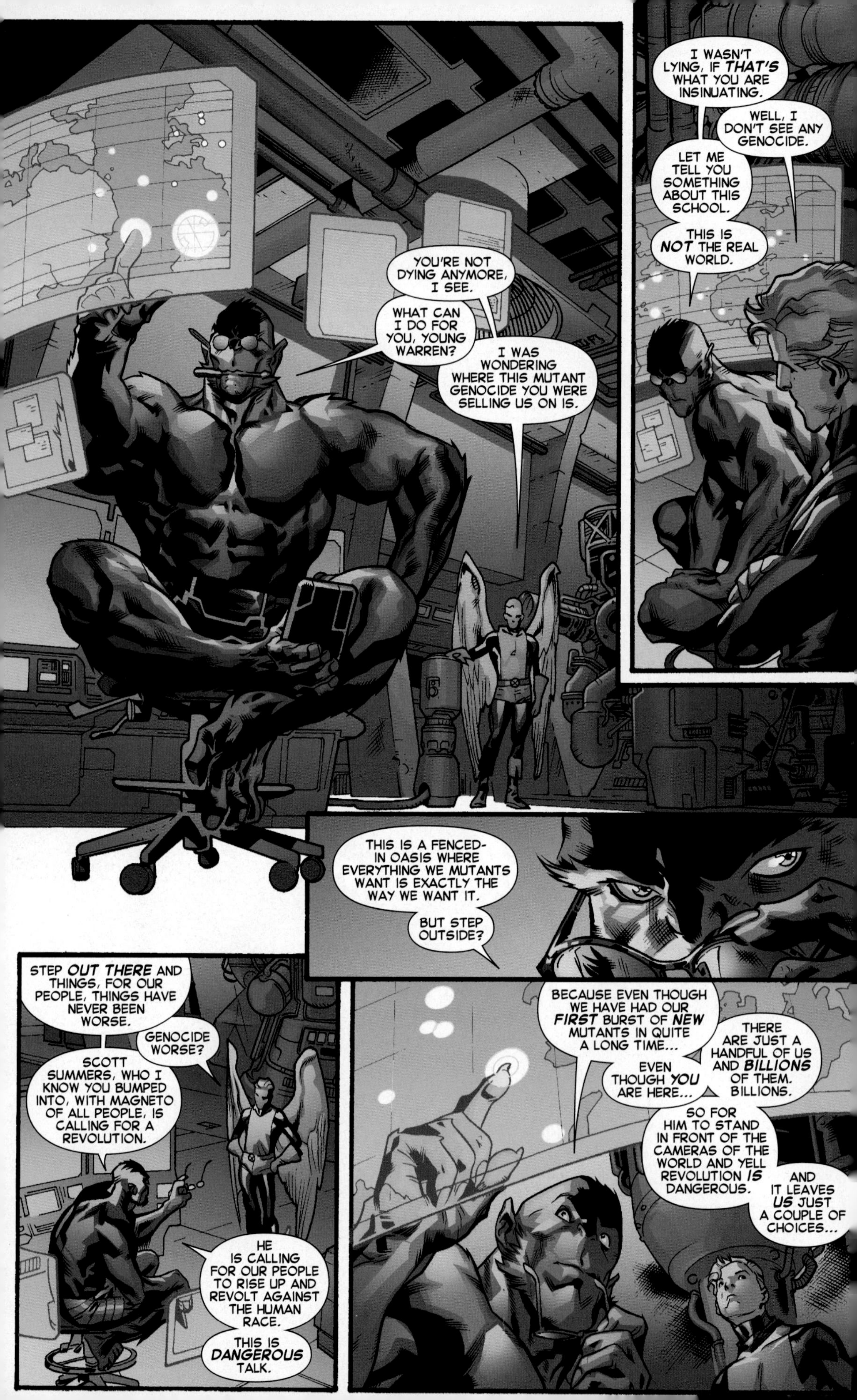
YOU'RE NOT DYING ANYMORE, I SEE.
WHAT CAN I DO FOR YOU, YOUNG WARREN?
I WAS WONDERING WHERE THIS MUTANT GENOCIDE YOU WERE SELLING US ON IS.
I WASN'T LYING, IF THAT'S WHAT YOU ARE INSINUATING.
WELL, I DON'T SEE ANY GENOCIDE.
LET ME TELL YOU SOMETHING ABOUT THIS SCHOOL.
THIS IS NOT THE REAL WORLD.
THIS IS A FENCED-IN OASIS WHERE EVERYTHING WE MUTANTS WANT IS EXACTLY THE WAY WE WANT IT.
BUT STEP OUTSIDE?
STEP OUT THERE AND THINGS, FOR OUR PEOPLE, THINGS HAVE NEVER BEEN WORSE.
GENOCIDE WORSE?
SCOTT SUMMERS, WHO I KNOW YOU BUMPED INTO, WITH MAGNETO OF ALL PEOPLE, IS CALLING FOR A REVOLUTION.
HE IS CALLING FOR OUR PEOPLE TO RISE UP AND REVOLT AGAINST THE HUMAN RACE.
THIS IS DANGEROUS TALK.
BECAUSE EVEN THOUGH WE HAVE HAD OUR FIRST BURST OF NEW MUTANTS IN QUITE A LONG TIME...
EVEN THOUGH YOU ARE HERE...
THERE ARE JUST A HANDFUL OF US AND BILLIONS OF THEM. BILLIONS.
SO FOR HIM TO STAND IN FRONT OF THE CAMERAS OF THE WORLD AND YELL REVOLUTION IS DANGEROUS.
AND IT LEAVES US JUST A COUPLE OF CHOICES...

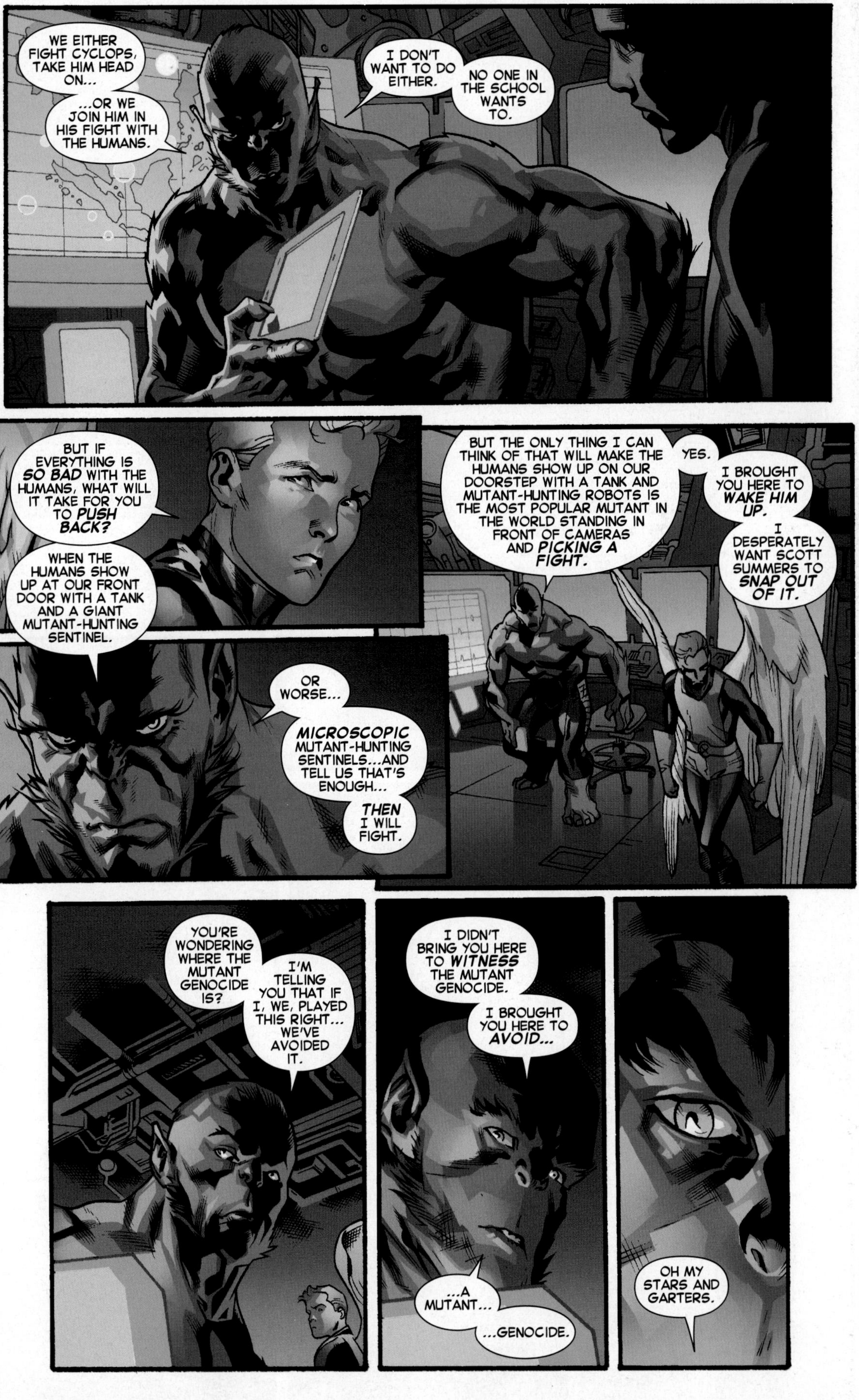
WE EITHER FIGHT CYCLOPS, TAKE HIM HEAD ON...
...OR WE JOIN HIM IN HIS FIGHT WITH THE HUMANS.
I DON'T WANT TO DO EITHER.
NO ONE IN THE SCHOOL WANTS TO.
BUT IF EVERYTHING IS SO BAD WITH THE HUMANS, WHAT WILL IT TAKE FOR YOU TO PUSH BACK?
WHEN THE HUMANS SHOW UP AT OUR FRONT DOOR WITH A TANK AND A GIANT MUTANT-HUNTING SENTINEL.
OR WORSE...
MICROSCOPIC MUTANT-HUNTING SENTINELS...AND TELL US THAT'S ENOUGH...
THEN I WILL FIGHT.
BUT THE ONLY THING I CAN THINK OF THAT WILL MAKE THE HUMANS SHOW UP ON OUR DOORSTEP WITH A TANK AND MUTANT-HUNTING ROBOTS IS THE MOST POPULAR MUTANT IN THE WORLD STANDING IN FRONT OF CAMERAS AND PICKING A FIGHT.
YES.
I BROUGHT YOU HERE TO WAKE HIM UP.
I DESPERATELY WANT SCOTT SUMMERS TO SNAP OUT OF IT.
YOU'RE WONDERING WHERE THE MUTANT GENOCIDE IS?
I'M TELLING YOU THAT IF I, WE, PLAYED THIS RIGHT... WE'VE AVOIDED IT.
I DIDN'T BRING YOU HERE TO WITNESS THE MUTANT GENOCIDE.
I BROUGHT YOU HERE TO AVOID...
...A MUTANT...
...GENOCIDE.
OH MY STARS AND GARTERS.

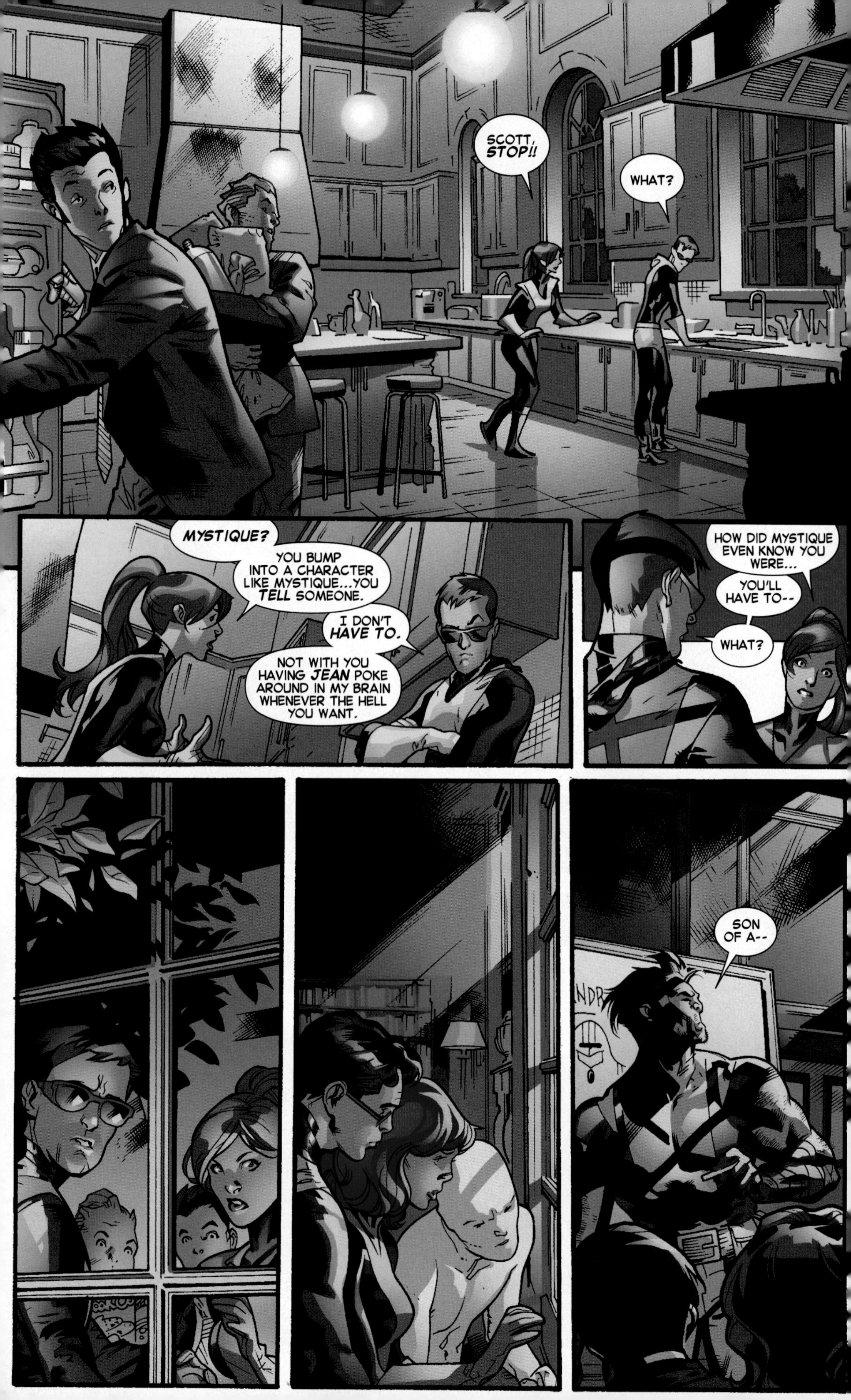
SCOTT, STOP!!
WHAT?
MYSTIQUE?
YOU BUMP INTO A CHARACTER LIKE MYSTIQUE...YOU TELL SOMEONE.
I DON'T HAVE TO.
NOT WITH YOU HAVING JEAN POKE AROUND IN MY BRAIN WHENEVER THE HELL YOU WANT.
HOW DID MYSTIQUE EVEN KNOW YOU WERE...
YOU'LL HAVE TO--
WHAT?
SON OF A--

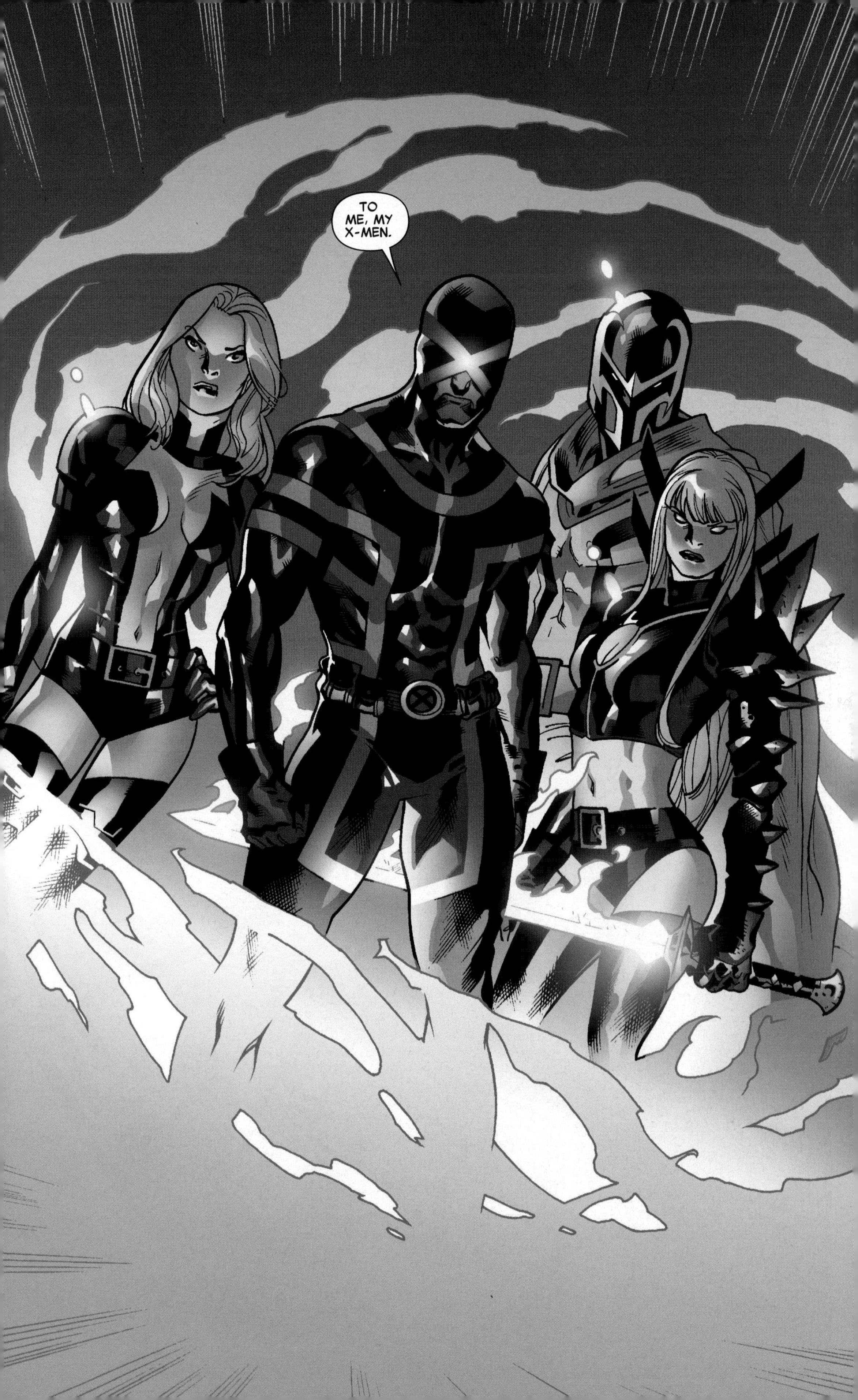
TO ME, MY X-MEN.

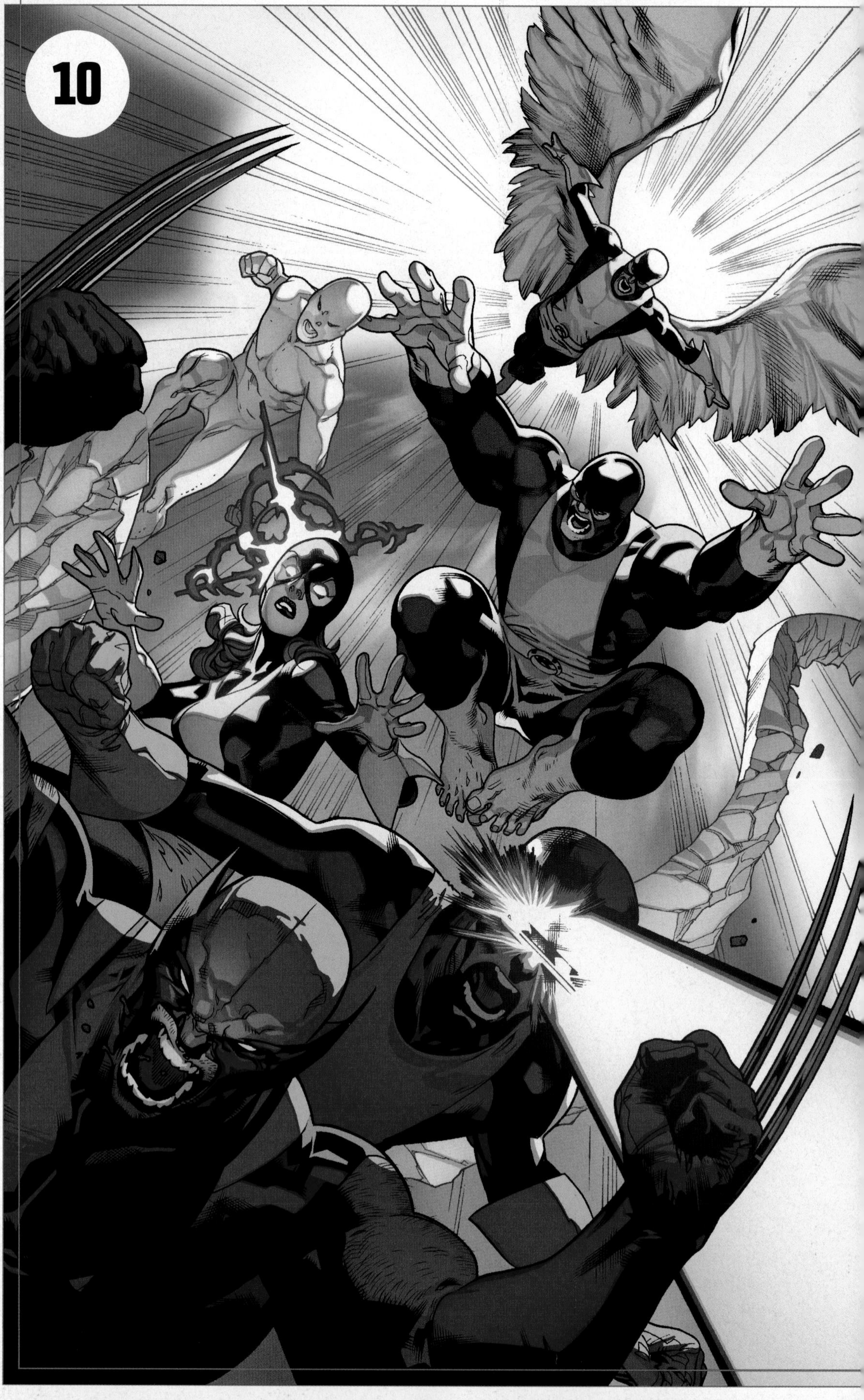
10

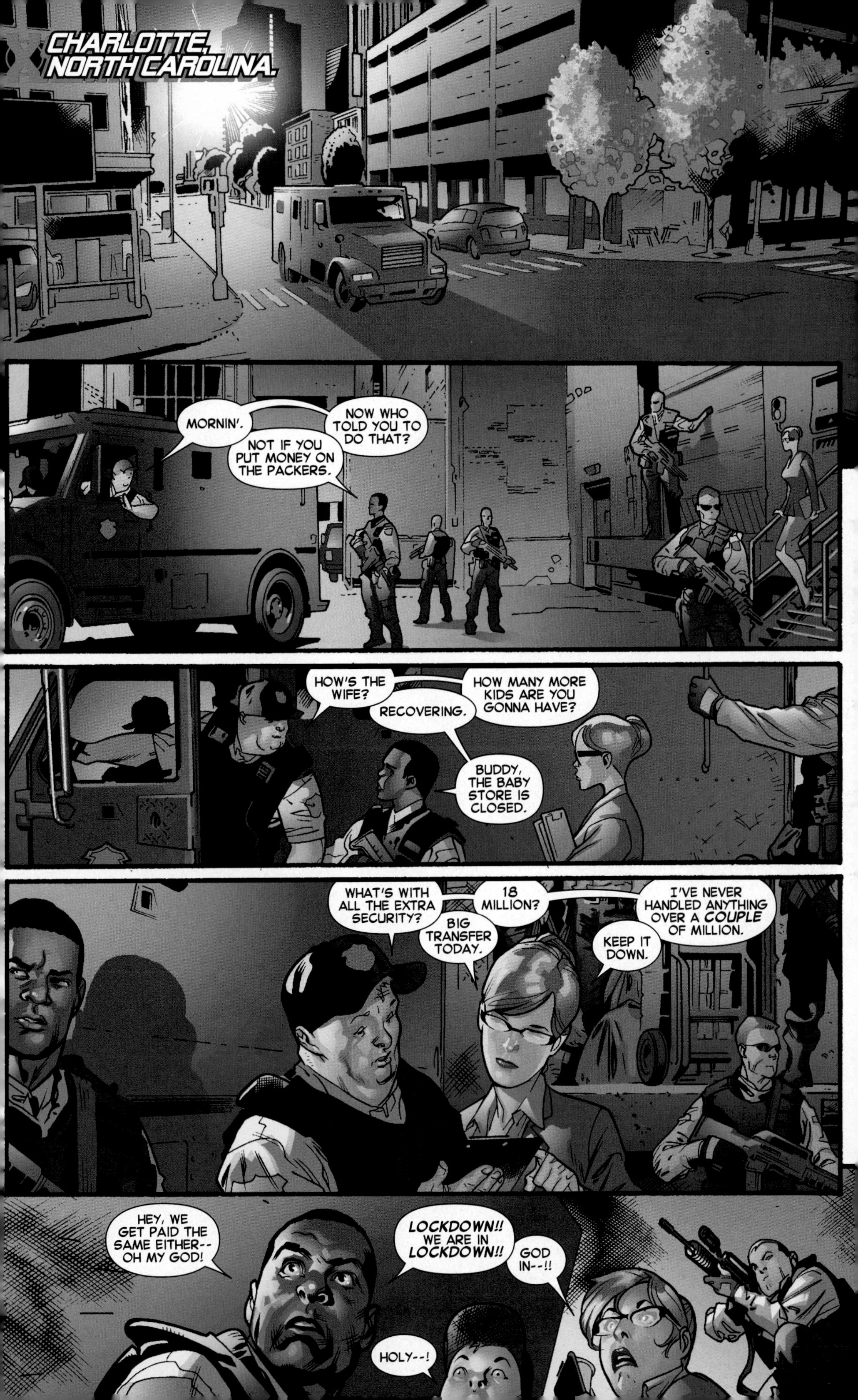
CHARLOTTE, NORTH CAROLINA.
MORNIN'.
NOW WHO TOLD YOU TO DO THAT?
NOT IF YOU PUT MONEY ON THE PACKERS.
HOW'S THE WIFE?
RECOVERING.
HOW MANY MORE KIDS ARE YOU GONNA HAVE?
BUDDY, THE BABY STORE IS CLOSED.
WHAT'S WITH ALL THE EXTRA SECURITY?
BIG TRANSFER TODAY.
18 MILLION?
I'VE NEVER HANDLED ANYTHING OVER A *COUPLE* OF MILLION.
KEEP IT DOWN.
HEY, WE GET PAID THE SAME EITHER-- OH MY GOD!
LOCKDOWN!! WE ARE IN *LOCKDOWN!!*
GOD IN--!!
HOLY--!

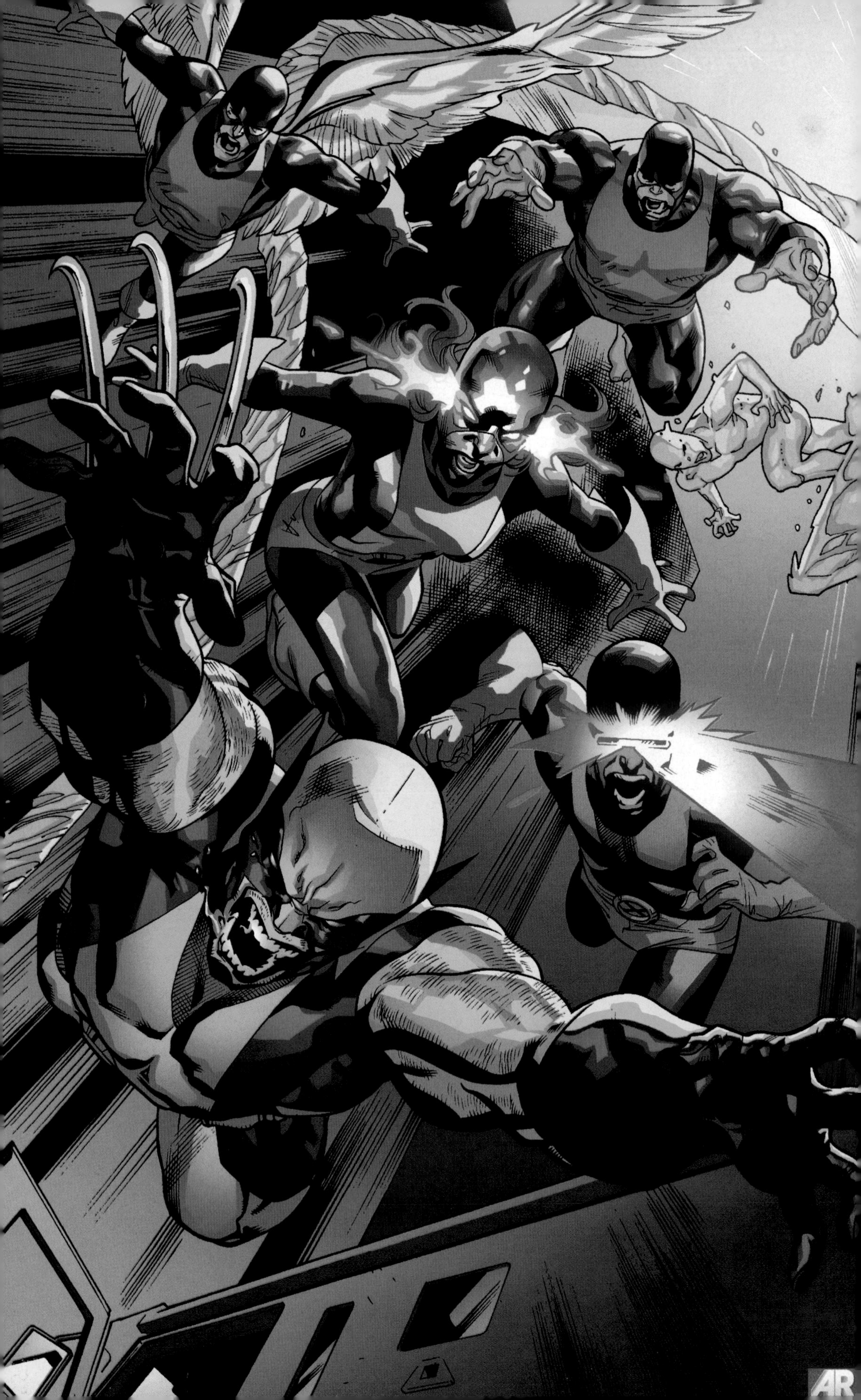

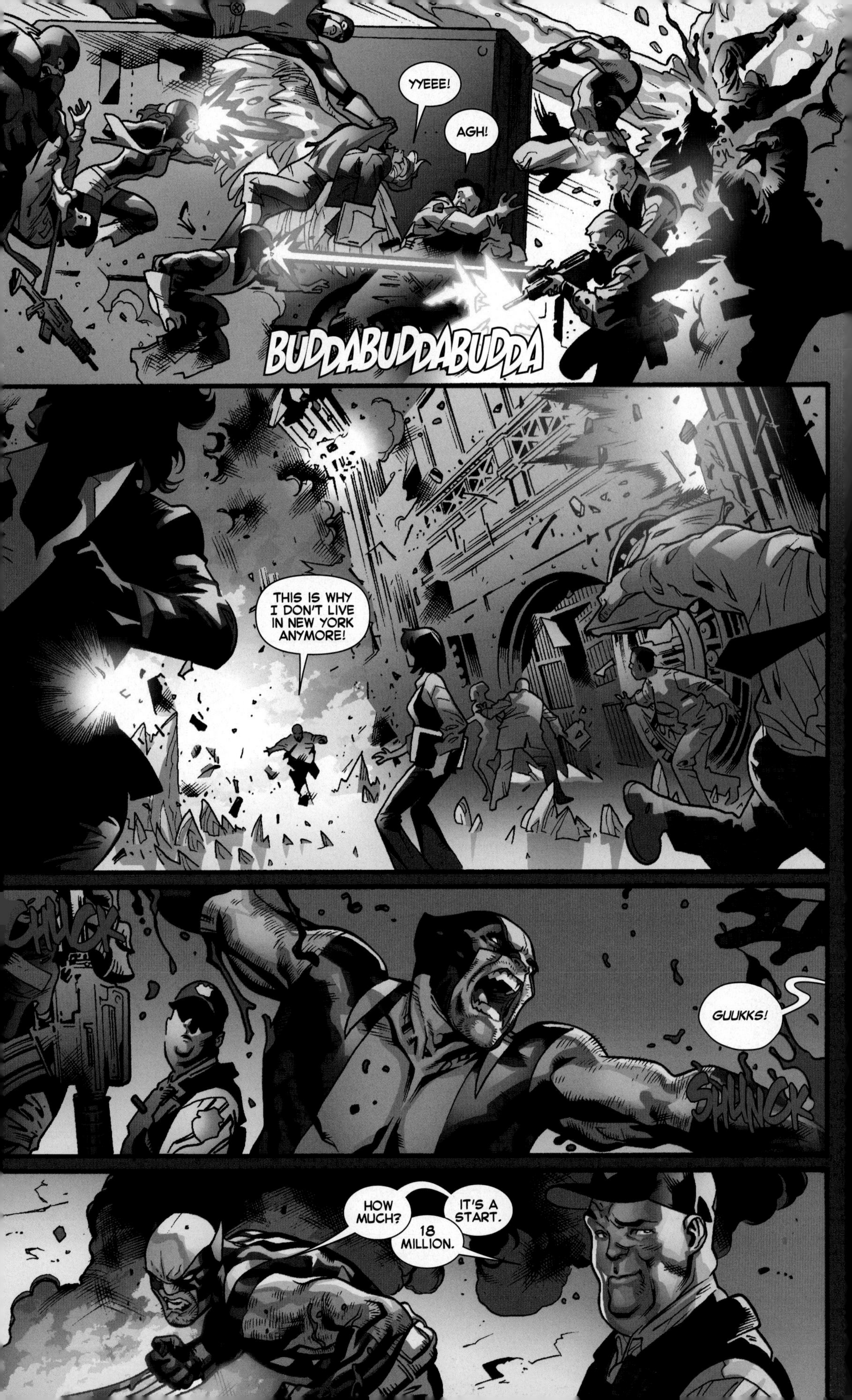
YYEEE!
AGH!
BUDDABUDDABUDDA
THIS IS WHY I DON'T LIVE IN NEW YORK ANYMORE!
CHUCK
GUUKKS!
SHUNCK
HOW MUCH?
18 MILLION.
IT'S A START.

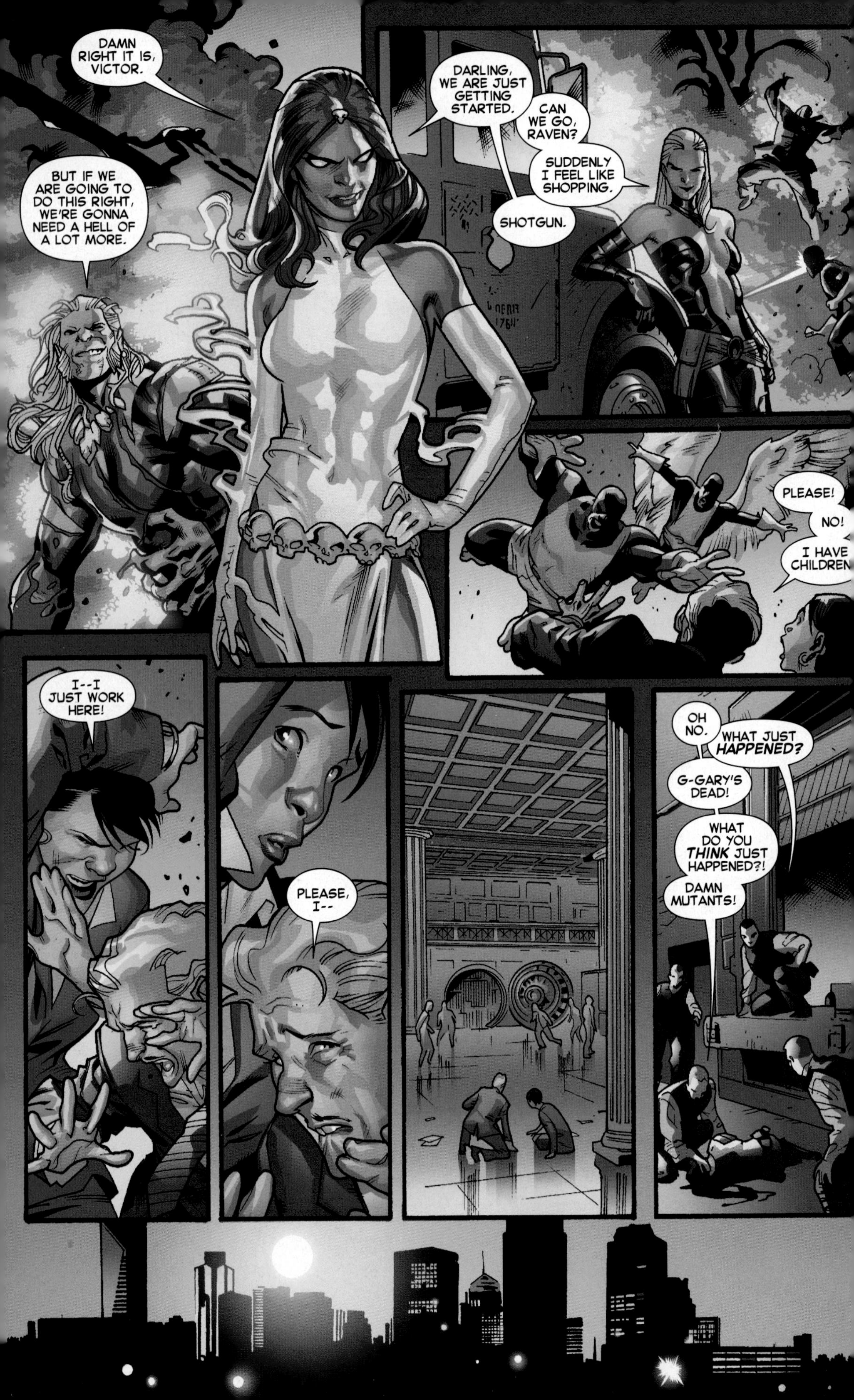
DAMN RIGHT IT IS, VICTOR.
BUT IF WE ARE GOING TO DO THIS RIGHT, WE'RE GONNA NEED A HELL OF A LOT MORE.
DARLING, WE ARE JUST GETTING STARTED.
CAN WE GO, RAVEN?
SUDDENLY I FEEL LIKE SHOPPING.
SHOTGUN.
PLEASE!
NO!
I HAVE CHILDREN
I--I JUST WORK HERE!
PLEASE, I--
OH NO.
WHAT JUST *HAPPENED?*
G-GARY'S DEAD!
WHAT DO YOU *THINK* JUST HAPPENED?!
DAMN MUTANTS!

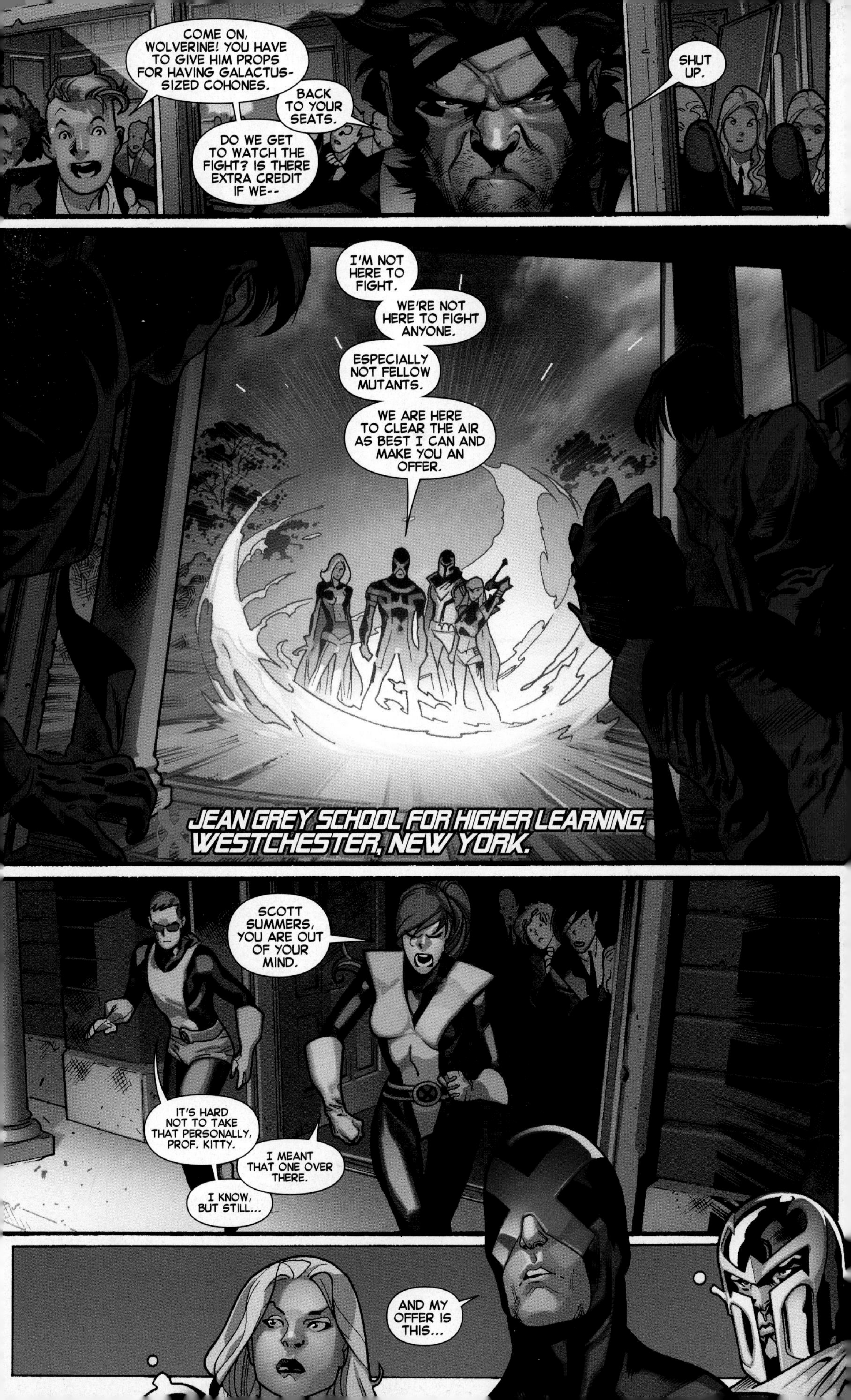
COME ON, WOLVERINE! YOU HAVE TO GIVE HIM PROPS FOR HAVING GALACTUS-SIZED COHONES.
DO WE GET TO WATCH THE FIGHT? IS THERE EXTRA CREDIT IF WE--
BACK TO YOUR SEATS.
SHUT UP.
I'M NOT HERE TO FIGHT.
WE'RE NOT HERE TO FIGHT ANYONE.
ESPECIALLY NOT FELLOW MUTANTS.
WE ARE HERE TO CLEAR THE AIR AS BEST I CAN AND MAKE YOU AN OFFER.
JEAN GREY SCHOOL FOR HIGHER LEARNING. WESTCHESTER, NEW YORK.
SCOTT SUMMERS, YOU ARE OUT OF YOUR MIND.
IT'S HARD NOT TO TAKE THAT PERSONALLY, PROF. KITTY.
I MEANT THAT ONE OVER THERE.
I KNOW, BUT STILL...
AND MY OFFER IS THIS...

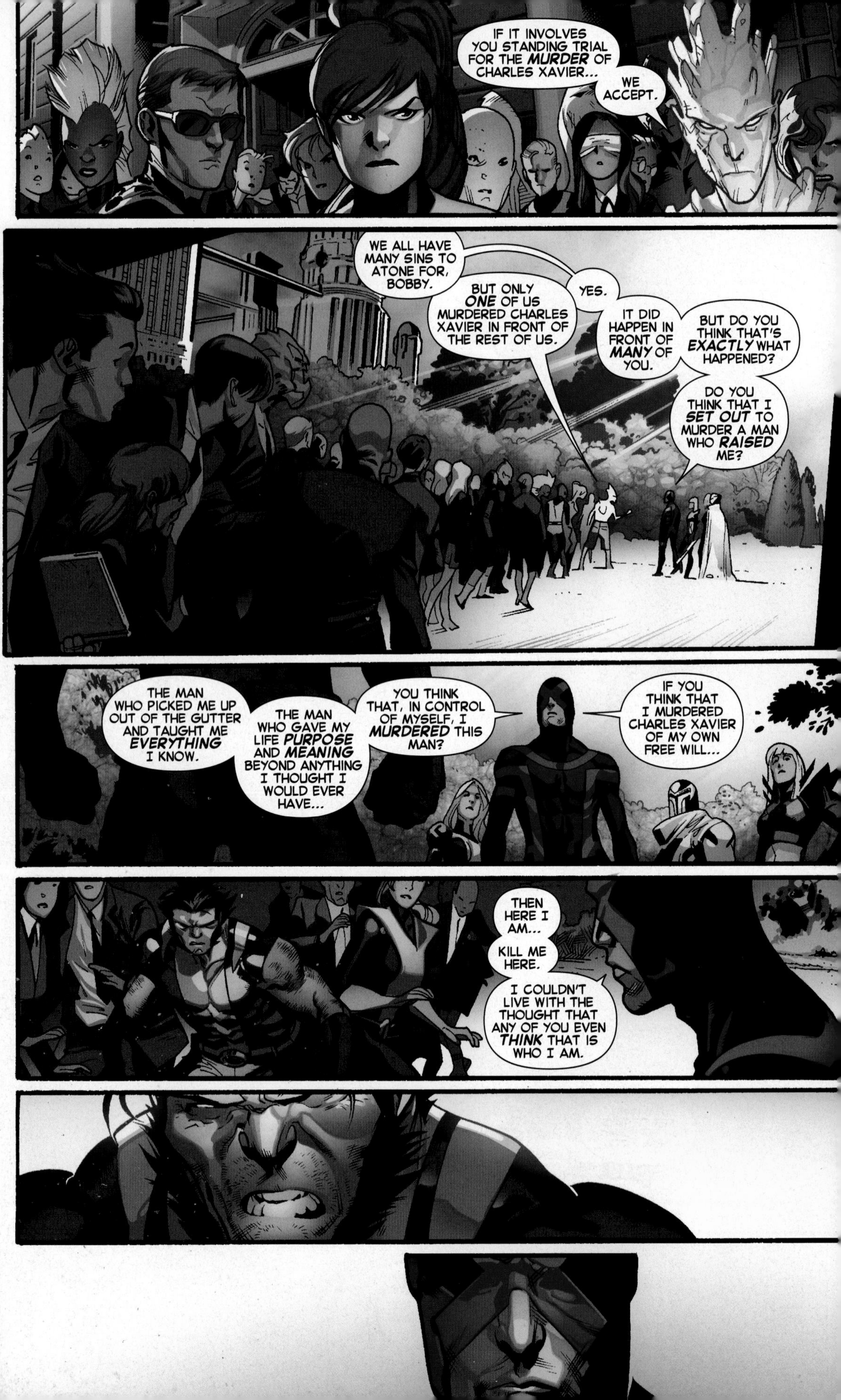
IF IT INVOLVES YOU STANDING TRIAL FOR THE MURDER OF CHARLES XAVIER...
WE ACCEPT.
WE ALL HAVE MANY SINS TO ATONE FOR, BOBBY.
BUT ONLY ONE OF US MURDERED CHARLES XAVIER IN FRONT OF THE REST OF US.
YES.
IT DID HAPPEN IN FRONT OF MANY OF YOU.
BUT DO YOU THINK THAT'S EXACTLY WHAT HAPPENED?
DO YOU THINK THAT I SET OUT TO MURDER A MAN WHO RAISED ME?
THE MAN WHO PICKED ME UP OUT OF THE GUTTER AND TAUGHT ME EVERYTHING I KNOW.
THE MAN WHO GAVE MY LIFE PURPOSE AND MEANING BEYOND ANYTHING I THOUGHT I WOULD EVER HAVE...
YOU THINK THAT, IN CONTROL OF MYSELF, I MURDERED THIS MAN?
IF YOU THINK THAT I MURDERED CHARLES XAVIER OF MY OWN FREE WILL...
THEN HERE I AM...
KILL ME HERE.
I COULDN'T LIVE WITH THE THOUGHT THAT ANY OF YOU EVEN THINK THAT IS WHO I AM.

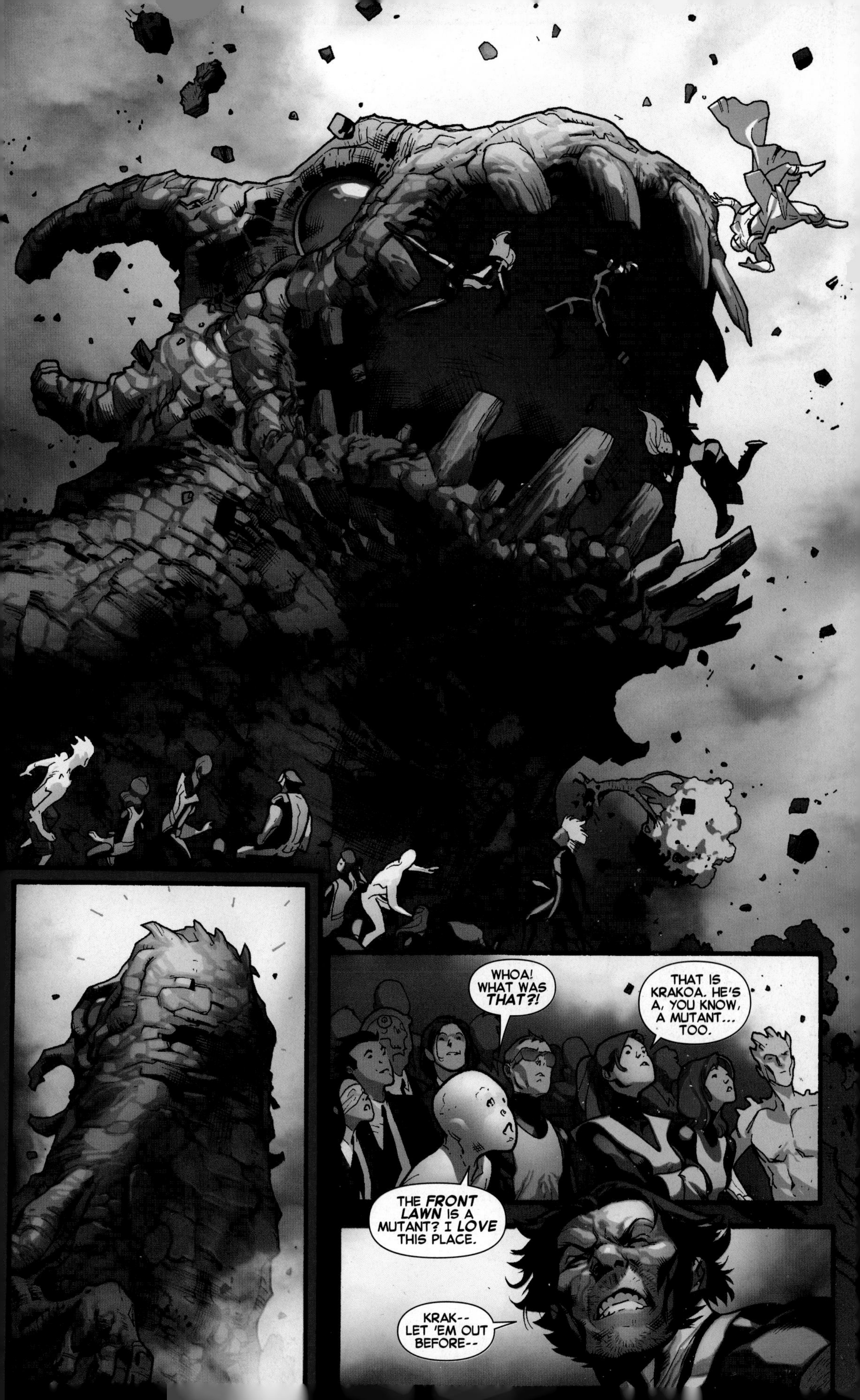
WHOA! WHAT WAS THAT?!
THAT IS KRAKOA. HE'S A, YOU KNOW, A MUTANT... TOO.
THE FRONT LAWN IS A MUTANT? I LOVE THIS PLACE.
KRAK-- LET 'EM OUT BEFORE--

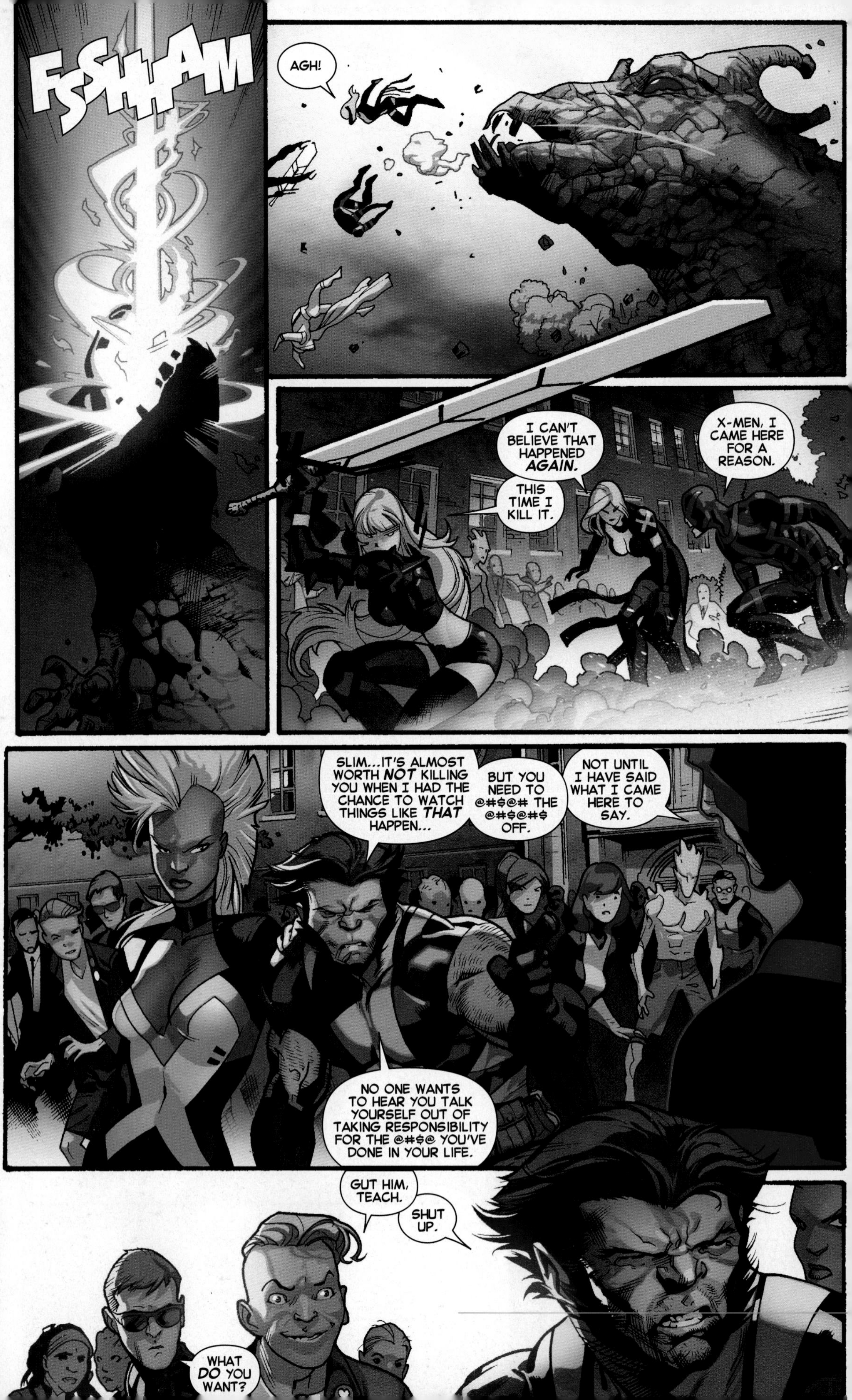
FSSHHAM
AGH!
I CAN'T BELIEVE THAT HAPPENED AGAIN.
THIS TIME I KILL IT.
X-MEN, I CAME HERE FOR A REASON.
SLIM...IT'S ALMOST WORTH NOT KILLING YOU WHEN I HAD THE CHANCE TO WATCH THINGS LIKE THAT HAPPEN...
BUT YOU NEED TO @#$@# THE @#$@#$ OFF.
NOT UNTIL I HAVE SAID WHAT I CAME HERE TO SAY.
NO ONE WANTS TO HEAR YOU TALK YOURSELF OUT OF TAKING RESPONSIBILITY FOR THE @#$@ YOU'VE DONE IN YOUR LIFE.
GUT HIM, TEACH.
SHUT UP.
WHAT DO YOU WANT?

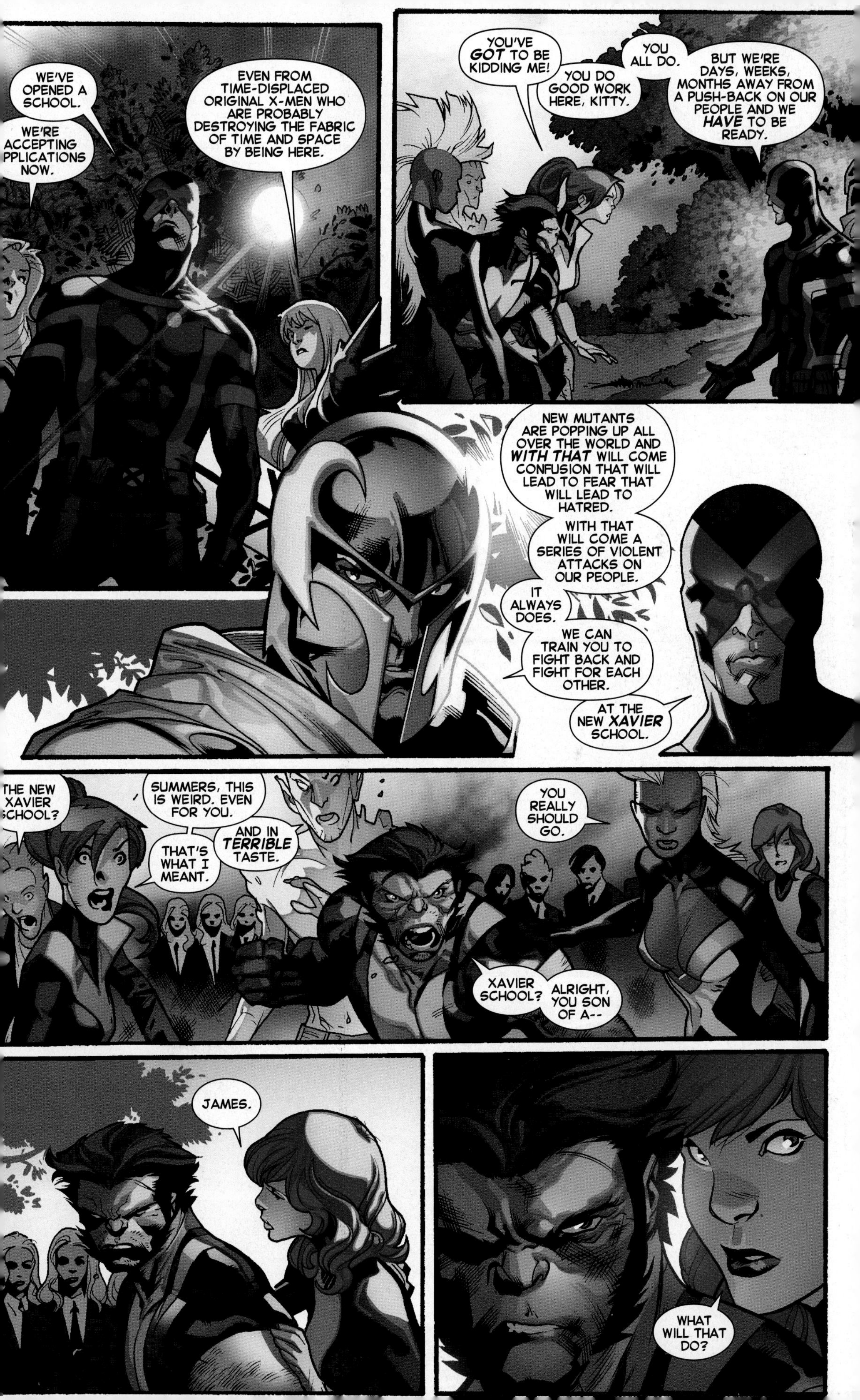
WE'VE OPENED A SCHOOL.
WE'RE ACCEPTING PPLICATIONS NOW.
EVEN FROM TIME-DISPLACED ORIGINAL X-MEN WHO ARE PROBABLY DESTROYING THE FABRIC OF TIME AND SPACE BY BEING HERE.
YOU'VE GOT TO BE KIDDING ME!
YOU DO GOOD WORK HERE, KITTY.
YOU ALL DO.
BUT WE'RE DAYS, WEEKS, MONTHS AWAY FROM A PUSH-BACK ON OUR PEOPLE AND WE HAVE TO BE READY.
NEW MUTANTS ARE POPPING UP ALL OVER THE WORLD AND WITH THAT WILL COME CONFUSION THAT WILL LEAD TO FEAR THAT WILL LEAD TO HATRED.
WITH THAT WILL COME A SERIES OF VIOLENT ATTACKS ON OUR PEOPLE.
IT ALWAYS DOES.
WE CAN TRAIN YOU TO FIGHT BACK AND FIGHT FOR EACH OTHER.
AT THE NEW XAVIER SCHOOL.
THE NEW XAVIER SCHOOL?
SUMMERS, THIS IS WEIRD. EVEN FOR YOU.
THAT'S WHAT I MEANT.
AND IN TERRIBLE TASTE.
YOU REALLY SHOULD GO.
XAVIER SCHOOL?
ALRIGHT, YOU SON OF A--
JAMES.
WHAT WILL THAT DO?

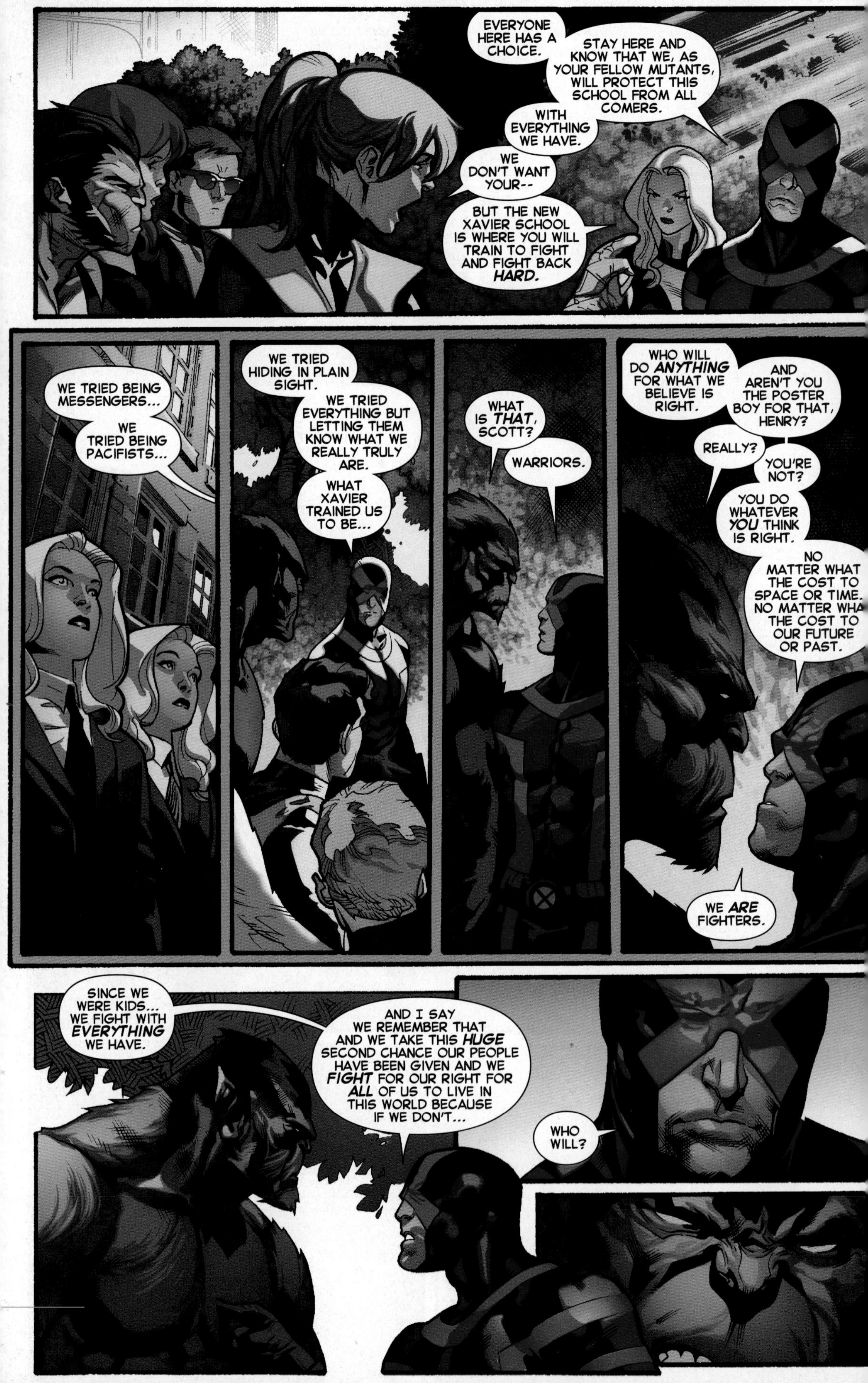
EVERYONE HERE HAS A CHOICE.
STAY HERE AND KNOW THAT WE, AS YOUR FELLOW MUTANTS, WILL PROTECT THIS SCHOOL FROM ALL COMERS.
WITH EVERYTHING WE HAVE.
WE DON'T WANT YOUR--
BUT THE NEW XAVIER SCHOOL IS WHERE YOU WILL TRAIN TO FIGHT AND FIGHT BACK HARD.
WE TRIED BEING MESSENGERS...
WE TRIED BEING PACIFISTS...
WE TRIED HIDING IN PLAIN SIGHT.
WE TRIED EVERYTHING BUT LETTING THEM KNOW WHAT WE REALLY TRULY ARE.
WHAT XAVIER TRAINED US TO BE...
WHAT IS THAT, SCOTT?
WARRIORS.
WHO WILL DO ANYTHING FOR WHAT WE BELIEVE IS RIGHT.
AND AREN'T YOU THE POSTER BOY FOR THAT, HENRY?
REALLY?
YOU'RE NOT?
YOU DO WHATEVER YOU THINK IS RIGHT.
NO MATTER WHAT THE COST TO SPACE OR TIME. NO MATTER WHA THE COST TO OUR FUTURE OR PAST.
WE ARE FIGHTERS.
SINCE WE WERE KIDS... WE FIGHT WITH EVERYTHING WE HAVE.
AND I SAY WE REMEMBER THAT AND WE TAKE THIS HUGE SECOND CHANCE OUR PEOPLE HAVE BEEN GIVEN AND WE FIGHT FOR OUR RIGHT FOR ALL OF US TO LIVE IN THIS WORLD BECAUSE IF WE DON'T...
WHO WILL?

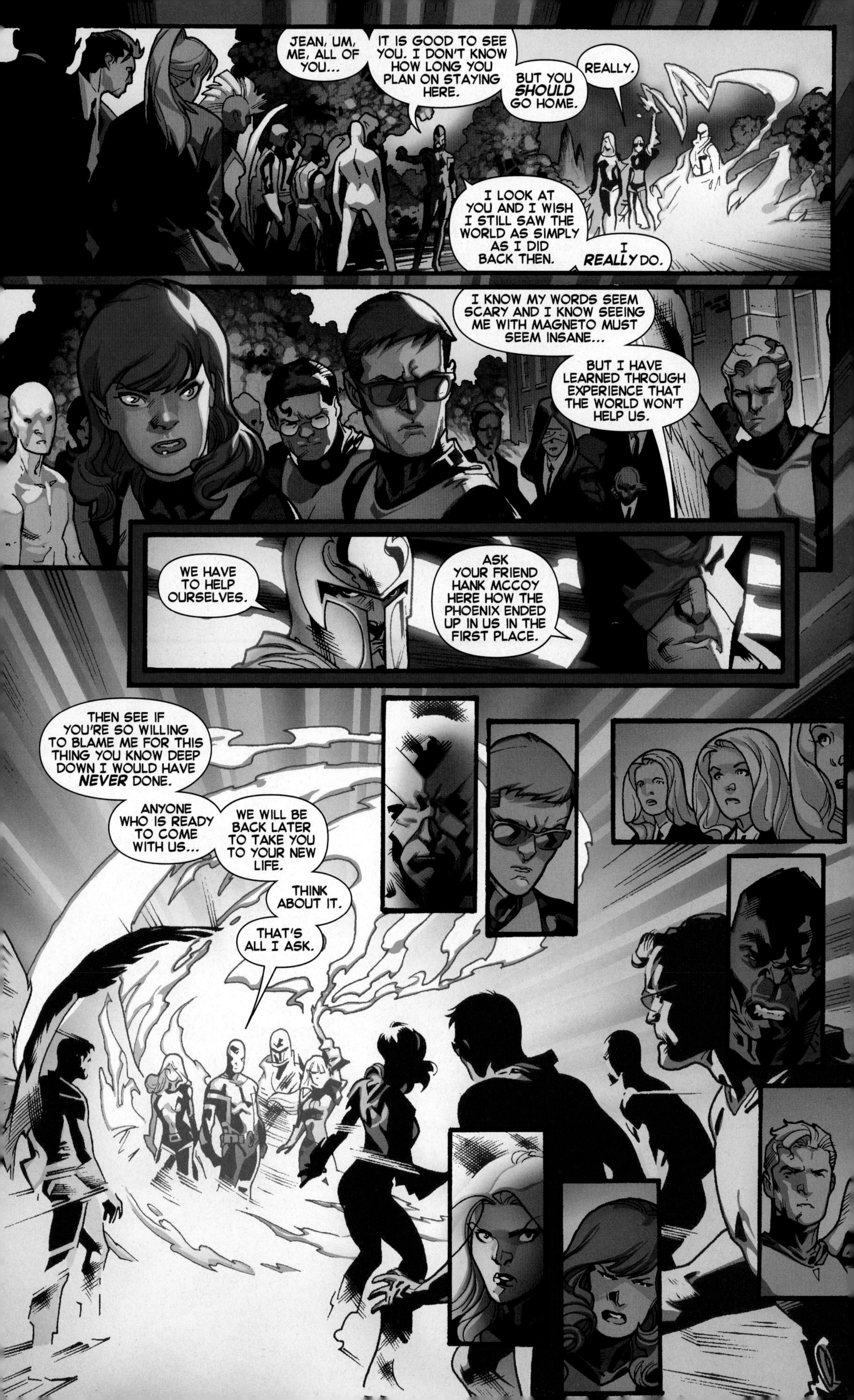

JEAN, UM, ME, ALL OF YOU...
IT IS GOOD TO SEE YOU. I DON'T KNOW HOW LONG YOU PLAN ON STAYING HERE.
BUT YOU SHOULD GO HOME.
REALLY.
I LOOK AT YOU AND I WISH I STILL SAW THE WORLD AS SIMPLY AS I DID BACK THEN.
I REALLY DO.
I KNOW MY WORDS SEEM SCARY AND I KNOW SEEING ME WITH MAGNETO MUST SEEM INSANE...
BUT I HAVE LEARNED THROUGH EXPERIENCE THAT THE WORLD WON'T HELP US.
WE HAVE TO HELP OURSELVES.
ASK YOUR FRIEND HANK MCCOY HERE HOW THE PHOENIX ENDED UP IN US IN THE FIRST PLACE.
THEN SEE IF YOU'RE SO WILLING TO BLAME ME FOR THIS THING YOU KNOW DEEP DOWN I WOULD HAVE NEVER DONE.
ANYONE WHO IS READY TO COME WITH US...
WE WILL BE BACK LATER TO TAKE YOU TO YOUR NEW LIFE.
THINK ABOUT IT.
THAT'S ALL I ASK.

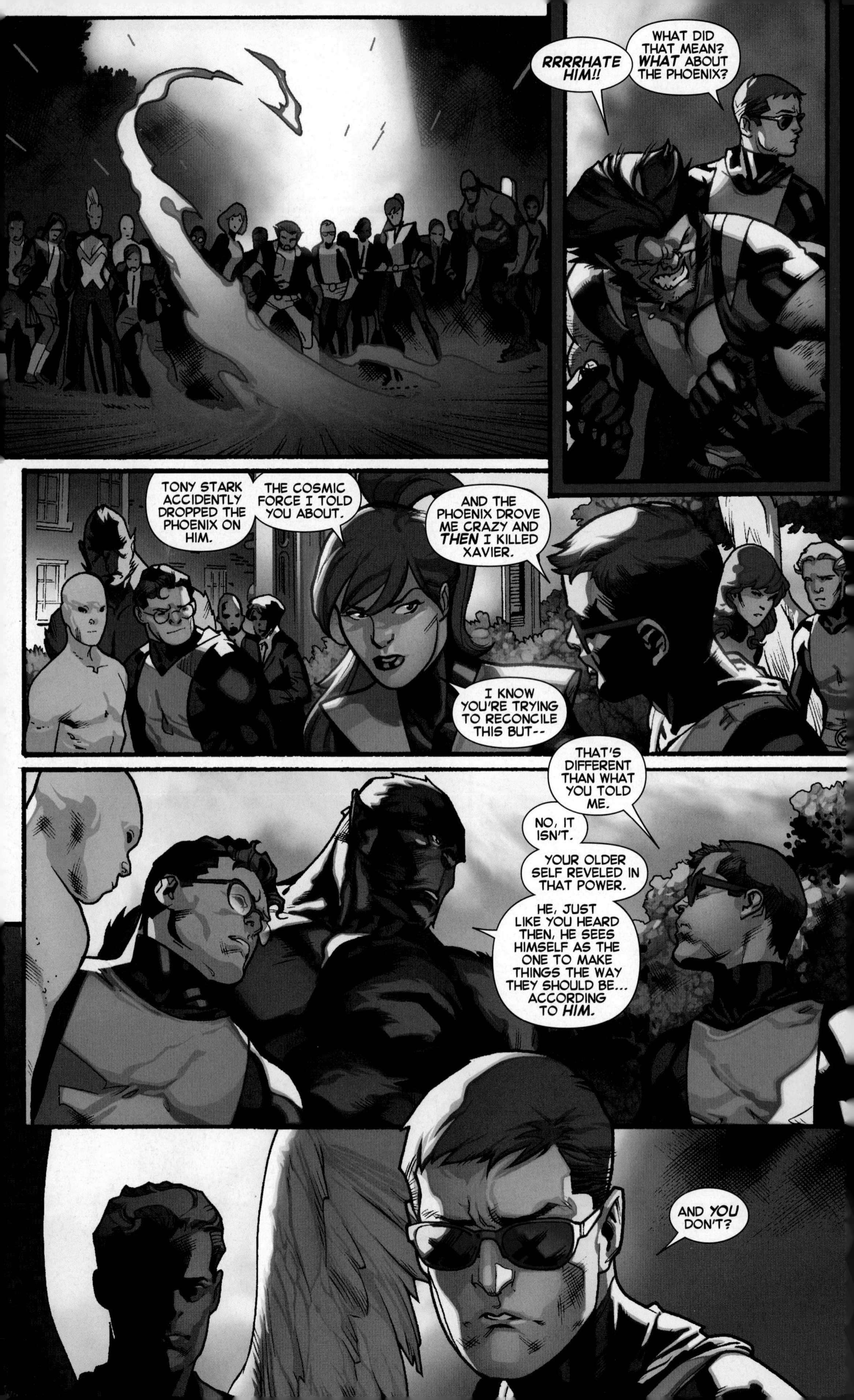
RRRRHATE HIM!!
WHAT DID THAT MEAN? WHAT ABOUT THE PHOENIX?
TONY STARK ACCIDENTLY DROPPED THE PHOENIX ON HIM.
THE COSMIC FORCE I TOLD YOU ABOUT.
AND THE PHOENIX DROVE ME CRAZY AND THEN I KILLED XAVIER.
I KNOW YOU'RE TRYING TO RECONCILE THIS BUT--
THAT'S DIFFERENT THAN WHAT YOU TOLD ME.
NO, IT ISN'T.
YOUR OLDER SELF REVELED IN THAT POWER.
HE, JUST LIKE YOU HEARD THEN, HE SEES HIMSELF AS THE ONE TO MAKE THINGS THE WAY THEY SHOULD BE... ACCORDING TO HIM.
AND YOU DON'T?

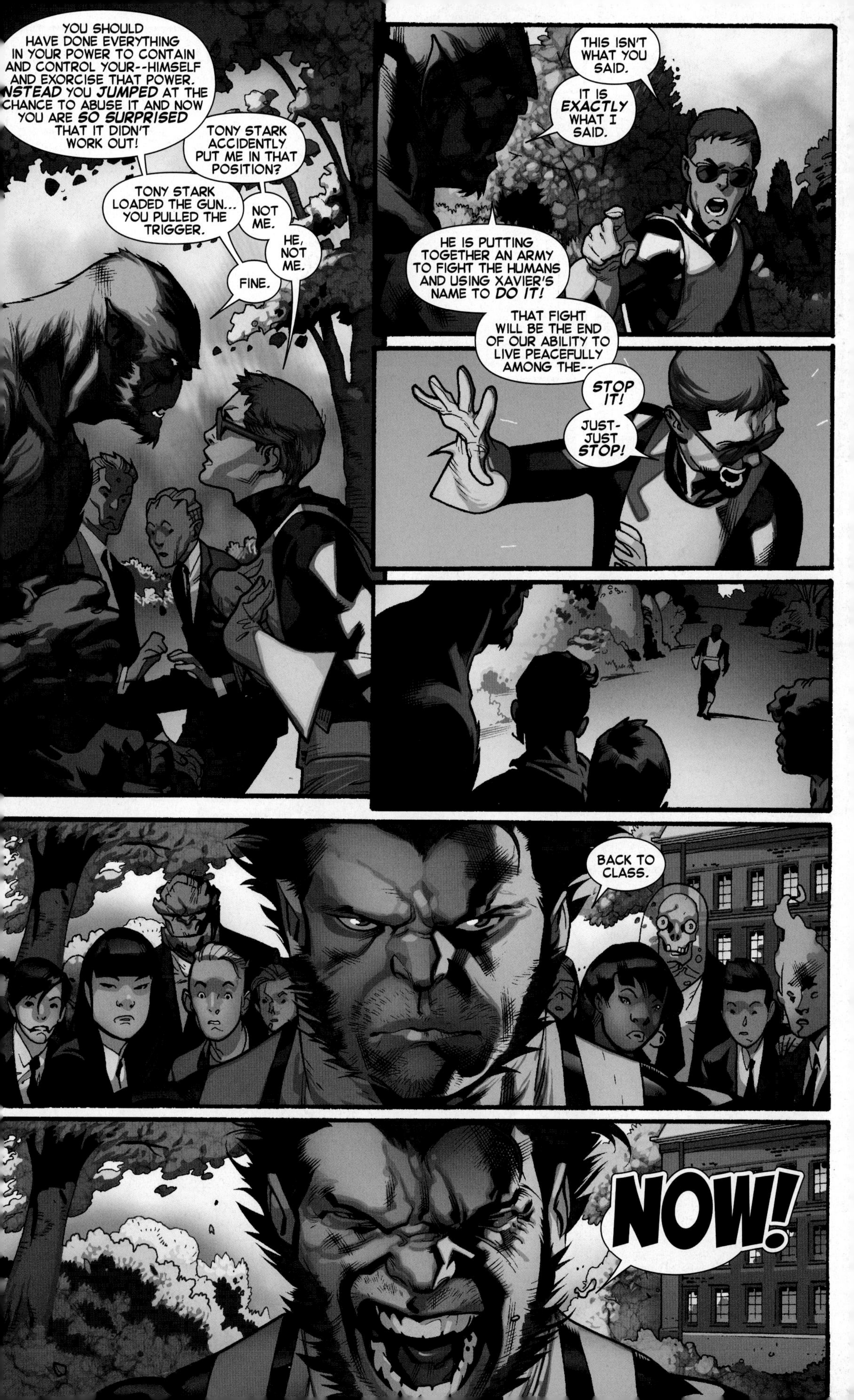
YOU SHOULD HAVE DONE EVERYTHING IN YOUR POWER TO CONTAIN AND CONTROL YOUR--HIMSELF AND EXORCISE THAT POWER. NSTEAD YOU JUMPED AT THE CHANCE TO ABUSE IT AND NOW YOU ARE SO SURPRISED THAT IT DIDN'T WORK OUT!
TONY STARK ACCIDENTLY PUT ME IN THAT POSITION?
TONY STARK LOADED THE GUN... YOU PULLED THE TRIGGER.
NOT ME.
HE, NOT ME.
FINE.
THIS ISN'T WHAT YOU SAID.
IT IS EXACTLY WHAT I SAID.
HE IS PUTTING TOGETHER AN ARMY TO FIGHT THE HUMANS AND USING XAVIER'S NAME TO DO IT!
THAT FIGHT WILL BE THE END OF OUR ABILITY TO LIVE PEACEFULLY AMONG THE--
STOP IT!
JUST-JUST STOP!
BACK TO CLASS.
NOW!

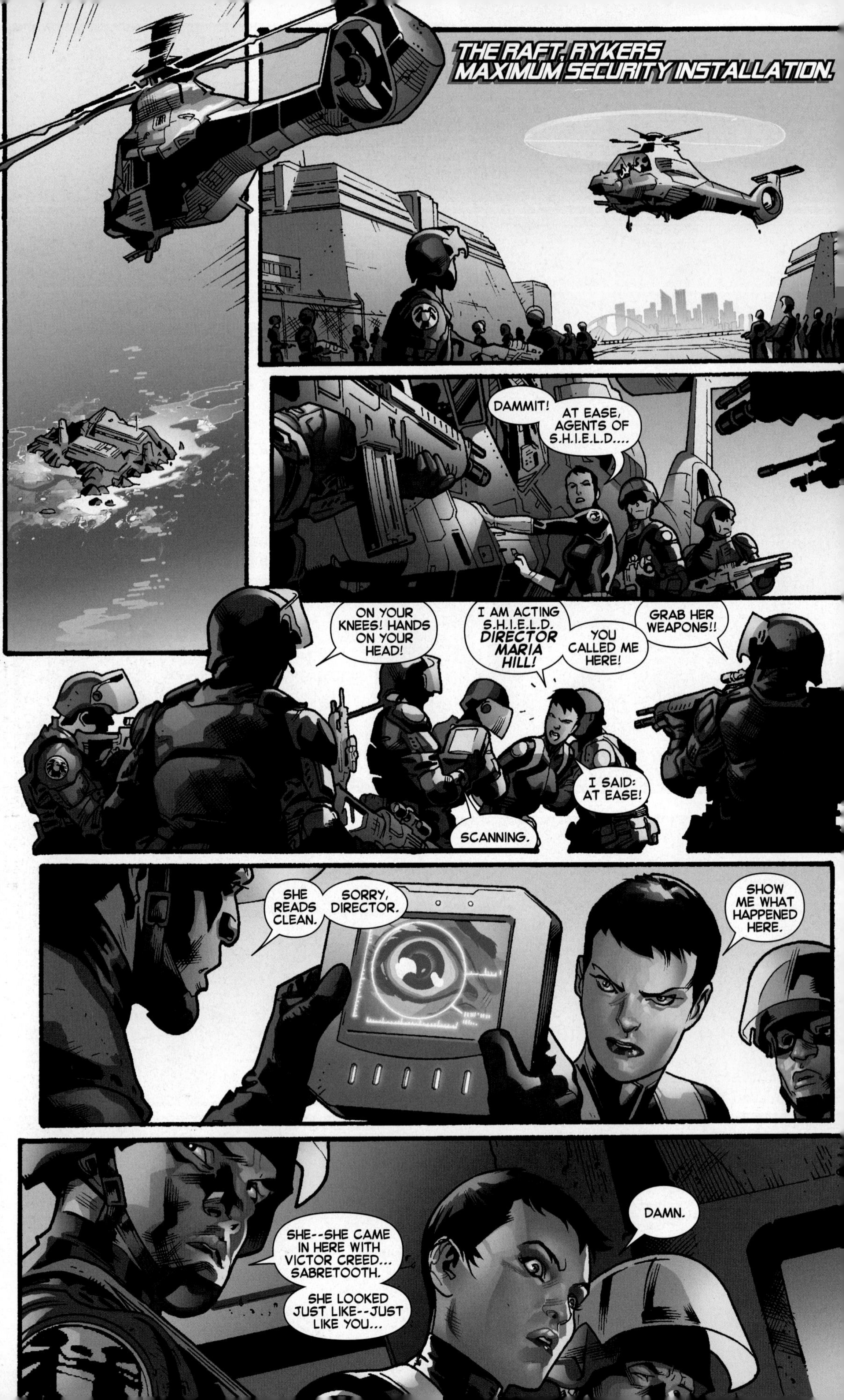

THE RAFT, RYKERS MAXIMUM SECURITY INSTALLATION.
DAMMIT!
AT EASE, AGENTS OF S.H.I.E.L.D....
ON YOUR KNEES! HANDS ON YOUR HEAD!
I AM ACTING S.H.I.E.L.D. DIRECTOR MARIA HILL!
YOU CALLED ME HERE!
GRAB HER WEAPONS!!
I SAID: AT EASE!
SCANNING.
SHE READS CLEAN.
SORRY, DIRECTOR.
SHOW ME WHAT HAPPENED HERE.
SHE--SHE CAME IN HERE WITH VICTOR CREED... SABRETOOTH.
SHE LOOKED JUST LIKE--JUST LIKE YOU...
DAMN.

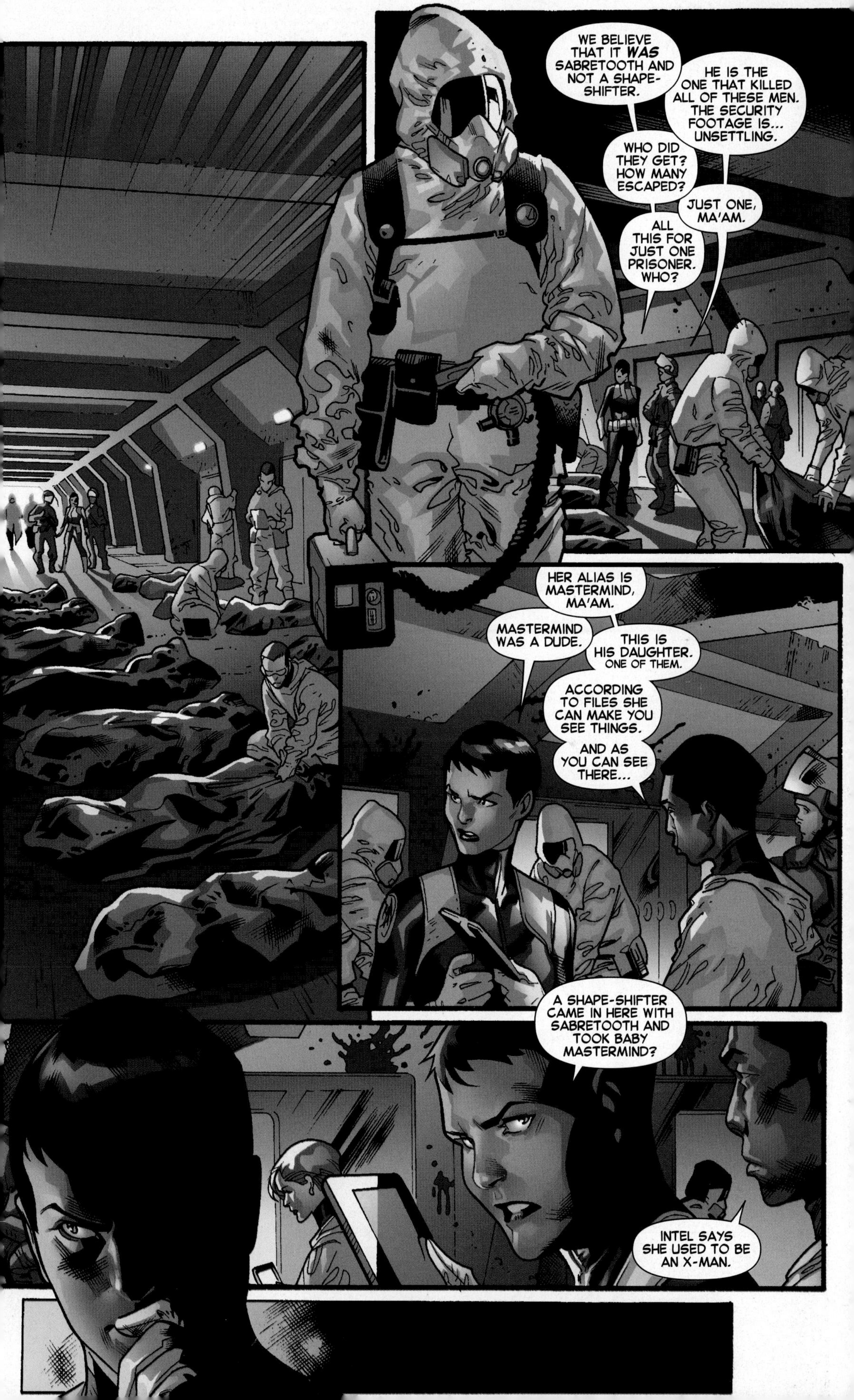

WE BELIEVE THAT IT *WAS* SABRETOOTH AND NOT A SHAPE-SHIFTER.
HE IS THE ONE THAT KILLED ALL OF THESE MEN. THE SECURITY FOOTAGE IS... UNSETTLING.
WHO DID THEY GET? HOW MANY ESCAPED?
JUST ONE, MA'AM.
ALL THIS FOR JUST ONE PRISONER. WHO?
HER ALIAS IS MASTERMIND, MA'AM.
MASTERMIND WAS A DUDE.
THIS IS HIS DAUGHTER. ONE OF THEM.
ACCORDING TO FILES SHE CAN MAKE YOU SEE THINGS.
AND AS YOU CAN SEE THERE...
A SHAPE-SHIFTER CAME IN HERE WITH SABRETOOTH AND TOOK BABY MASTERMIND?
INTEL SAYS SHE USED TO BE AN X-MAN.

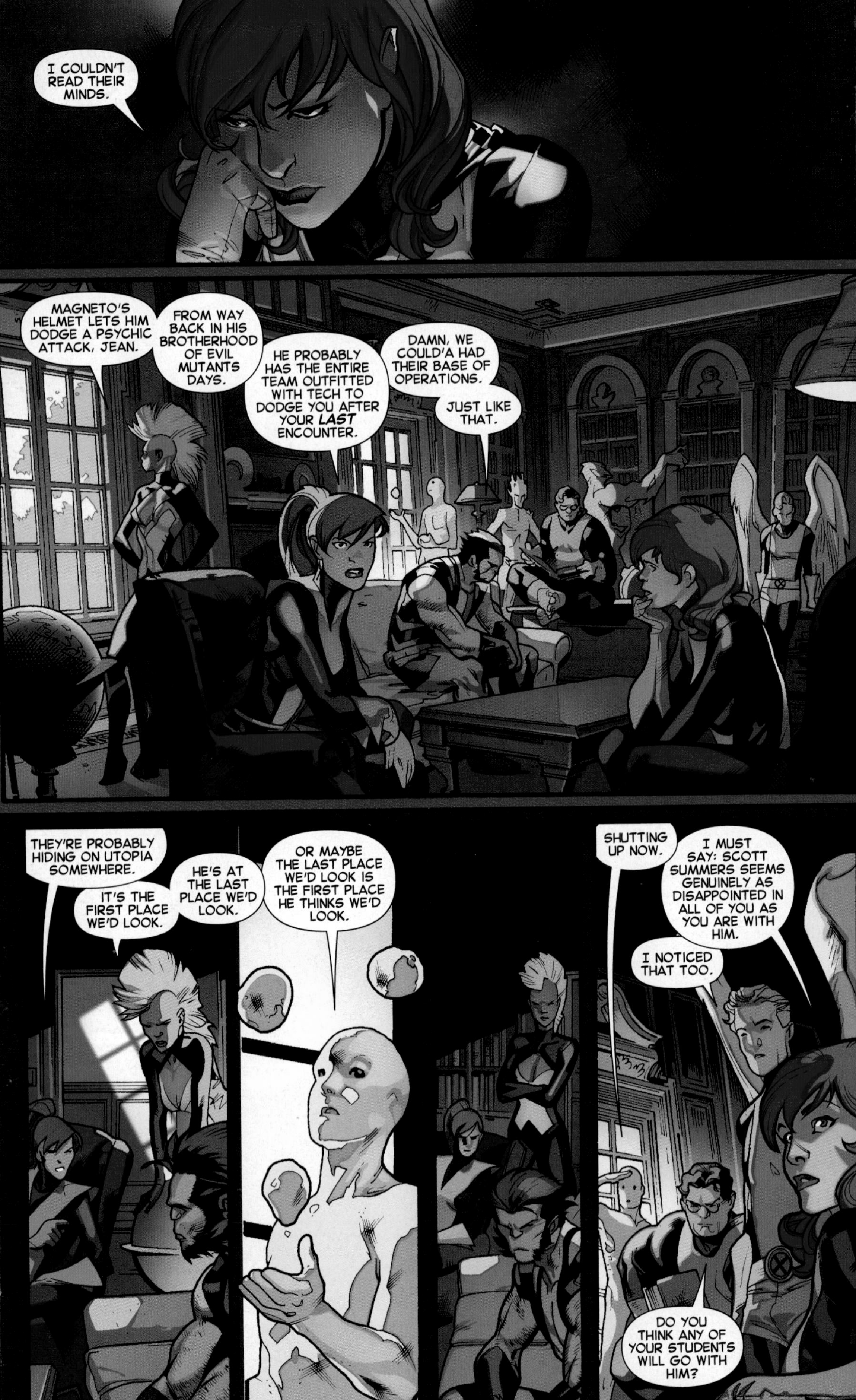

I COULDN'T READ THEIR MINDS.
MAGNETO'S HELMET LETS HIM DODGE A PSYCHIC ATTACK, JEAN.
FROM WAY BACK IN HIS BROTHERHOOD OF EVIL MUTANTS DAYS.
HE PROBABLY HAS THE ENTIRE TEAM OUTFITTED WITH TECH TO DODGE YOU AFTER YOUR LAST ENCOUNTER.
DAMN, WE COULD'A HAD THEIR BASE OF OPERATIONS.
JUST LIKE THAT.
THEY'RE PROBABLY HIDING ON UTOPIA SOMEWHERE.
IT'S THE FIRST PLACE WE'D LOOK.
HE'S AT THE LAST PLACE WE'D LOOK.
OR MAYBE THE LAST PLACE WE'D LOOK IS THE FIRST PLACE HE THINKS WE'D LOOK.
SHUTTING UP NOW.
I MUST SAY: SCOTT SUMMERS SEEMS GENUINELY AS DISAPPOINTED IN ALL OF YOU AS YOU ARE WITH HIM.
I NOTICED THAT TOO.
DO YOU THINK ANY OF YOUR STUDENTS WILL GO WITH HIM?

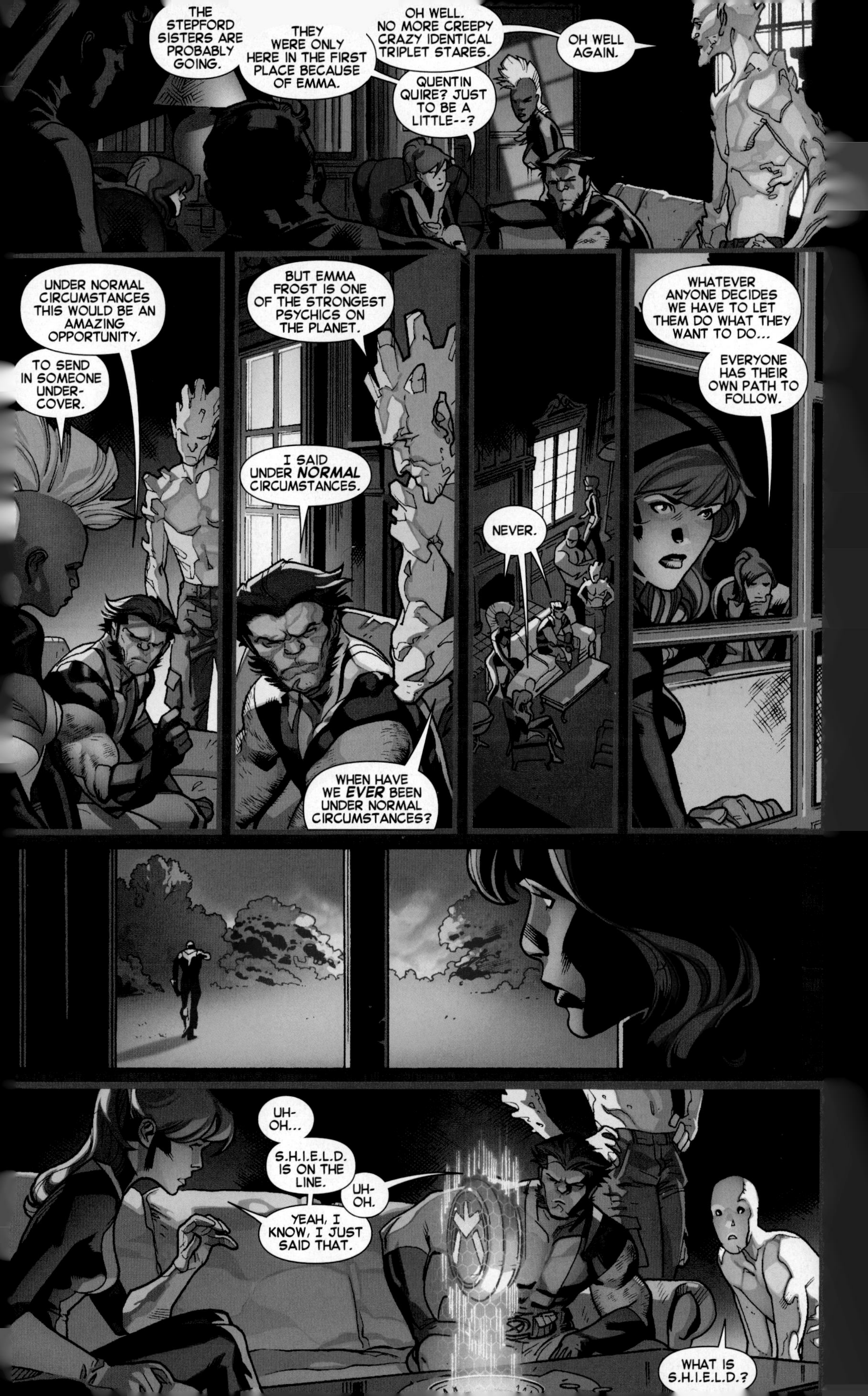

THE STEPFORD SISTERS ARE PROBABLY GOING.
THEY WERE ONLY HERE IN THE FIRST PLACE BECAUSE OF EMMA.
OH WELL. NO MORE CREEPY CRAZY IDENTICAL TRIPLET STARES.
QUENTIN QUIRE? JUST TO BE A LITTLE--?
OH WELL AGAIN.
UNDER NORMAL CIRCUMSTANCES THIS WOULD BE AN AMAZING OPPORTUNITY.
TO SEND IN SOMEONE UNDER-COVER.
BUT EMMA FROST IS ONE OF THE STRONGEST PSYCHICS ON THE PLANET.
I SAID UNDER NORMAL CIRCUMSTANCES.
WHEN HAVE WE EVER BEEN UNDER NORMAL CIRCUMSTANCES?
NEVER.
WHATEVER ANYONE DECIDES WE HAVE TO LET THEM DO WHAT THEY WANT TO DO...
EVERYONE HAS THEIR OWN PATH TO FOLLOW.
UH-OH...
S.H.I.E.L.D. IS ON THE LINE.
UH-OH.
YEAH, I KNOW, I JUST SAID THAT.
WHAT IS S.H.I.E.L.D.?

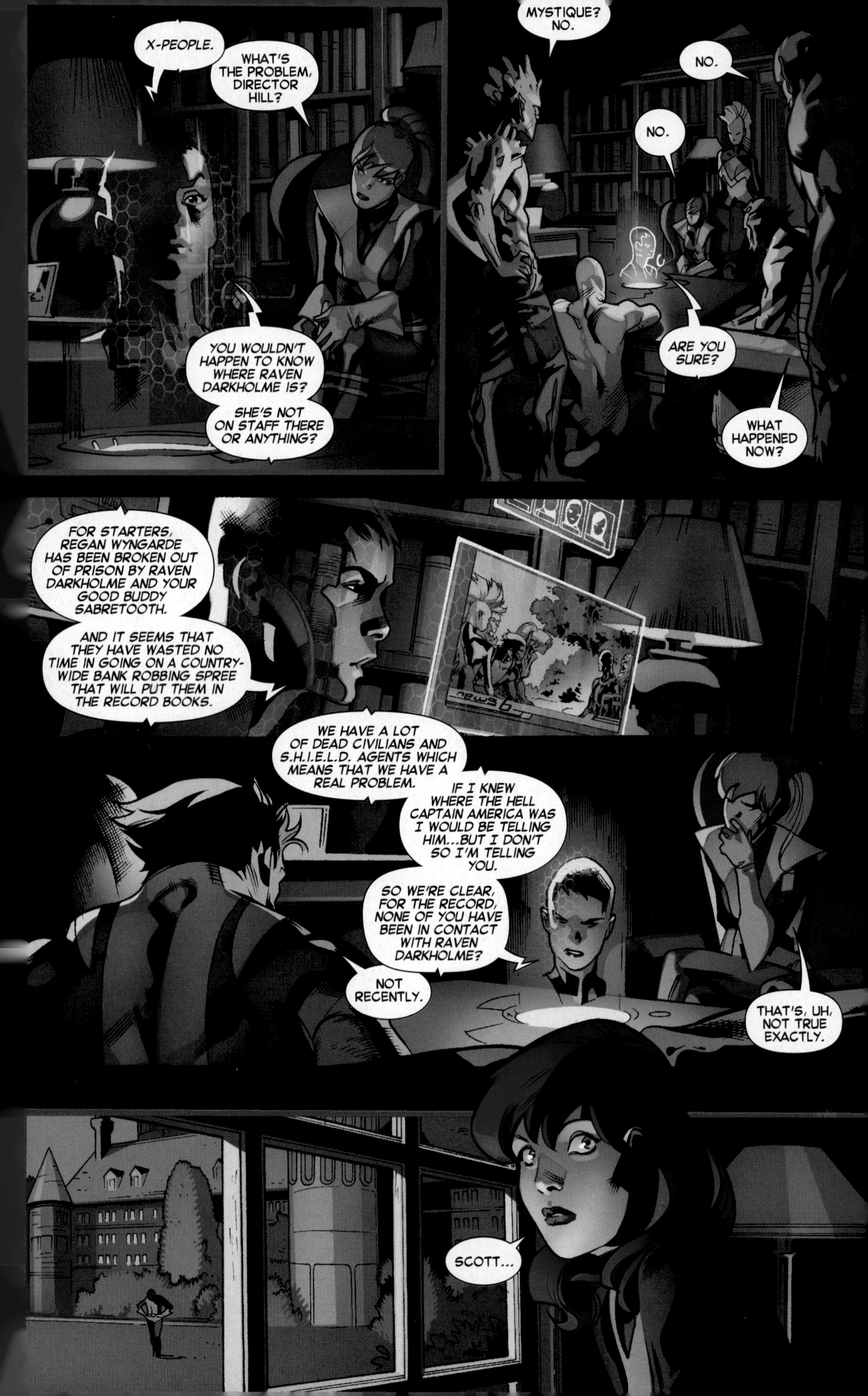

X-PEOPLE.
WHAT'S THE PROBLEM, DIRECTOR HILL?
YOU WOULDN'T HAPPEN TO KNOW WHERE RAVEN DARKHOLME IS?
SHE'S NOT ON STAFF THERE OR ANYTHING?
MYSTIQUE? NO.
NO.
NO.
ARE YOU SURE?
WHAT HAPPENED NOW?
FOR STARTERS, REGAN WYNGARDE HAS BEEN BROKEN OUT OF PRISON BY RAVEN DARKHOLME AND YOUR GOOD BUDDY SABRETOOTH.
AND IT SEEMS THAT THEY HAVE WASTED NO TIME IN GOING ON A COUNTRY-WIDE BANK ROBBING SPREE THAT WILL PUT THEM IN THE RECORD BOOKS.
WE HAVE A LOT OF DEAD CIVILIANS AND S.H.I.E.L.D. AGENTS WHICH MEANS THAT WE HAVE A REAL PROBLEM.
IF I KNEW WHERE THE HELL CAPTAIN AMERICA WAS I WOULD BE TELLING HIM...BUT I DON'T SO I'M TELLING YOU.
SO WE'RE CLEAR, FOR THE RECORD, NONE OF YOU HAVE BEEN IN CONTACT WITH RAVEN DARKHOLME?
NOT RECENTLY.
THAT'S, UH, NOT TRUE EXACTLY.
SCOTT...

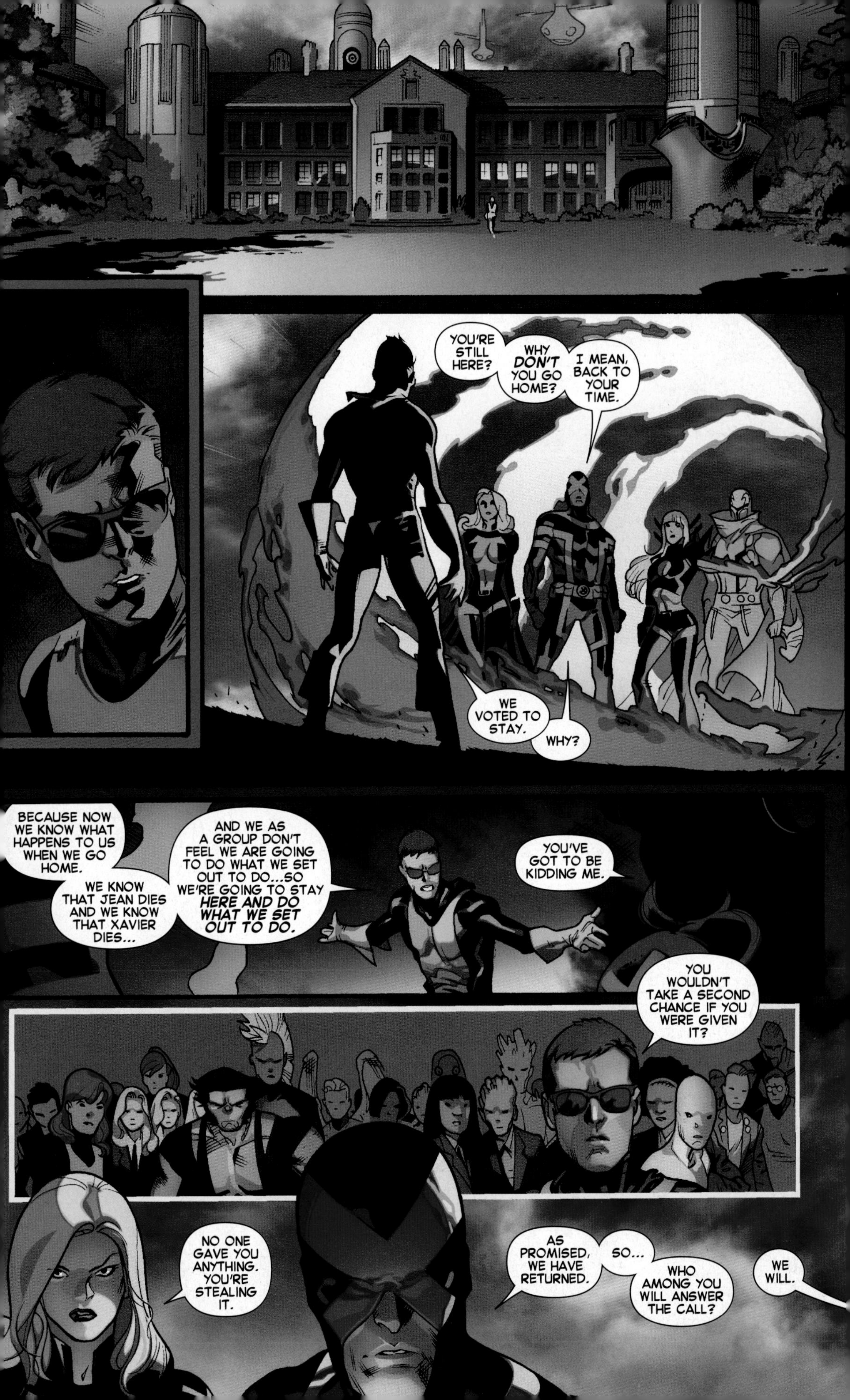
YOU'RE STILL HERE?
WHY DON'T YOU GO HOME?
I MEAN, BACK TO YOUR TIME.
WE VOTED TO STAY.
WHY?
BECAUSE NOW WE KNOW WHAT HAPPENS TO US WHEN WE GO HOME.
WE KNOW THAT JEAN DIES AND WE KNOW THAT XAVIER DIES...
AND WE AS A GROUP DON'T FEEL WE ARE GOING TO DO WHAT WE SET OUT TO DO...SO WE'RE GOING TO STAY HERE AND DO WHAT WE SET OUT TO DO.
YOU'VE GOT TO BE KIDDING ME.
YOU WOULDN'T TAKE A SECOND CHANCE IF YOU WERE GIVEN IT?
NO ONE GAVE YOU ANYTHING. YOU'RE STEALING IT.
AS PROMISED, WE HAVE RETURNED.
SO...
WHO AMONG YOU WILL ANSWER THE CALL?
WE WILL.

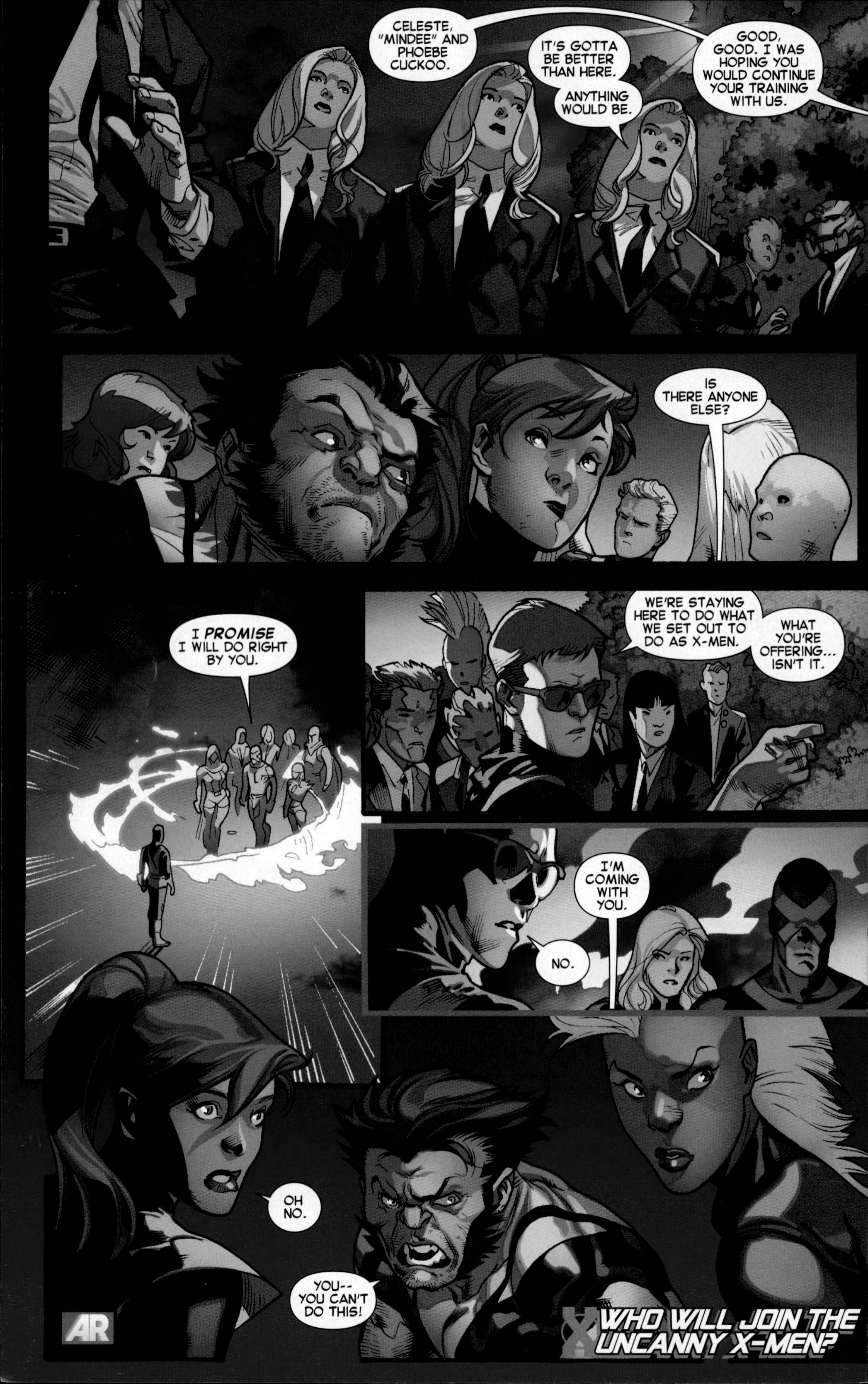
CELESTE, "MINDEE" AND PHOEBE CUCKOO.
IT'S GOTTA BE BETTER THAN HERE.
ANYTHING WOULD BE.
GOOD, GOOD. I WAS HOPING YOU WOULD CONTINUE YOUR TRAINING WITH US.
IS THERE ANYONE ELSE?
I PROMISE I WILL DO RIGHT BY YOU.
WE'RE STAYING HERE TO DO WHAT WE SET OUT TO DO AS X-MEN.
WHAT YOU'RE OFFERING... ISN'T IT.
I'M COMING WITH YOU.
NO.
OH NO.
YOU-- YOU CAN'T DO THIS!
AR
WHO WILL JOIN THE UNCANNY X-MEN?

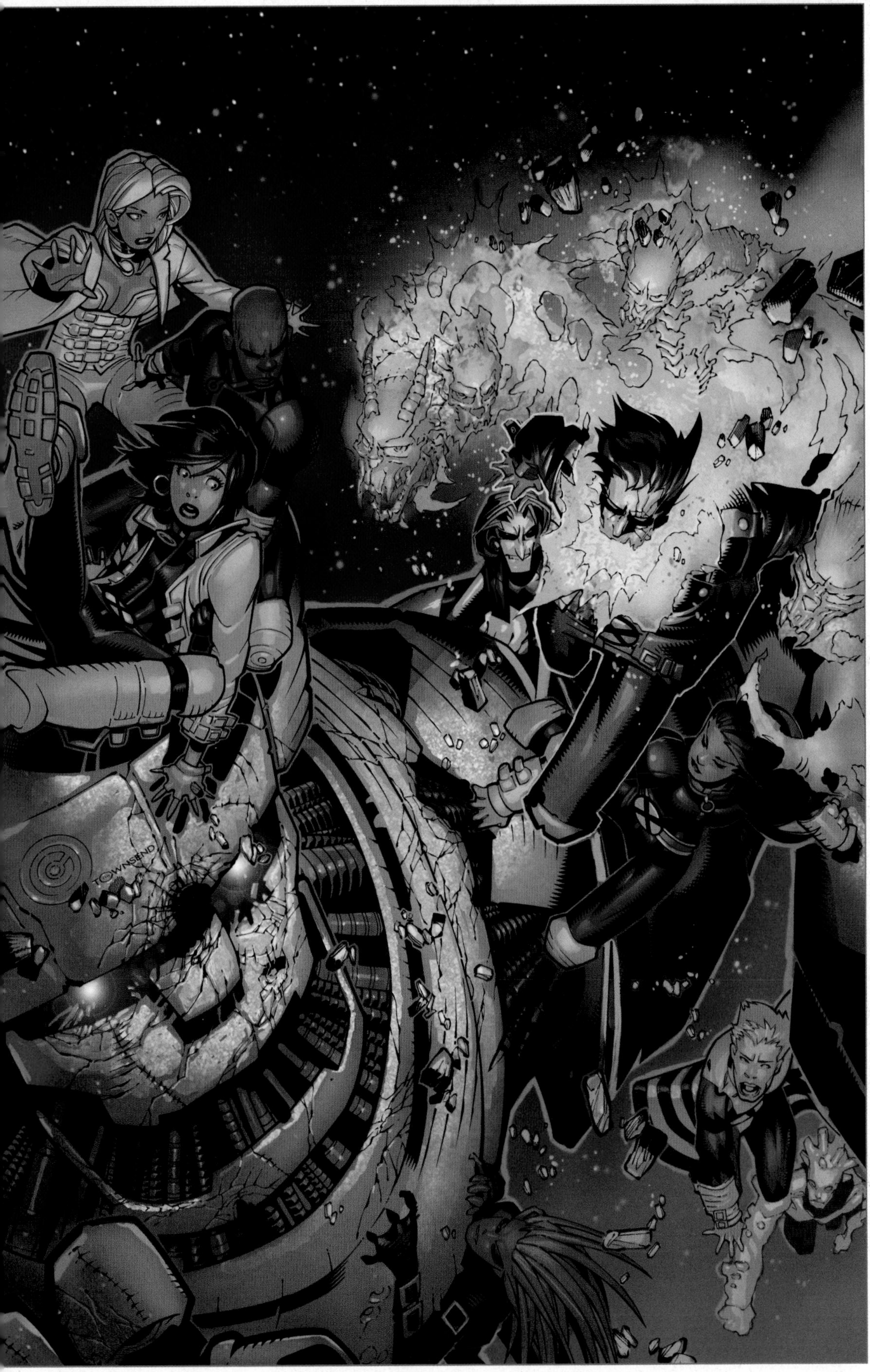
TOWNSEND

ALL-NEW X-MEN #6 X-MEN 50TH ANNIVERSARY VARIANT

BY CHRIS BACHALO & TIM TOWNSEND

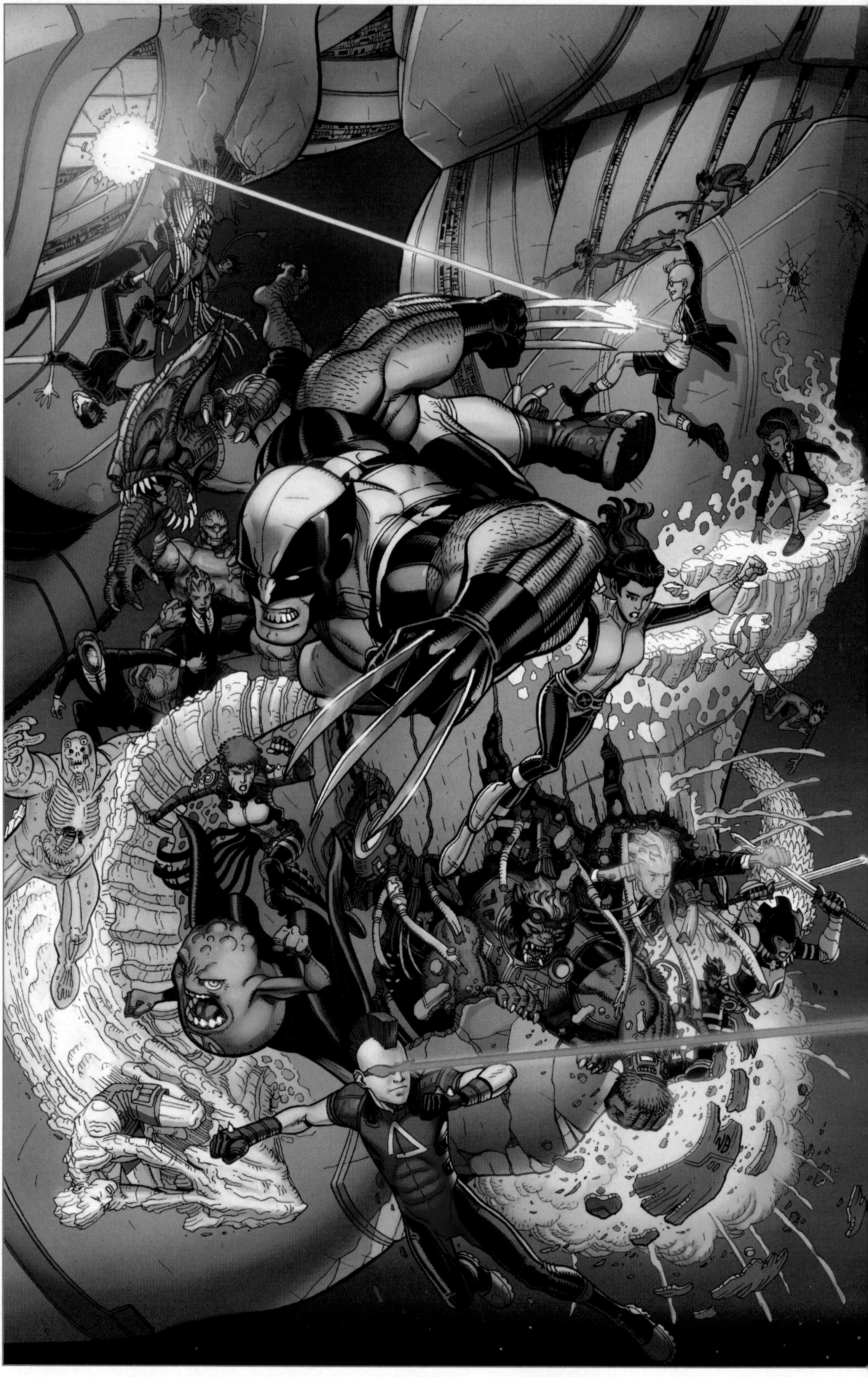

ALL-NEW X-MEN #7 X-MEN 50TH ANNIVERSARY VARIANT
BY NICK BRADSHAW & JASON KEITH

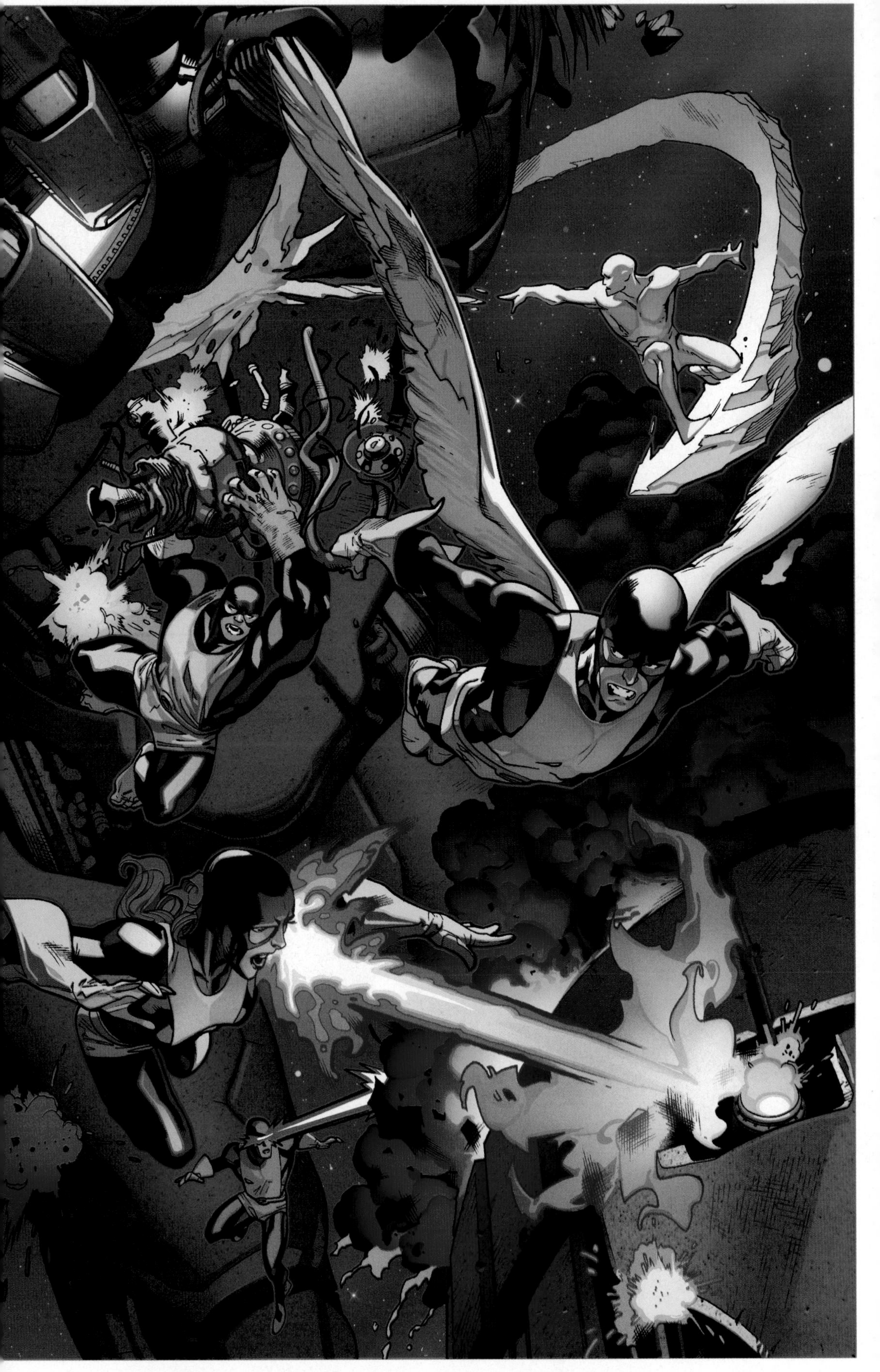

ALL-NEW X-MEN #8 X-MEN 50TH ANNIVERSARY VARIANT
BY STUART IMMONEN, WADE VON GRAWBADGER & MARTE GRACIA

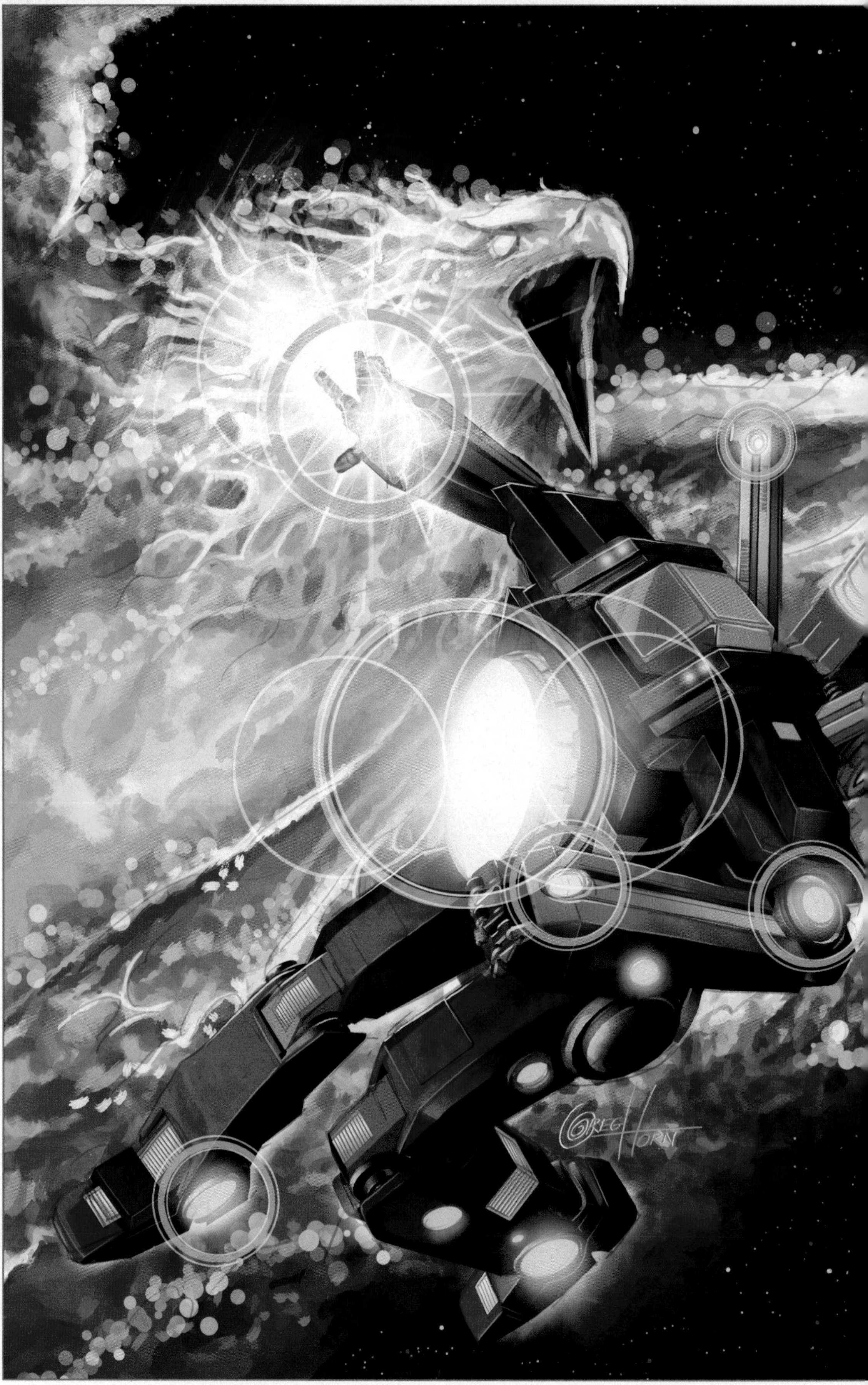
GREG HORN

ALL-NEW X-MEN #10 MANY ARMORS OF IRON MAN VARIANT
BY GREG HORN

ART PROCESS & COMMENTARY WITH DAVID MARQUEZ

I thought it might be interesting, as part of the "behind the scenes" material, to give readers a look into the editorial and review process of a few pages that underwent some changes before the final image. Marvel Comics are by nature very collaborative, and the input made by editors and writers regarding the art is incredibly important. So...

#6, PAGE 5, PANEL 1

This page was an awesome opportunity to draw the huge cast of the Jean Grey School. To take some of the edge off an already very complex page and panel, I leaned pretty heavily on one of my favorite tools for digital art creation: SketchUp. It's a great tool that allows a user to intuitively build 3D models that I use extensively in my workflow.

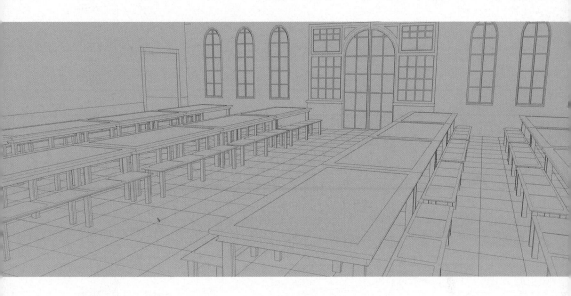

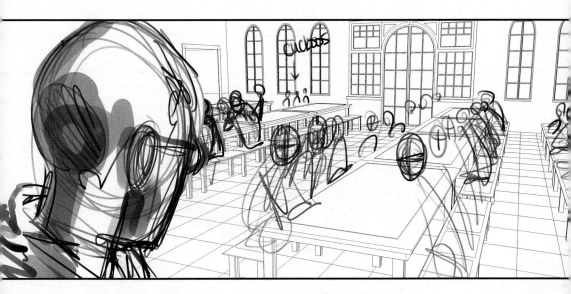

For this scene, I created a model of the cafeteria, added some brick texture to the walls and started populating the tables with all the colorful characters from the school.

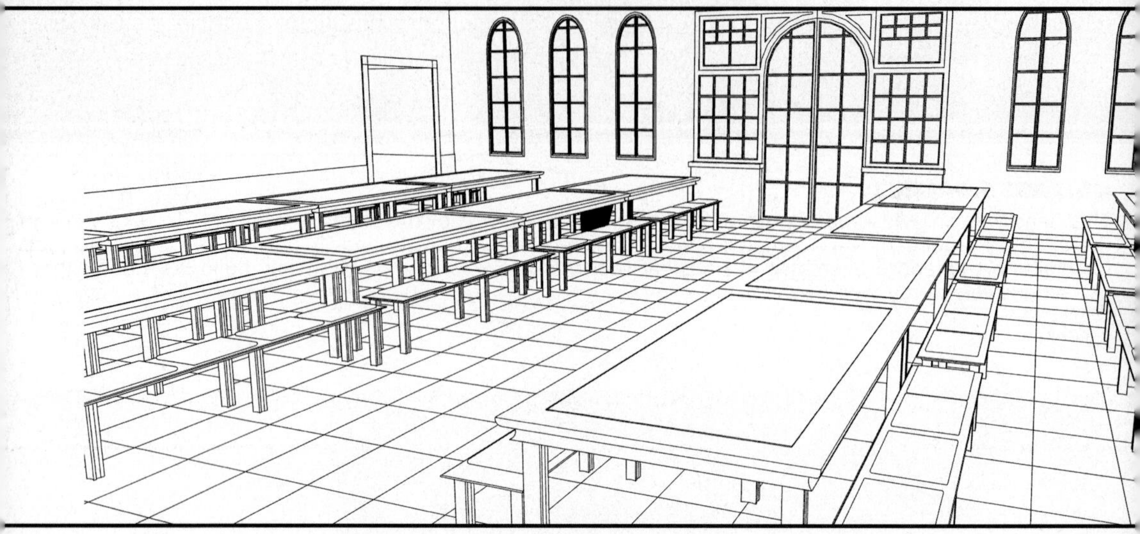

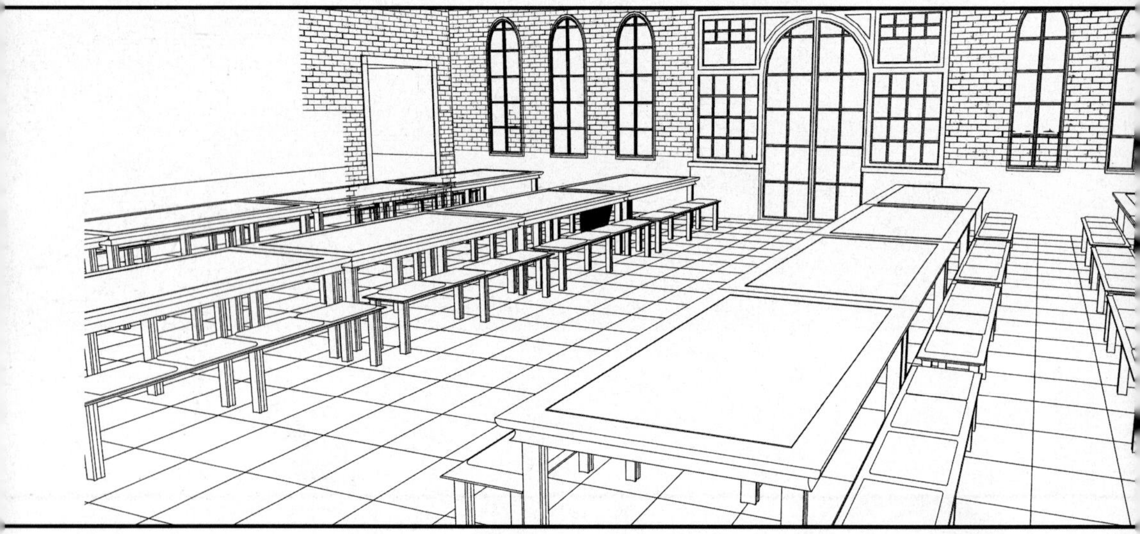

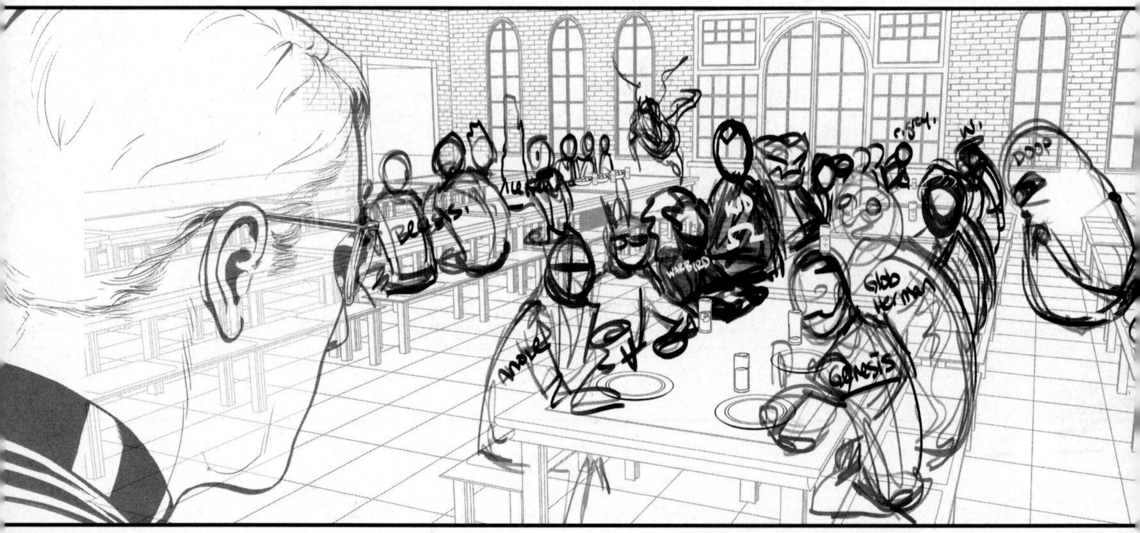
Anole
Wingbird
Glob Herman
Genesis
Doop

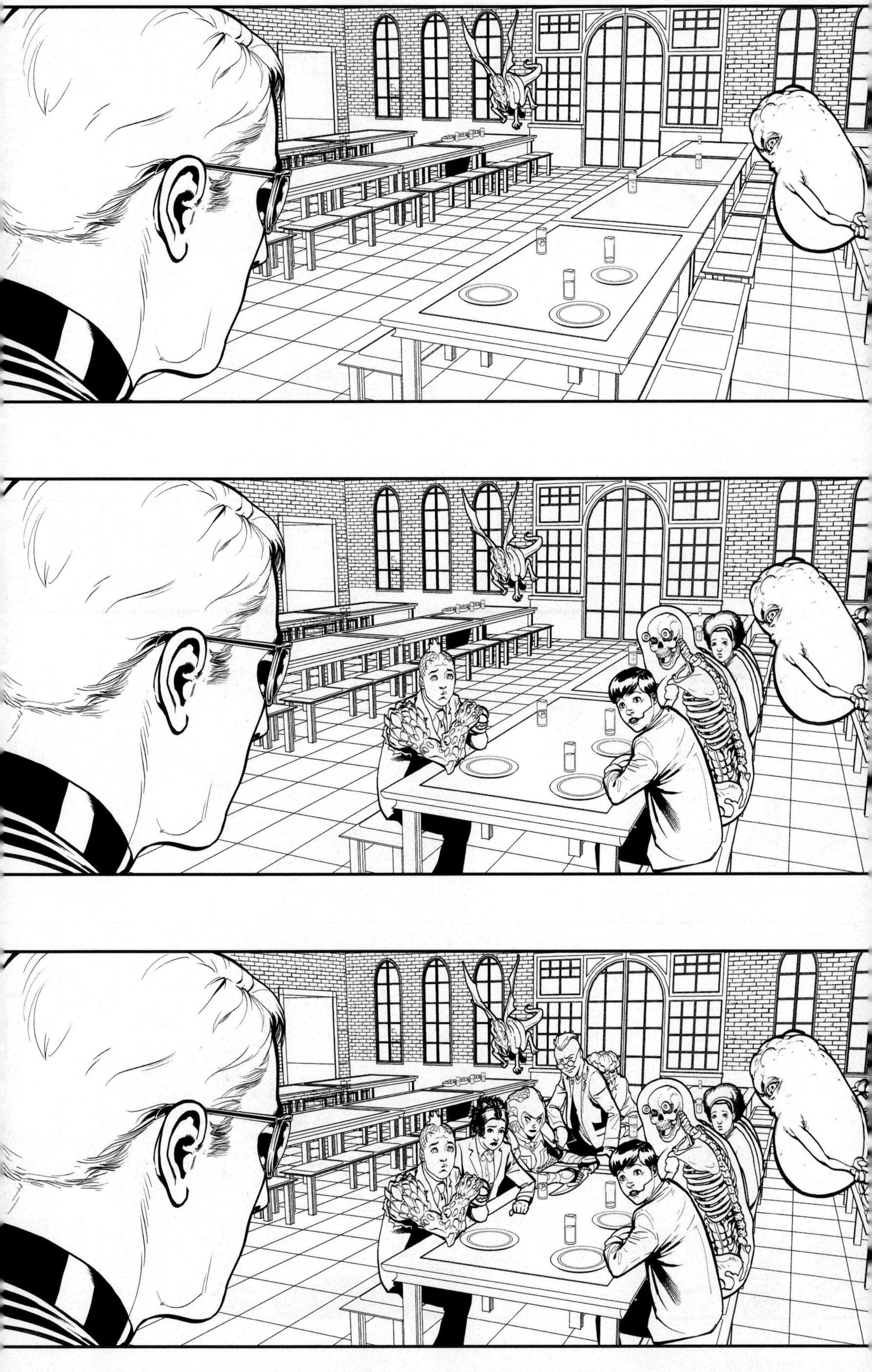

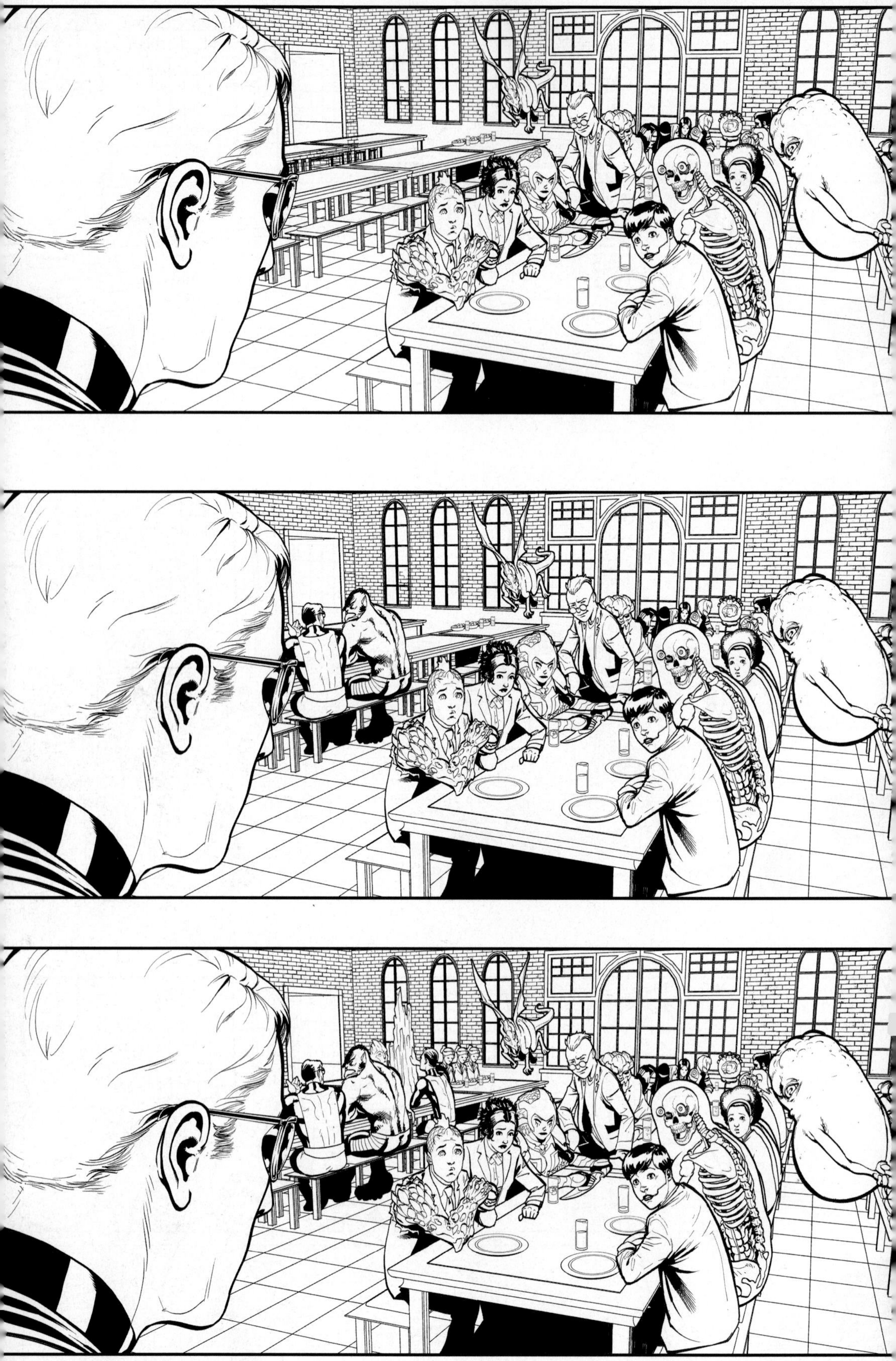

HUGE kudos go to editors Nick and Jordan for providing me with an official school roster to make sure I didn't mess it up!

#6, PAGE 3

This was a tricky page since it's important to keep the gore level low in a Marvel comic, while still portraying the ferocity and viciousness Wolverine is capable of. In the first version of this panel, I drew Jean after being slashed so I wouldn't have to explicitly show the wound she received, but editors Nick and Jordan, as well as Brian, all made the excellent point that we really should be able to see her face and reaction to sell the moment.

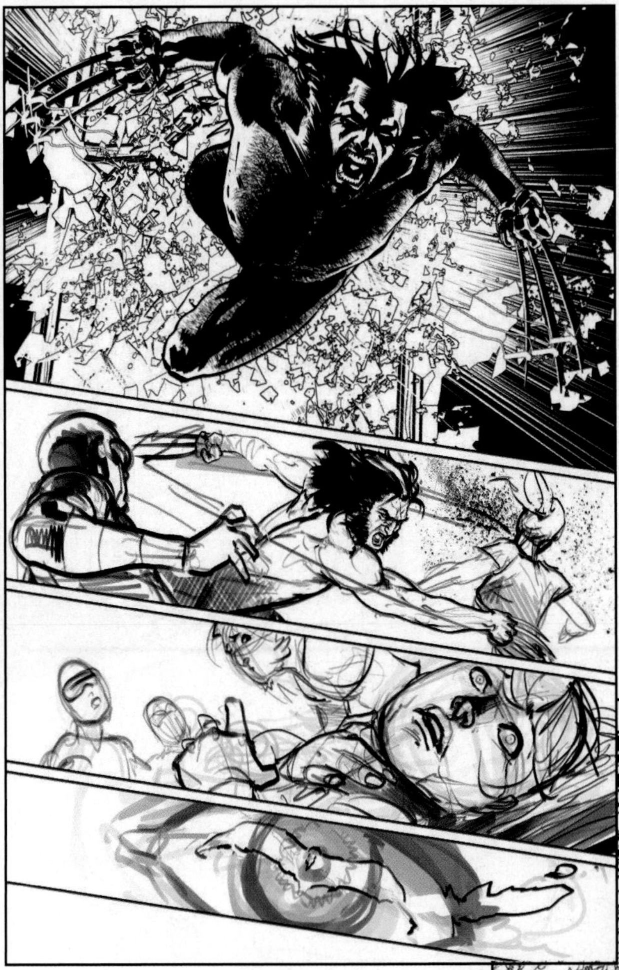

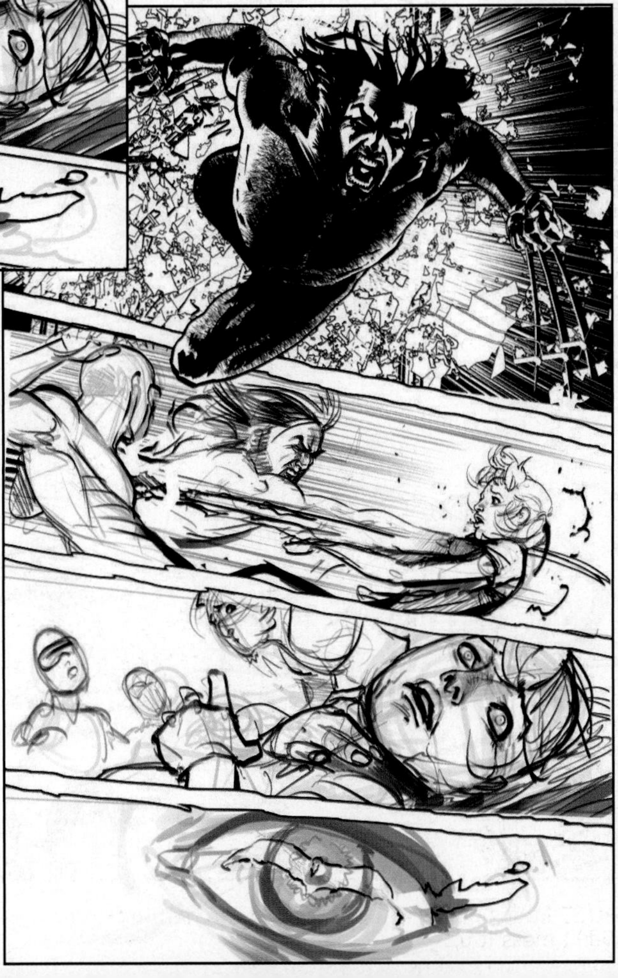

In version two — which ended up being the final version — we got to see her face, with her hair and shoulder hiding the worst of the damage, while showing the claws popping out behind her head give the sense of just how terrible Wolverine's strike was.

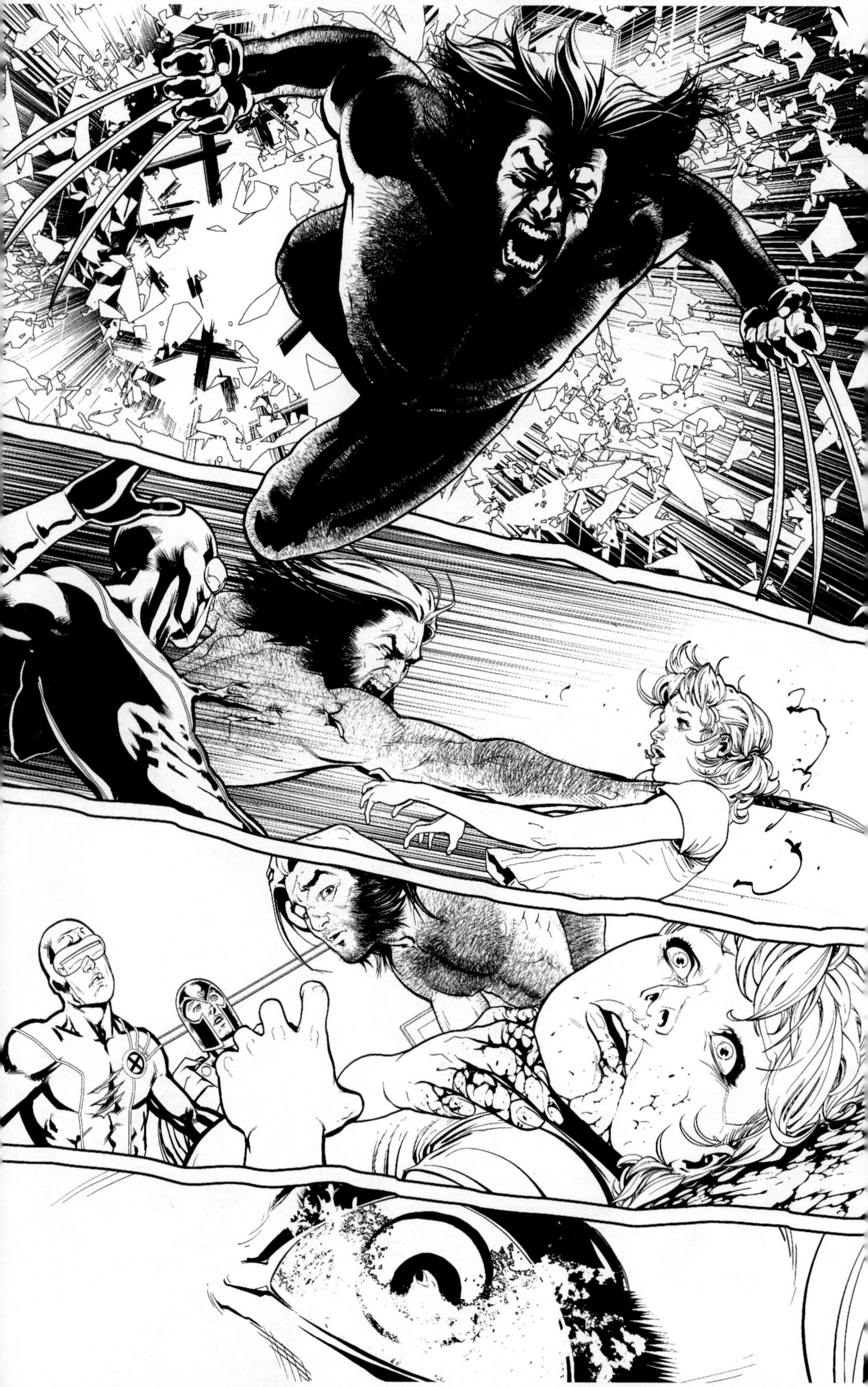

#8, PAGE 4

My original layout for this panel was meant to evoke WW2-era propaganda posters, with Madam Hydra against a backdrop of Hydra exoskeletons flying in formation. The rest of the team was afraid that the extreme low angle would obscure her face too much, so in the revised sketch I inched the "camera" up just enough so we could still see her, while also giving us the sense of power that low-angle shots offer.

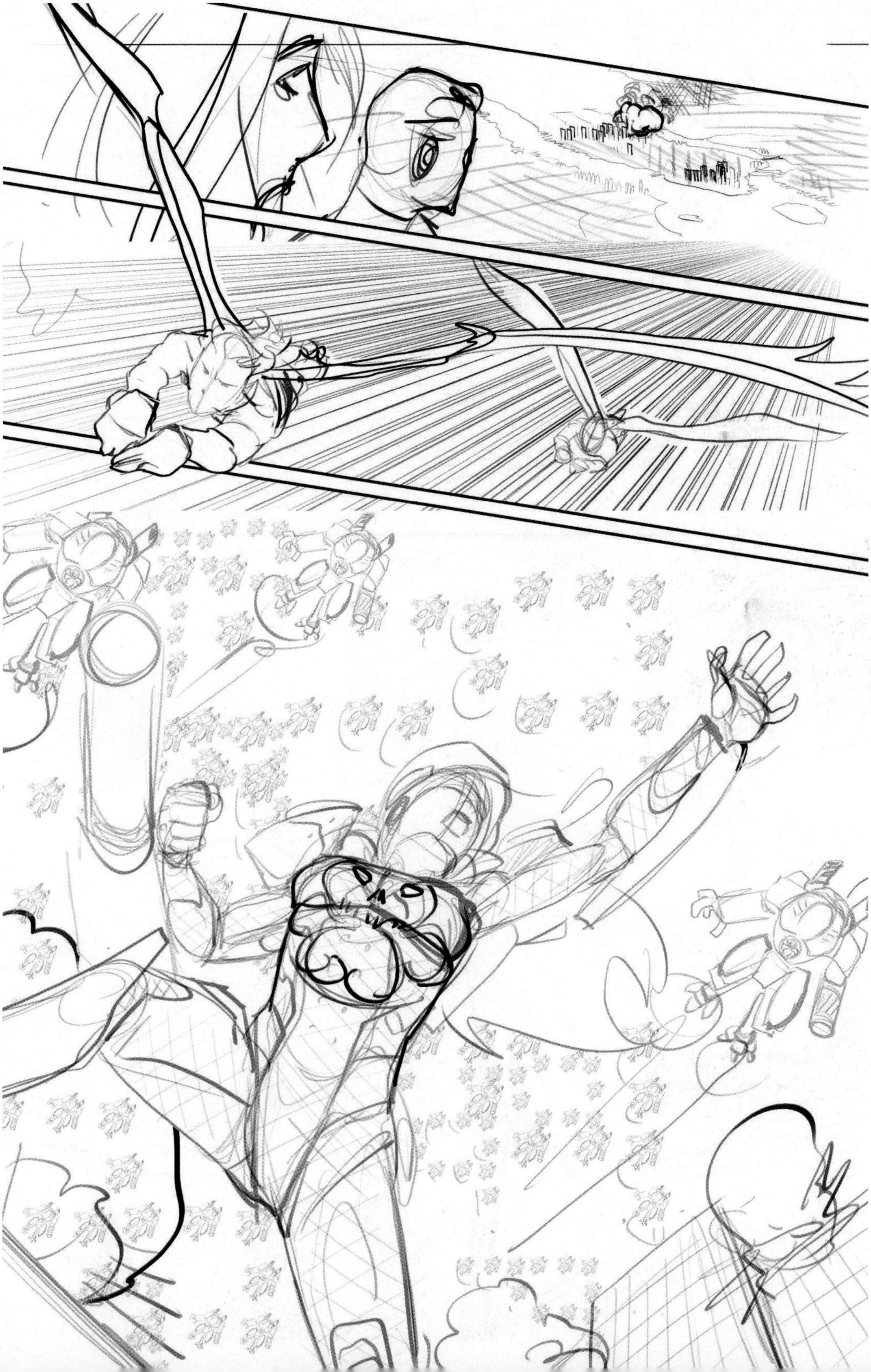

An unexpected consequence of changing the angle, though, was that we wouldn't be looking quite s directly up into the sky, and so I dropped in the building behind her to give a sense of scale and verticalit

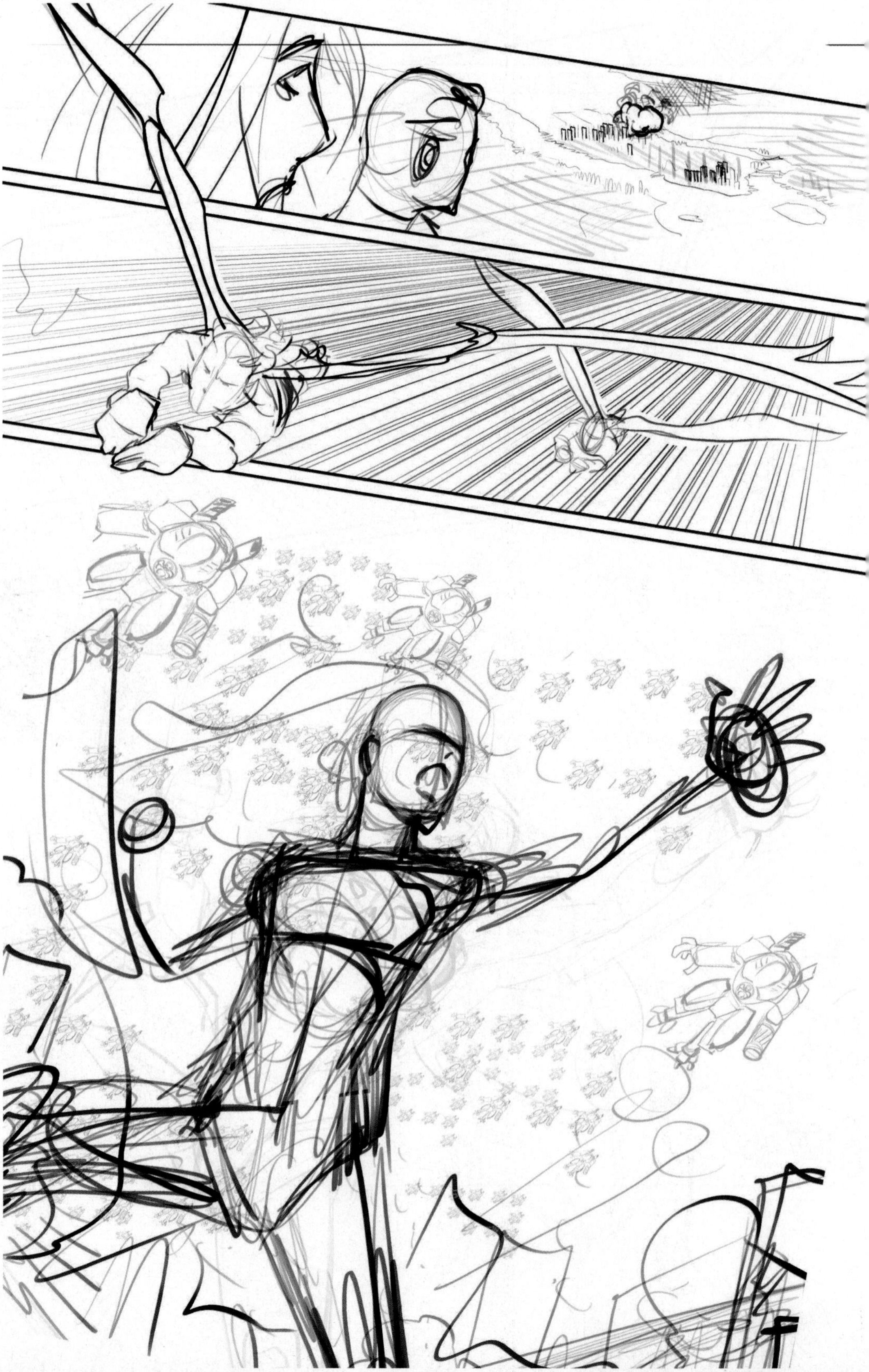

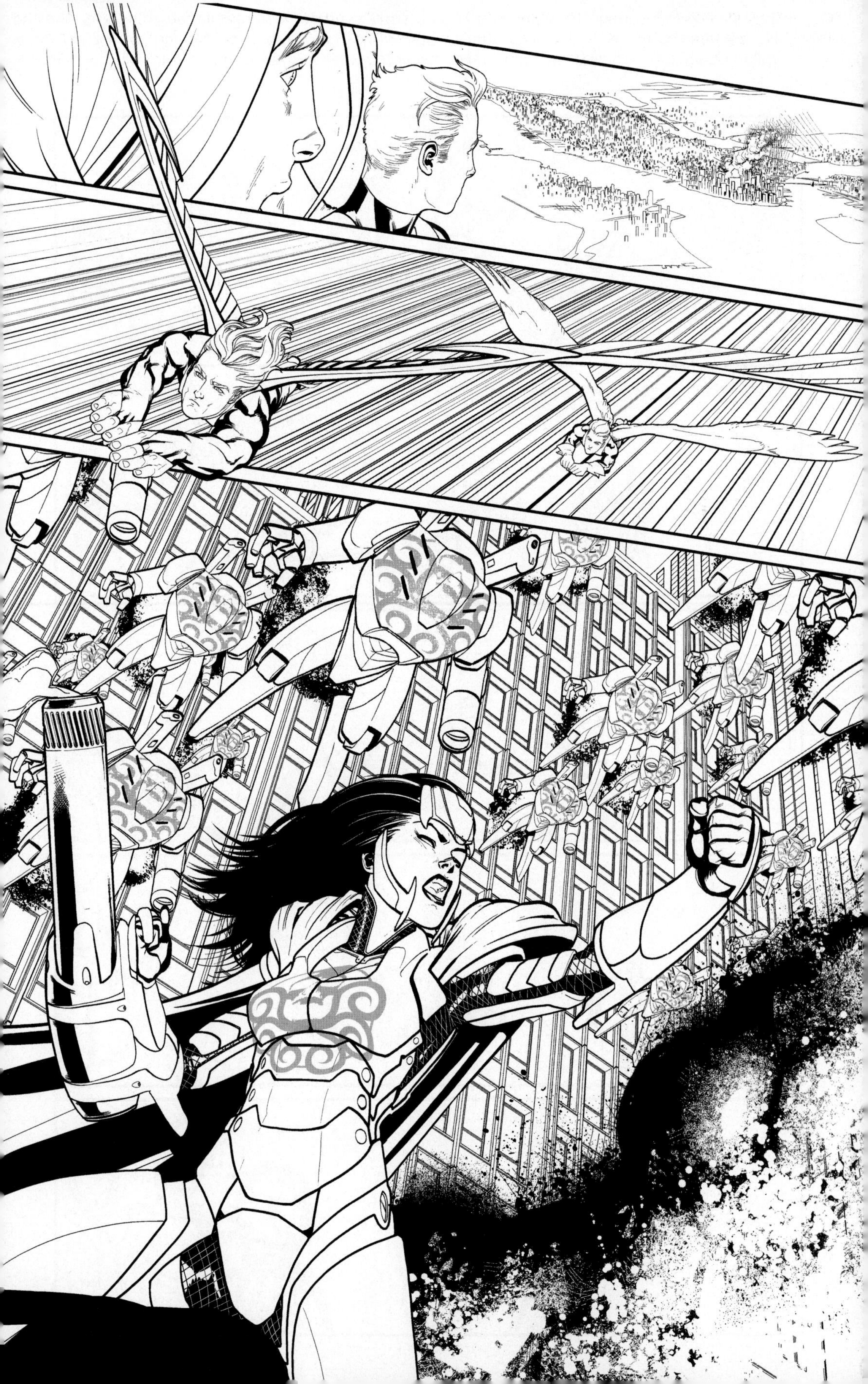

#8, PAGE 16

This was an incredibly fun page to draw. Brian has a such a gift for writing hilarious dialogue, and th
relationship between Kitty and Bobby is so fun to play with. This was a case, though, where my initi
layout, while visually functional, really didn't take into account leaving enough space for all the dialogu

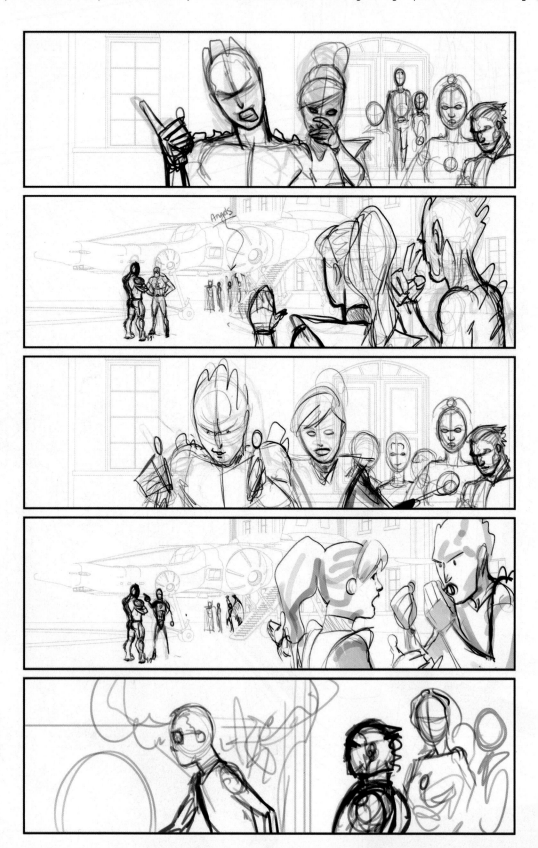

The collaborative nature of comics — between writer and artist, and also between words and pictures — can be seen right on the page. Tall panels can, among many other things, give dialogue room to breathe.

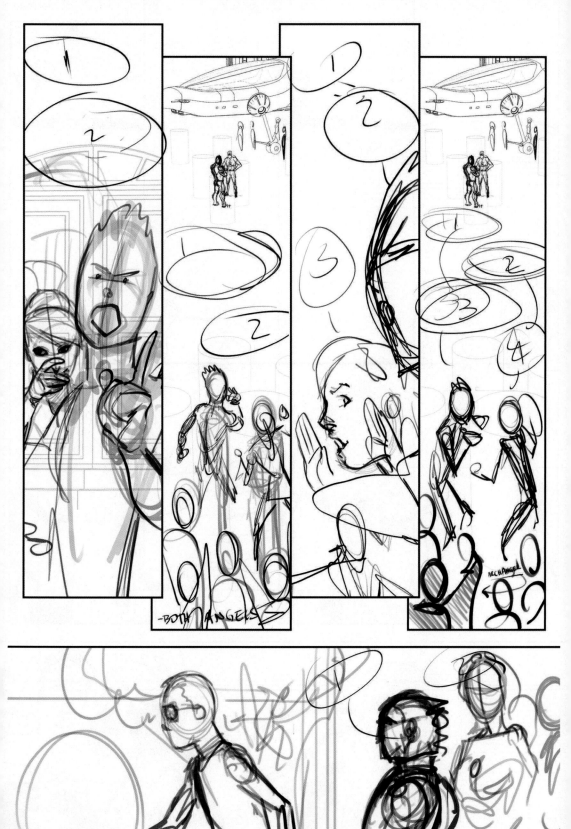

FINAL INKS

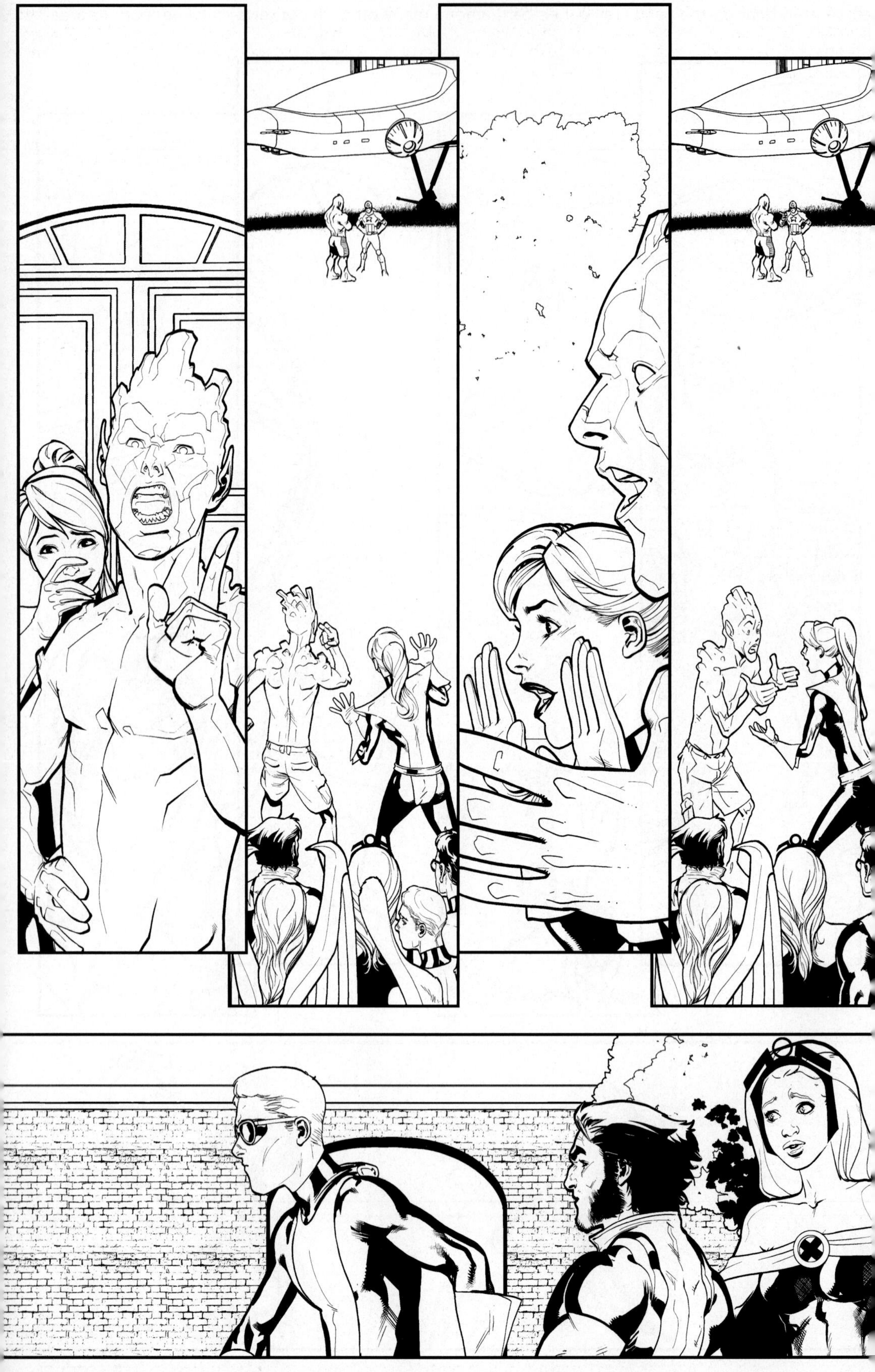

The last page of the issue — and the last page of my three-issue run on *All-New X-Men* — and such a huge moment for Jean. We really needed to get this page right. There was a lot of back-and-forth discussion between Nick, Jordan, Brian and myself about how to sell the moment that Jean takes charge, and possibly begins down a very dark path. There were two really important things to show here: Jean's imposing presence, and the stunned — and horrified — reaction of her teammates.

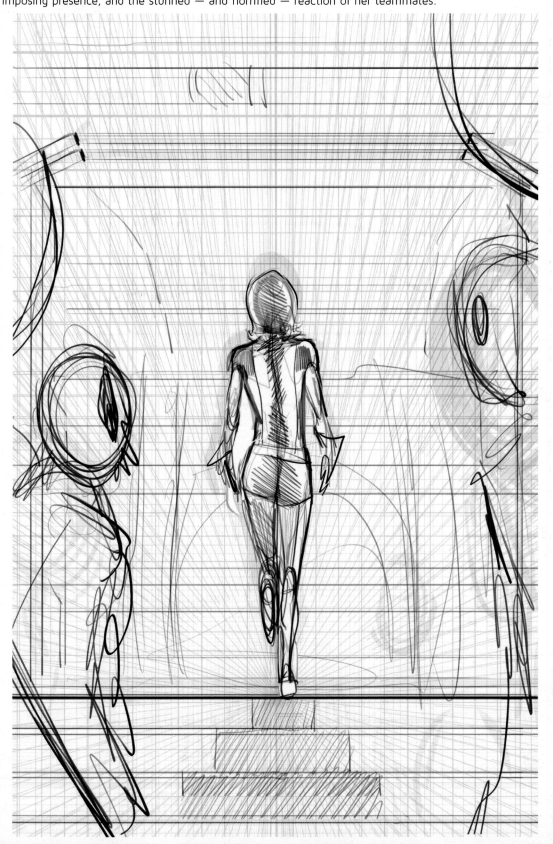

As you can see from all the sketches, most of initial drawings were really focused on Jean, without showing much of the other X-Men.

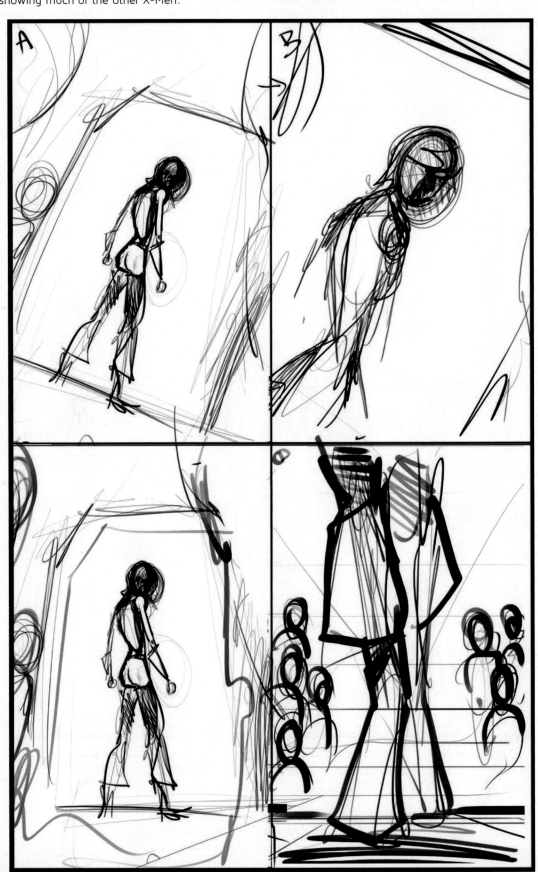

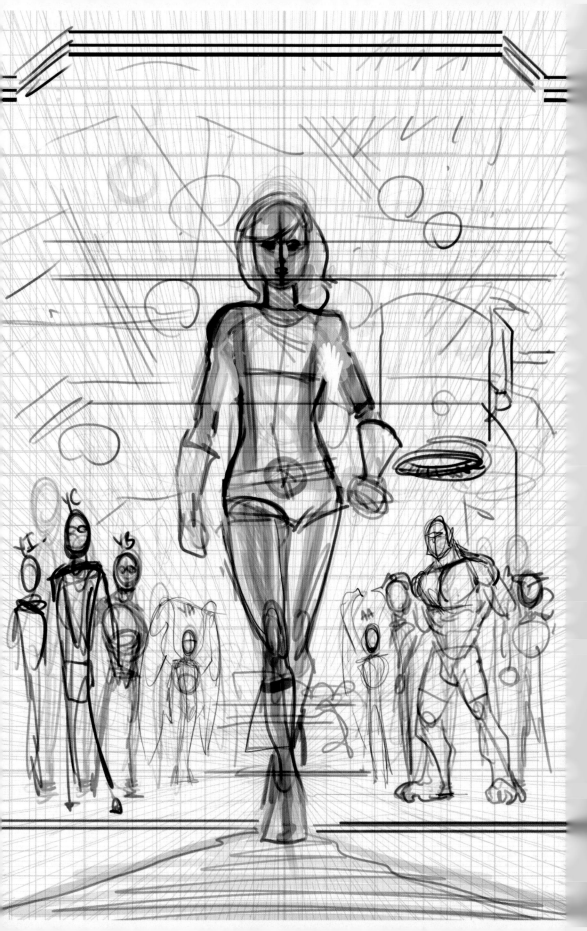

In the final version of the page, we drastically increased Jean's size, letting her dominate the page while also giving us a clear look at of all the X-Men, and how each of them reacts differently to what this person they love so much has said and done, and what it might mean for all of their futures.

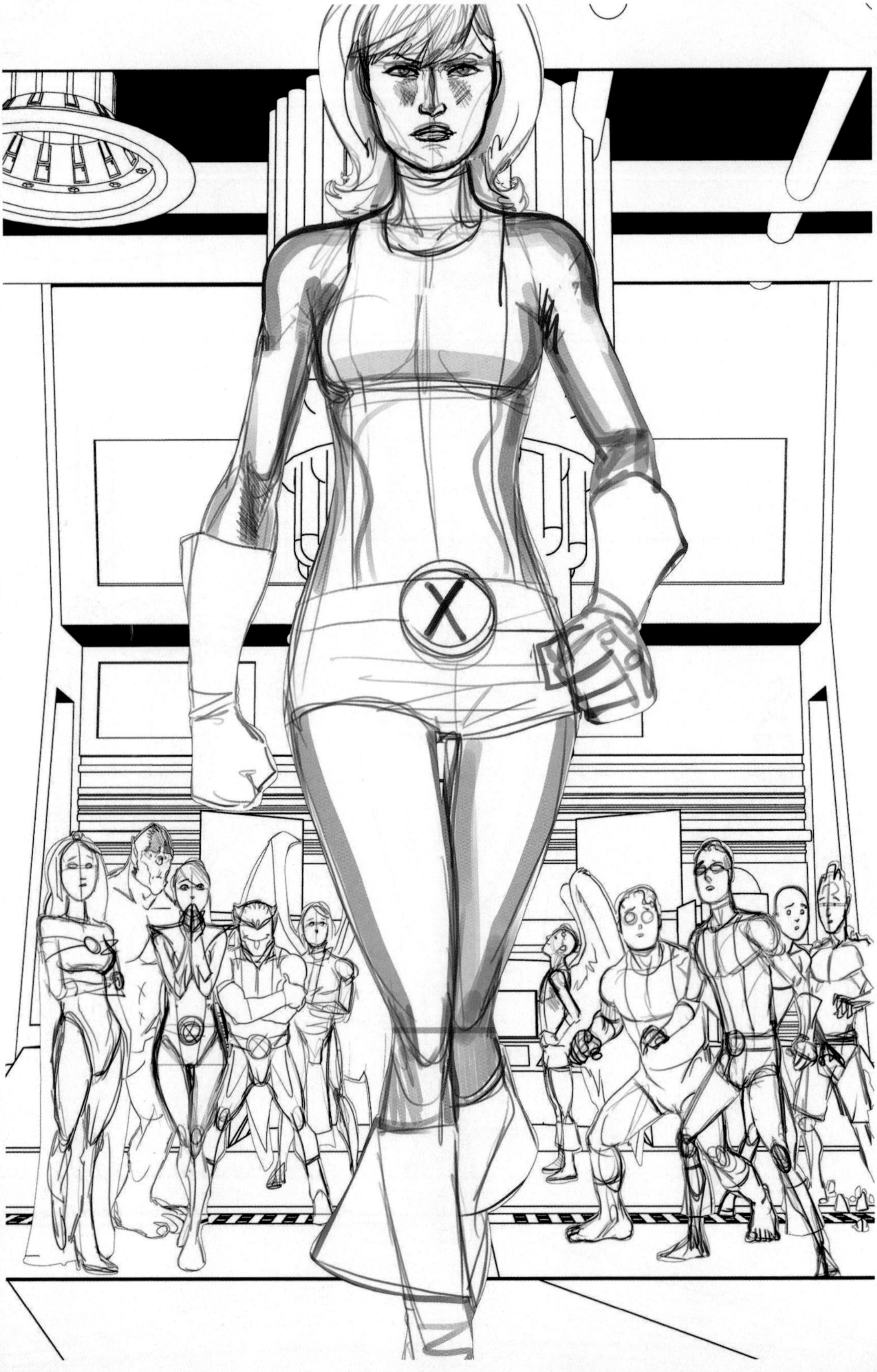

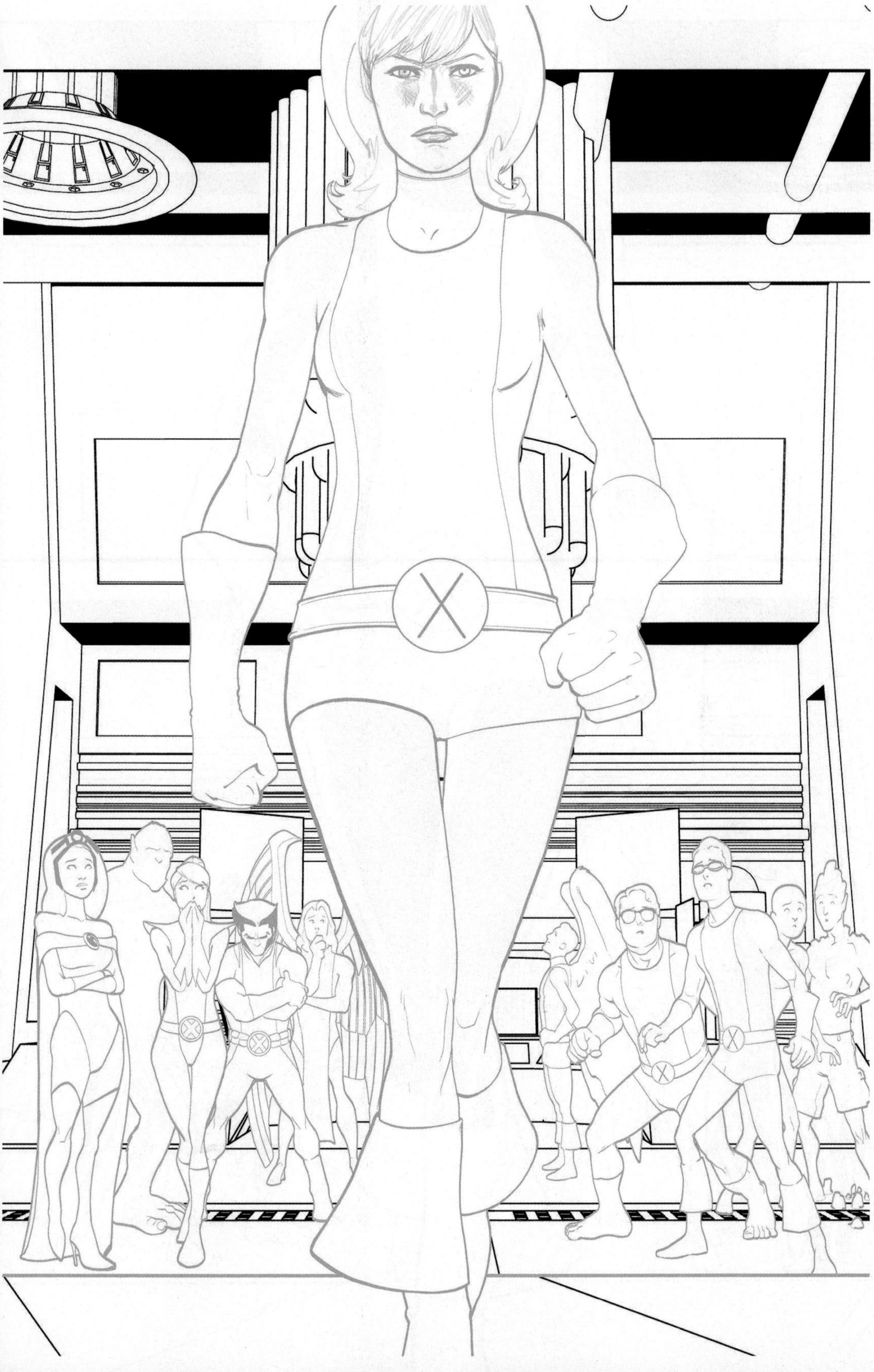

FINAL INKS

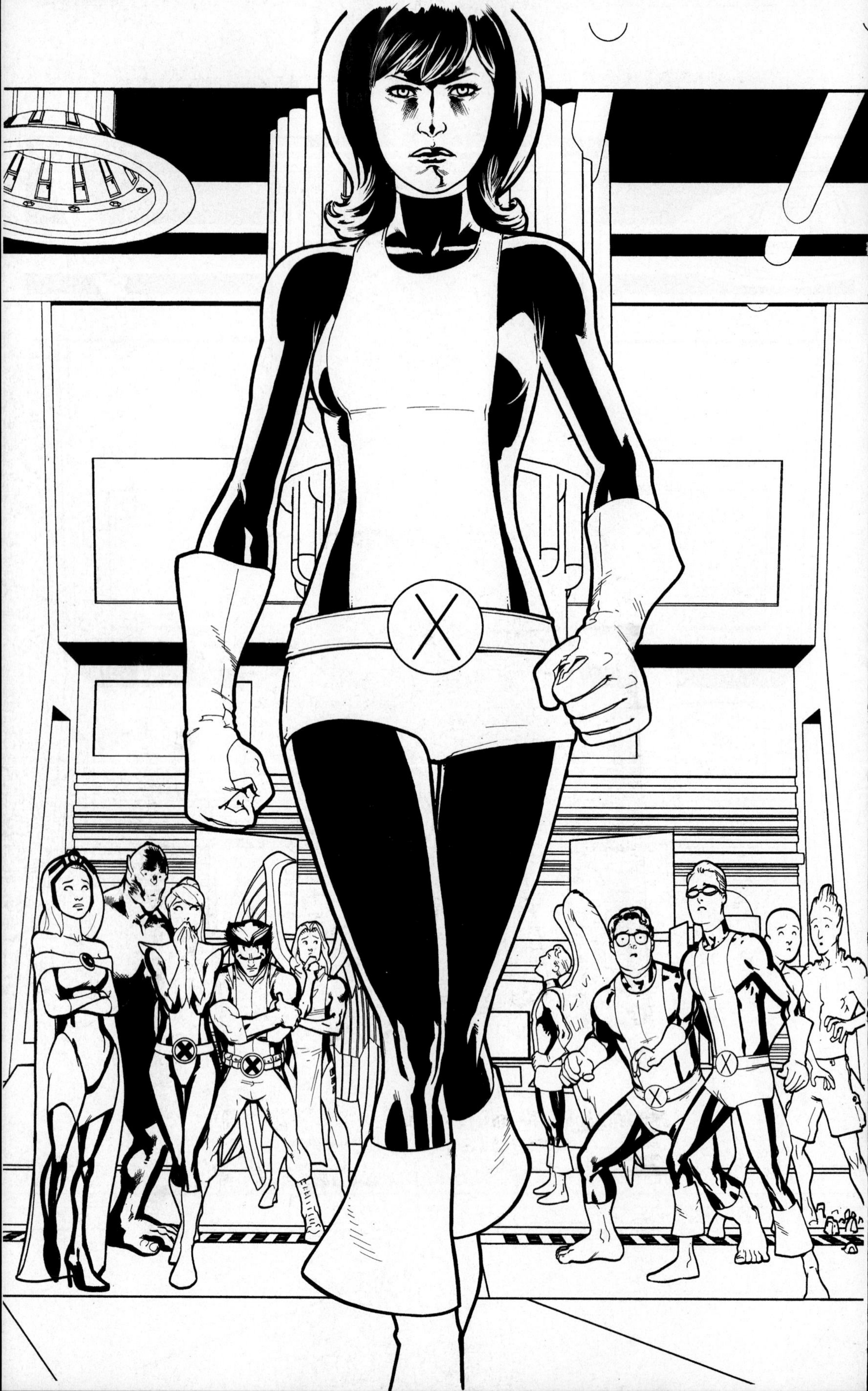

TO ACCESS THE FREE *MARVEL AUGMENTED REALITY APP* THAT ENHANCES AND CHANGES THE WAY YOU EXPERIENCE COMIC

1. Download the app for free via marvel.com/ARapp

2. Launch the app on your camera-enabled Apple iOS® or Android™ device*

3. Hold your mobile device's camera ove any cover or panel with the **AR** graph

4. Sit back and see the future of comics in action!

*Available on most camera-enabled Apple iOS® and Android™ devices. Content subject to change and availability.

X ALL·NEW X·MEN AR INDEX